Refiguring Identity in Corporate Times

For my late father, Mario Vella

Refiguring Identity in Corporate Times

Or Rediscovering Oneself in a Consumer Culture

David Vella

LIVERPOOL UNIVERSITY PRESS

First published 2023 by
Liverpool University Press
4 Cambridge Street
Liverpool L69 7ZU

British Library Cataloguing in Publication Data
A CIP catalogue record for this book is available from the British Library.

Library of Congress Cataloging-in-Publication Data
To be applied for.

Paperback ISBN 978-1-78976-187-0

Typeset & designed by Sussex Academic Press, Brighton & Eastbourne.
Printed and bound by CPI Group (UK) Ltd, Croydon CR0 4YY.

Contents

Contents

Contents

Contents

The Age of Identity

The Contemporary Need to be Ourselves

The contemporary new conformity

The late twentieth and early twenty-first centuries, or what thinkers tend to call 'late modernity', 'hypermodernity', 'liquid modernity', or 'postmodernity', are often characterized by the decline of all 'grand narratives'[1] and their social scripts that organize knowledge and explain experience. In the human sciences and the arts, this absence has by now become a staple feature that virtually defines our times. State-sanctioned public institutions, we are told, have withdrawn their role of providing us and in many ways enforcing an overarching cultural narrative that interprets who we are and our role in life. In the West for the most part, religion, Marxism, and beliefs in providential reason and universal progress have ceased to capture the public's imagination and motivate their reflection and mode of conduct. Hypermodern times, Gilles Lipovetsky claims, generate 'the loss of fixed guide-lines, the disappearance of secular utopias, and an individualist disintegration of the social bond'.[2]

The rapid advances in science and technology may have given us the chance to increase control over our life and yet their knowledge has mostly failed to serve as substitute for the life directives of the past metanarratives. In their absence, it is expected that *we*, each and every one of us as individuals, devise our own personal structural interpretation of ourselves and our experiences. As Philip A. Mellor and Chris Shilling point out in 'Modernity, Self-Identity and the Sequestration of Death' (1993), we are now alone with the task of establishing and maintaining values to guide us and make sense out of our daily lives.[3]

The dissolution of universalizing schemes of meaning and the social glue they provided has pushed toward an atomization of society where sense-making of 'big' subjects such as life purpose and morality has become privatized. What Charles Taylor calls the 'massive subjective turn of modern culture'[4] draws attention to the formation of a society where every individual is expected to be their own centre of action in life planning and behaviour.

The emphasis of our culture on constructing our own future has paradoxically generated, however, its own share of conformity and dependence. It would not be far off the mark to pin this down on an existentialist reasoning of a Sartrean type where the prospect of freedom and responsibility induces disorientation and insecurity, compelling many to escape to socially accepted personalities, to adopt 'bad faith'. The independence that comes with 'freedom from', as Erich Fromm would say, isolates us, placing us in a state of loneliness and doubt as to the manner of our relatedness with the world. In an effort to suppress the emergent anguish, we impose on ourselves conformity with socially approved, popular modes of being.[5] Assistance is sought in various channels that profess to know the kind of mindframe and conduct we are to possess if we are to discover our true self. Adverts, talkshows, self-help books, certain types of psychotherapies, lifestyle magazines, celebrity news, Instagram influencers, fitness regimes, various spiritual workshops, and so on, often offer us *readymade personas* we can take up or combine according to our tastes. As Fromm points out, we give ourselves aims that are commonly endorsed by our culture because that is easier than having to figure out what we really want. To task ourselves with finding our own purpose and projects, he states, 'it is necessary to realize that to know what one really wants is not comparatively easy, as most people think, but one of the most difficult problems any human being has to solve [...]'.[6] For many of us, escape to readymade selves is the quickfix answer to the uncertainty of not knowing what to like, what to believe and value, what to do, who to be.

Perhaps the irresistible appeal of conformity concerns also the relief from having to be accountable to our own coherent picture of the world with the consequences this might entail. We do not want to be held at fault for the actions we take. 'Modern man', Fromm writes, 'is ready to take great risks when he tries to achieve the aims which are supposed to be "his" but he is deeply afraid of taking the risk and the responsibility of giving himself his own aims'.[7] As Jean-Paul Sartre would remind us, acknowledging our independent role in the formation of our projects can be intimidating and frightening in the ineradicable consciousness that our decisions might not be the 'right' ones, that we might not have the courage to maintain them.[8]

At the same time, our reliance on the security that mainstream life-strategies provide can paradoxically exacerbate our insecurity. As Fromm stresses, our commitment to a life script manufactured by others might not eventually satisfy our distinct needs. It might be incapable of expressing our authentic self, propagating as a result more self-doubt and uncertainty.[9] Furthermore, the readymade life directives we opt for can often conflict with others. Zygmunt Bauman in *Postmodern Ethics* (1993) remarks on circumstances where the experts and followers of different lifeguides, as well as different versions of the same lifeguide, may 'clash and contradict each other, each claiming the authority the others deny'.[10] The convenience of not having to make our own choices on how to live is here eroded as we find ourselves once more accountable for which instructions we are to follow and which ones to discredit. Relative to the big decisions we ran away from, this subsequent disorienting situation is not any easier to resolve. The diversity of instructions displayed for us, the speed with which they can change and differ into more updated and improved versions, can overwhelm and intimidate – which accentuates ever further the freedom and responsibility that predicate our selections. However much we would like to conform, we cannot ever really be true 'conformists'. 'Each act of obedience', Bauman writes, 'is, and cannot but be, an act of disobedience; and with no authority strong enough or bold enough to disavow all the others and claim monopoly, it is not clear the disobeying of which one is a "lesser evil"'.[11]

Ours is the time of pluralism. With so many lifeguides competing for our attention, we cannot but view even our most convincing options as fundamentally ambivalent. What to do in what situation, who to be at what point in life have never been as indeterminate. Contemporary society, Bauman states, 'offer[s] us freedom of choice never before enjoyed, but also cast[s] us into a state of uncertainty never before so agonizing'.[12]

The lifeguides on offer may be miscellaneous but they are yet all *commodified* by the market as any other product for sale. Behind their production and promotion often stand multinational corporate companies with the sole aim of increasing their demand and

3

supply. What this means is that the gurus and disciples that assist with the dissemination of mainstream lifeguides intentionally or unintentionally service the profit motives of such companies. Their offers are constituted by the same *values* of the consumer culture in general. Like any other item on the market, they pose as so many cures to be *finally happy*. Their purpose is for our exclusive personal enjoyment. Their promise is of a quick and easy but supposedly deep and transformative satisfaction, when in actuality it often amounts to short-lived feelgood sensations. The inadequacy felt in their effects, however, inclines us to purchase other commodities that claim in turn that they can deliver better on their promise.

When we choose to adopt the lifeguides that are scripted and rescripted by the consumer culture, ideals and behaviour related to what transcends the self, that is, whatever concerns our care for other living beings, society, politics, and the environment, tend to be marginalized or sometimes completely ignored. They become as Bauman stresses, 'a waste of time, since they are irrelevant to individual happiness'.[13] If market products are designed to sensually stimulate in order to sell, then, Bregham Dalgliesh reminds us, they divorce us from our social contexts and bifurcate us from others, 'who become mere asides to our individual fulfilment [...]'.[14] Taylor likewise points out that our societal responsibilities or the demands of our ties with anything that is outside our self-reflexive desires and ambitions are drastically sidelined in importance, if not completely foregone.[15]

The concern with self-identity: Definitions (Giddens, Bauman)

At the heart of our search for compelling lifeguides is our obsessive concern with identity. Our preoccupation is inevitable for a society of individuals who are undecided on how they are going to understand themselves and the world around them, even when they do. This work is an indepth exploration of the issue of self-identity. It is fitting that we begin by establishing a basic and coherent definition of what the concept entails for some current eminent thinkers.

'Identity' in 'self-identity' refers to the constancy of the self over time. Unlike the self as a generic phenomenon, the constancy in focus is required to coincide with our awareness. As Giddens

4

explains, 'It is what the individual is conscious "of" in the term "self-consciousness"'.[16] In self-identity, we are conscious of ourselves as continuous in time by way of a routine *interpretation through a biography* of our perpetual construction. What we experience daily is reflexively integrated and organized within a life-story that consciously or unconsciously premises our behaviour on most occasions. 'A person with a reasonably stable sense of self-identity', Giddens states, 'has a feeling of biographical continuity which she is able to grab reflexively and, to a greater or lesser degree, communicate to other people'.[17] At the same time, we must always be ready to reassess and alter our story to address unforeseeable and unprecedented events that impact on our life. Self-identity is a never-ending work in progress.

Giddens characterizes the self-identity phenomenon as both fragile and robust. It can be fragile because the biography we choose to hold on to is only one version of so many alternatives. Our regular awareness of this can easily erode our conviction in who we define ourselves as being. The implacable what-if possibilities that our self-hermeneutics could have been better and more satisfactory in any way can become a source of much doubt and insecurity.[18]

Our identity can also be robust because we can paradoxically still choose to hold firm to our biography despite all odds. The opposition we face from an external environment might hardly, if at all, affect our conviction in the self-story and values that we have formulated. As Giddens points out, a strong belief in the integrity of our self-understanding signifies a consistent loyalty to a particular definition of ourselves that 'filters out' in our day-to-day activities any threats to its coherence.[19]

Giddens further adds that we also reinforce constancy in our identity by reflexively structuring what is to come in accordance to its perspective. Not only does our identity 'rework' past events but it also integrates into its biographical narrative the future by viewing it in terms of the projects that derive from our underlying self-beliefs. We craft our own version of a future by plotting and mobilizing a course of actions.[20] Strategic life-planning helps reassure us that our sense of the self matters, that it will endure.

What is really revealed in the fragile and robust tendencies of identity, however, is not an inherent stability but rather an intrinsic *aspiration* for such stability. Self-identity acts on behalf of an *ideal* of an enduring essence of the self that we hope others will acknowledge and recognize us by. It is a longing for an actuality that it has to necessarily pretend is already in existence if it is to survive against all odds. As Bauman explains, it therefore represents less of a noun denoting a collection of traits belonging to a material entity and more of an active verb denoting an ambitious enterprise. What the enterprise indicates above all is a need that is contingent on the contemporary absence of any 'truths' regarding our nature and place in the world. The very idea of identity with its indissociable determination to be a fact is a *reaction* to the uncertainty pervading our society. It is the protective product of deep-set vulnerability. Bauman confirms our predicament in the following:

> One thinks of identity whenever one is not sure of where one belongs; that is, one is not sure how to place oneself among the evident variety of behavioural styles and patterns, and how to make sure that people around would accept this placement as right and proper, so that both sides would know how to go on in each other's presence. 'Identity' is a name given to the escape sought from that uncertainty […]. Identity is a critical projection of what is demanded and/or sought upon what is or, more exactly still, an oblique assertion of the inadequacy or incompleteness of the latter.[21]

What this work sets out to do: The refiguring identity as an alternative to consumerist identities

The concept of self-identity defined so far belongs strictly to personal subjectivity and there has been no mention as yet of another form that is prevalent in the West of the late twentieth and twenty-first centuries. Some choose to define themselves in accordance to a subculture, which embeds them in a mindset and conduct that is shared by a certain group of people bonded by one or more common traits.

Popular cultural identities are mostly oriented around gender, religion, race, sexual orientation, and historical memory, related especially to nationality. As Lipovetsky indicates, the turn toward cultural self-definition is evidenced in today's upsurge of demands for such social groups to be respected in their distinctness from other groups. Just as we seek recognition for the self-identities we construct and/or adopt as individuals, so are these communities fighting to be recognized for their own.[22]

Despite the important role that cultural identities play in any study on contemporary identity as well as their unmistakable increase in popularity in the West, their subject will not be the focus of this work. Our primary concern is with the individualist identities sponsored by the market especially because of their ubiquity in our societies. It is clear that these life-strategies have become so integral to our day-to-day existence that they have almost assumed a *normative status* as standards and guides. Without exception, our exposure to their seductions is insistent, most notably through the public media whose influence on our unconscious is undeniable. Not only would an indepth study of these identities disclose the nature of the consumer culture that saturates our everyday life but by extension it would also shed some light on the psychology and behaviour of many people living in Western societies insofar as they follow their prescriptions. And who does not to some extent?

Refiguring Identity in Corporate Times is above all a creative and productive response to the popular life-strategies of our consumer culture. It sketches the schema of an alternative way how we can build an identity that operates in part outside this culture. This schema, which I call the 'refiguring identity', can inaugurate a self-assessing relationship that allows the consumerist life-strategies to be pursued insofar as their practices are beneficial to our character. What the relationship seeks to prevent is an unquestioning conformation to these life-strategies on account of their inherent narcissistic and hedonistic values. The refiguring identity's purpose is to empower us to create our own inimitable vision of life from our personal needs. It accomplishes this by defining our self as originally bonded to a *call to be authentic*.

The refiguring identity model sees the call as constituting *the ground of ethics*. The call emerges from what is good and just. The authenticity it is a summoning of is therefore not oriented toward solipsism of any kind. It does not posit the self as the absolute subject of concern. It enjoins us rather to be susceptible to our close and far environment. It tells us that our affirmation of the outside is inseparable from the discovery and expression of our truest self. The process of finding who we really are must go by way of our solicitude to the world we live in. As a result, the journey toward our self-realization inherently motivates us to act on behalf of that world in order to make it a better place where we can dwell. The search for our singularity is thus endowed with the highest purpose. It becomes by turns a fundamental right and duty.

If the consumerist identities are usually centred on self-care, our faith in the call can help us expand our circle of care to include anything that is not us. While the former are focused on our personal welfare, the latter enlists us to find intrinsic value in our external environment and commit ourselves to it, most especially in relation to other people and their social institutions. We incorporate their welfare *as part of our own*. By drawing our attention on our sense of responsibility beyond personal matters to include the societal as well, the refiguring identity model to be introduced helps ensure that our self-development is more integral and fulfilling than that promised by the consumerist life-strategies. Its structural narrative is meant to pave the way for ways of understanding ourselves that can assist us in living a potentially fuller and more diverse life.

The refiguring identity as a hermeneutic-phenomenology of conscience

The ideas explored in *Refiguring Identity in Corporate Times* are highly influenced by the works of Jean Baudrillard, Paul Ricoeur, and Zygmunt Bauman. On the one hand, Baudrillard's and Bauman's insightful study of today's consumerist life-strategies especially has proved crucial for my own approach to the subject. On the other hand, the alternative identity model proposed will be loosely based on Ricoeur's constitutive conditions of conscience as a dimension of passivity in *Oneself as Another* (1990).

Though the subject of self-identities is typically treated by the discipline of psychology, it will be here approached philosophically on account of the refiguring identity model's structure as a *hermeneutic-phenomenology of conscience*. Its narrative predicates itself on a belief in an inner voice that summons us to an ethical mode of interpretation that can be especially significant for events that are more foreign to our worldview than usual. It inaugurates an ideal way of understanding existence as irreducibly different from us whereby we can develop a vision and praxis that aspire toward a better future for everyone.

An underlying suggestion of the refiguring identity model is the persuasion that its narrative structure of conscience expresses the foundation of our being. Its emplotment, that is, articulates a *fundamental ontology* (or preontology) that we are always already embedded in even if our attention is usually absorbed by our day-to-day routines and egotistic projects. Consequently, its more basic purpose is to re-attune us to our inner voice – which it endeavours to do in two interrelated ways. It orients us toward the scheme of an objective for a better future of solidarity and justice through which we can signify our own idiosyncratic objectives. It also orients our motives by reference to five character qualities or what it describes as 'virtues'. In its narrative, these two components are described as follows: the voice of conscience directs our conduct toward a better future by enjoining us to practice five virtues.

It is the refiguring identity's conviction that to live through our conscience – or its definition of 'conscience' – is to live in the most authentic way that is available for us. To hear and answer to our conscience is to hear and answer to our most original self.

In view of what it attempts to accomplish, our exploration of the refiguring identity will best be served by the philosophical approaches of hermeneutic-phenomenology, phenomenological ethics, and virtue ethics. My study of consumerist life-strategies will be rooted in the sociology of late modernity as well as cultural theory. Whereas my investigations on the latter will employ a predominantly descriptive and critical mode of writing, a jointly descriptive and prescriptive mode will be employed for my study of the former.

Chapter 1 sets the stage by presenting five of the most mainstream, consumerist life-strategies of our times, which many unquestioningly adopt as identities. A contrast between them and the structuration of a typical self-identity, however, makes evident their predominant lifestyle character. Turning them or confusing them with identities entails a suppression of our authenticity.

Chapter 2 charts the narrative of the self that is peculiar to the refiguring identity. At its heart is the call of conscience through which our originary self is configured. The call summons us to live the good life with and for others in just institutions. The three components that are seen to construe this futural state of being are described in their innate development from one another.

Chapter 3 focuses on the shared nature of the five virtues that thematize the refiguring identity's story. They are seen as providing a more integral and fulfilling understanding of our life in contrast to those values advanced by consumerist life-strategies that are seen, nonetheless, to bear an uncanny resemblance to them. In their narrowed-down perspective, targeted especially to indulge hedonistic and narcissistic needs, the mainstream values' relationship with the virtues is seen to comprise the faux reality character of Baudrillardian simulations. The role of the virtues is to co-constitute the sincerest, most empathic and effective ethical-hermeneutical decisions toward experience. In so doing, they direct us toward more insightful personal understandings of the good life.

What follows from chapter 4 to 8 is a separate account of each virtue. Explained by reference to eminent philosophical works, the virtues' particular modes of engagement with the world are extensively traced out. A comparison with the corresponding values embedded in the consumerist life-strategies is also investigated in order to demonstrate how the virtues represent an augmented and authentic version of them.

Chapter 9 presents the worst-case scenario of episodes whose extreme suffering deprives us of our sense-making capacities. These events have often gone under the title of 'limit-experiences' in philosophy and critical and cultural theory. The question is raised as to whether the refiguring identity model remains efficacious in such instances. What is demonstrated is that the most basic foundations of its conscience narrative can still be maintained, and that while some of its virtues do indeed lose their credibility as a result, the others are reinforced.

The Conclusion argues that it is perhaps inadvisable to discard today's commercial life-strategies altogether from our life. In promoting our wellbeing, several of their practices should not be abandoned. The sketch of a relationship between them and the refiguring identity model is thus charted where either one can inform the other for a certain life equilibrium to be reached.

Turning Lifestyles into Identities

The Distinction between Two Self-Narratives

The myth of self-transformation in consumer culture

Contemporary society allegedly offers us the freedom to make sense of who we are and what we want to do with our life and yet, ironically, many of us tend to blindly conform to prepackaged life-strategies produced and/or appropriated by the market. Erich Fromm's diagnosis in *The Fear of Freedom* (1941) remains highly relevant to this day. We are insistently told and we believe strongly in being ourselves and yet many of us still do not express themselves sufficiently through their emotional and intellectual potential, what Fromm would call their 'spontaneous activity'.[1] Instead, we resort to the popular approval of life-scripts publicized across the public media. In belonging to a culture that is targeted to consume, these identity-types are essentially designed to maximize our spending to profit corporate companies.

A crucial strategy employed to this end is the mainstream identities' shared idealism on *self-transformation*. All of them pose as momentous life-altering journeys that will lead to our self-discovery. Predicating their discourses of salvation is a high estimation and prestige conferred on some species of change that can involve our habits, interests, appearance, relationships, perspective, and so on, in order to discover some unprecedented 'depth' and 'authenticity' about ourselves. 'You must change your life!' they warn in a gentle and friendly way. Sure enlightenment, we are told, comes by wiping out old orientations and building new ones.

Self-transformation as instructed by a consumer culture, however, does not come from within. It comes from *without*. It is

11

indissociably attached to the application of a certain product or service that is usually new and fashionable. It is on account of what we buy that our transformation can be realized. Our epiphany can only arrive on purchase of the *right* commodities. The commodities for sale in turn have a limited expiration date that will shortly be replaced by others that are more fashionable and 'improved' and that purport to transform us once more.[2] Insatiable possession is thus *rationalized*. Who we are is what we acquire.

The most popular identity-types of consumer culture that evangelize the myth of self-transformation through their diverse narratives can be differentiated into what I will call 'fashion', 'entrepreneurship', 'fitness', 'travel', and 'self-spirituality'. The first four are loosely derived from what Zygmunt Bauman in his essay, 'From Pilgrim to Tourist – or a Short History of Identity' (1996), describes as 'postmodern life strategies': metaphors for types or styles of practice that are popularly pursued in our times.[3]

The five mainstream life-strategies of consumer culture

The fashionista

The world of fashion is connected to an identity-type that is based on the frenzied pursuit of the latest vogues in aesthetic appearance, from clothes and accessories to hairstyles and beauty products. Fashion seduces by virtue of its *novelty*, which is seen in Gilles Lipovetsky's words, as an invitation for 'personal "liberation", as an experiment to be undertaken, an experience to be lived, a little adventure of the self'.[4] Buying that new dress or getting this new hairstyle is supposed to fulfil the promise of rejuvenation: becoming a new me, getting off to a fresh start, becoming younger. New wardrobes and cosmetics serve to 'make me over', to make me feel alive again. The new will set you free. This gives it a therapeutic function.[5]

Fashion's tenet is that the self can be recycled through innovative appearances. To put on untried products is equivalent to putting on untried selves, which we playact for ourselves and the public eye, and then dispose of whenever their glamour is lost and others catch our attention. To be our most authentic self, we must prove that we are always changing, adopting new skins and shedding them.

We are, according to Georg Simmel, in 'a permanent state of becoming',[6] carried by 'a self-perpetuating momentum that gathers energy while expending it [...]'.[7] Changing our looks, always looking different to be ourselves entails a celebration of what Lipovetsky calls the 'aesthetic cult of the self'.[8]

The everlasting experiment with our appearance is thus in fashion a flamboyant expression of our individuality. It is testimony to an affirmation of our autonomy and control, our mastery over aesthetic décor. Contemporary fashionistas often display these characteristics by adapting the current official looks to their own ideas. In their look, for example, they can integrate articles found in charity shops or that have long exceeded their expiration date. The legitimacy of their creative touch is the cultural inheritance of the second phase of modern fashion that started in the 1980s: what was known as 'open fashion' or *'le look'* in France. Open fashion encouraged the free invention of our self-image through a pick-and-mix of different clothing items and accessories, designs and styles, which could have also incorporated the most incompatible principles of appearances. *Le look*, Lipovetsky explains, invites us 'to decompartmentalize styles, to blend them, to do away with stereotypes and copies, to abandon rules and fossilized conventions [...]. What is valued is the deviation, the creative personality, the astonishing image [...]'.[9]

The contemporary scene is still faithful to the trends of open fashion in its acclaim of the combinatorial choice of elements taken from the vogue of the moment along with other forms, styles, and materials whose discontinuity from that vogue is taken as evidence that their choice has been purely ours. To be seductive in fashion hinges upon this individualist aesthetic. At the same time, however, the same scene prescribes that the display of individuality should be *understated*. Any playing around with the canonical aesthetic must never be excessive and explicit. Disobedience must always take place safely. Creativity must operate within the bounds of conformity. The process places the fashionista in close proximity to the fin-de-siècle dandy as described by Charles Baudelaire in his art criticism of the 1860s. In the section called 'The Dandy' in *The Painter of Modern Life*, Baudelaire explains that the passion driving the true dandy is '[a]bove all the burning need to develop originality within the ostensible boundaries of propriety'. To the dandy's way of thinking, perfection of one's toilette consists in 'absolute simplicity', which is 'the best way of distinguishing himself'.[10]

Originality must be only *minimally different* from the norm because the overall attitude we are often required to give off has to do with being relaxed, carefree, at ease, 'cool'.[11] We are not to show that we have invested so much time and energy in how we look. Just enough innovative boldness and we can risk breaking the consecrated laid-back impression. 'Being different' inasmuch as it betrays 'making an effort' is considered to be discordant, 'unsexy'. If we are to exhibit our individuality, we must do so under absolute discretion.[12]

Fashion, for Bauman, is also governed by normative constraints in that 'the desire to be distinct from the masses, to acquire a sense of individuality and originality' is always inevitably counterbalanced by a 'longing for a sense of belonging within a group or an agglomeration'.[13] 'Fashion', Georg Simmel reminds us in *Zur Psychologie der Mode*, 'is a particular form of life, which seeks to ensure a compromise between a tendency towards social equality and a tendency toward individual separateness'.[14] Two contradictory impulses thus drive the glamorous world of the fashionista. Insofar as we feel the need to distinguish ourselves from the crowd, we experiment with innovation. Insofar as we feel the simultaneous need to be socially accepted, however, the innovation we seek has to be marginal in character. Conforming to the dominant models and codes of fashion expresses the deep-set desire for approval.

The cohabitation of originality and conformity, however, is perpetually in tension, always requiring further renegotiation. If what is in vogue is also supposed to convey our sense of originality, and if all of us desire to be original, then what is considered to convey originality today tends to be quickly adopted by so many others that it becomes mainstream tomorrow, which compels in turn a search for newer looks that are in vogue, which are also as a result also quickly mainstreamed. 'Driven by the impulse to be different and to escape the crowds and the rat race', Bauman remarks, 'the mass pursuit of the latest fashion (of the very moment), quickly causes the current marks of distinction to become common, vulgar and trivial, and even the shortest lapse of attention, or even a momentary slowing down of the speed of prestidigitation may produce results opposite to those intended: the loss of individuality'.[15]

There is conclusively a particular logic of novelty and hyperindividualism that are peculiar to the fashion scene. Since the modern epoch, however, as Lipovetsky makes clear in *Empire of Fashion* (1987), this same logic has slipped out of its designated scene and has been increasingly pervading the consumer culture in general. Fashion is now *consummate*. It has permeated the very *structure* of the market. How the market operates in its production, distribution, and sales has become determined according to a psychology that used to be associated predominantly with fashion. What this means is that the popular identity-types produced today by the economy are also determined according to the laws of fashion.[16] Louis Cheskin's announcement in the 1950s is more relevant now than ever before: 'Every industry tries to emulate the women's fashion industry. This is the key to modern marketing'.[17] The four other identity-types that follow are therefore also centred on the codes of novelty and hyperindividualism as calibrated by the tempering codes of conformity.

The entrepreneur

Coinciding with the laws of fashion are the laws of entrepreneurship that have likewise been internalized by today's popular identity-types.[18] The life-strategy of the entrepreneur or the finance investor is today being promoted in various adverts on business-related courses and job vacancies, films and TV series on politics and/or the corporate world, rags-to-riches biographies, self-help books on the road to unlimited material and spiritual success, finance magazines, as well as the news, among other sources. According to the anthropologist, David Graeber, in America, the tendency to extol this role started off in the seventies with 'heroic CEOs [being] lionized in the media, their success largely measured by the number of employees they could fire'.[19]

At the same time, the new credo was that everyone should look at the world through the eyes of an investor – that's why, in the eighties, newspapers began firing their labor reporters, but ordinary TV news reports came to be accompanied by crawls at the bottom of the screen displaying the latest stock quotes. The common cant was that through participation in personal retirement funds and investment funds of one sort or another, everyone would come to own a piece of capitalism.[20]

In analogy with the fashion world, the world of entrepreneurship idolizes the value of novelty. It is the central constituent of the highly influential model of entrepreneurship as proposed by the Austrian economist, Joseph Alois Schumpeter, in his major work, *The Theory of Economic Development* (1911). Entrepreneurs, he claims, are the ones who innovate by taking a new idea and putting it into practice in the market. Innovations pertain to every aspect of business, ranging from new products to new methods of organization and management to the possession of a new source of supply of raw materials or semimanufactured goods. It is through the entrepreneurs' processes of innovation that capitalism profits and the economy rises.[21] Irma Adelman in *Theories of Economic Growth and Development* (1961) states that 'like the Marxian capitalist, who accumulates for the sake of accumulation, the Schumpeterian innovator, innovates, at least in part, for the sake of innovating'.[22]

Contemporary models of a successful entrepreneur character refer to numerous other qualities. ActionCOACH, for instance, a prominent business coaching franchise, sees confidence as a hallmark in the achievement of self-esteem and faith in our abilities, driving entrepreneurs to confront challenges by taking action. Entrepreneurs are also to take responsibility for any issue that arises in their firm. They are to treat all problems as if they are their own and resolve them with care and attention. In addition, they have to be able to communicate effectively and convincingly, to be passionate about learning, to be team players, and rely upon systems for solutions. They are required to design, implement, and perfect such systems before considering solutions related to human resources. Dedication, gregariousness, gratefulness, exemplariness, and fearlessness before risk and success are also highly desirable attributes.[23] *Personality Traits of Entrepreneurs: A Review of Recent Literature* (2018), mentions openness to experience, conscientiousness, extraversion, agreeableness, and emotional stability and even-temperedness as defining traits.[24]

In late twentieth and early twenty-first century society, the relevance of the entrepreneurs' life-strategy has expanded beyond the actual entrepreneurial position to include virtually all employees who are involved in the running of a business. In principle, every member of staff employed by a company, especially if corporate, is now expected to model their conduct on the values of the professional investor. Ideal candidates can now include both lead management positions, such as chief operating officer, marketing manager, and chief financial officer, and key personnel, such as quality control manager, safety manager, accountant, office manager, purchasing manager, and professional staff. Implemented to this end are processes of recruitment and socialization, such as programs of corporate culturism, human resource management, and total quality management. These programs are endorsed by various leading management gurus, corporate executives, and state mandarins, which explains their high popularity.

In 'Strength is Ignorance; Slavery is Freedom' (1993), Hugh Willmott illustrates that the most prominent values that business employees are asked to internalize are 'quality', 'flexibility', and 'value-added'. Implied in the triad, however, are various other values, such as 'efficiency', 'effectiveness', 'profitability' 'hardness', 'shrewdness', 'ambitiousness', 'innovativeness', and 'single-mindedness', among others, all of which are ultimately targeted toward capital accumulation for the firm.[25] Corporate culturism or cultural excellence, Paul du Gay maintains, 'is a struggle for identities, an attempt to enable all sorts of people, from highest executive to lowliest shop-floor employee, to see themselves reflected in the emerging conception of the enterprising organization and thus to come increasingly to identify with it'.[26] It refers to the mandate that we are to redefine the idea of the self in strict association with the firm's interests.

The fitness-seeker

The most popular identity-type of all five is fitness and its cult of the body. A cursory review of today's newspaper reports, television documentaries, advertisements, magazine articles, and internet sites will easily reveal the importance of the body's role in our society. It is also evident in the explosion of fitness gyms and clubs since the 1980s as well as the proliferation of information on how to avoid obesity and prevalent types of sickness such as coronary heart disease and some forms of cancer.[27] It is not far from the truth to claim that we live in a culture that often tends to interpret us according to the status of our body and the maintenance of a fit lifestyle.[28]

According to Cheryl L. Cole in 'Body Studies in the Sociology of Sport' (2002) and Brian Turner in *The Body and Society* (1996), the late twentieth and twenty-first century obsession with fitness and health is intimately related to several current health crises. The prevalent presence of deadly diseases such as AIDS, tuberculosis, strokes, cancer, and dementia among others have contributed significantly to the increase of anxieties surrounding the body. On the other hand, developments in medicine and technology in general have contributed to the perspective of sickness, ageing, and death as avoidable and contingent.[29]

Furthermore, as Turner makes clear, the transition from industrial capitalism toward a 'postindustrial culture' founded on a global economy, service industries, advertising, and consumerism, has brought about an unprecedented hypercommercialization of the body. One of the most successful markets in our times indeed concerns resources, activities, and commodities related to the improvement – the *drastic* improvement – of our bodies. Diets, self-help books, gym workout plans, health and fitness magazines and cosmetic products, and several spiritual practices, among others, are all promoted particularly with the intention of spectacularly transforming our physique. At the same time, this market and the mass media endorsing it, ignores and denies the *inevitability* of the ageing or diseased body, and in doing so, stigmatizes it.[30]

In *Liquid Modernity* (1999), Bauman defines 'fitness' by distinguishing it from what we call 'health'. Health, he remarks, was the proper and desirable state sought after by the early twentieth century societies of producers in the West. Health signified the physical standard we had to maintain in order to satisfy the responsibilities of our assigned role in society, which was namely attached to the workplace and the family. We were required to do our best to avoid illnesses and physical disabilities while keeping ourselves in a physical condition that would allow us to perform successfully on the job and help out at home. Being healthy was about avoiding excesses and '"sticking to the norm"' in order to *function* on a day-to-day basis. It signalled 'a state which can be more or less exactly described and precisely measured'. In fact it was 'clearly defined and circumscribed by modern medicine "in empirically testable and quantifiable terms"'.[31]

'Fitness', however, Bauman points out, belongs to a 'society of consumers'.[32] What motivates it is not *duty* as is often the case with health, but *desire*. Fitness is propelled by the aspiration to have the ideal physique and the purchase of any product and the implementation of any regimen that is believed to bring us closer and faster to that objective.[33] Louise Mansfield in *Gender, Power and Identities in the Fitness Gym* (2005) likewise sees 'fitness' as a way of life that ceaselessly and unconditionally strives to attain what is sometimes known as the 'body-beautiful' or the 'high-status body'. This is usually portrayed as a body that is lean, muscularly toned, and tight. Adverts, fashion magazines, fitness publications, as well as films and TV series in the West continuously expose us to images of people that embody this ideal just as personnel in the fitness, sport, and diet industries tend to extol and reinforce it in various ways.[34]

The prestige held by the high-status body is due to its association with the ideals of youth, (sexual) pleasure, success, vitality, self-esteem, and discipline. It is understood that whoever possesses this type of physique naturally possesses such qualities as well as inspiring them in others. Our self-value is thereby enhanced, which can in turn open up new life opportunities. To sport the high-status body is to bring favourable attention from all sides, which can in turn assist us greatly in landing the career of our dreams and/or find the love of our life.[35]

From dieting to yoga, from dancing to exercising, the path toward the high-status body is understood to involve a plurality of activities all designed to gradually sculpt our appearance in its image. The body is perceived as a site that can be worked on and worked out, open for construction and reconstruction, holding so many potentials that can be fulfilled. Physical information that differs from the model standard, such as flab, waist or thigh measurements that exceed this standard, the absence of a thigh-gap, aches, pains, wrinkles, etcetera, are interpreted as occasions for further productive action. Our self-esteem depends on our proximity to the criteria that underlie our objective.[36]

The traveller

Since the late twentieth century, the tourist industry has grown into a lucrative social phenomenon, marking a new type of consumer behaviour that has extended into a way of relating to the everyday world. In such works as *Globalization* (1998) and 'A Short History of Identity' (1996), Bauman sees in the traveller's mindframe, a reflection of the general mindframe that informs the contemporary Western quotidian life. He calls this interrelatedness, 'the tourist syndrome'.[37]

Fordist or post-Fordist, the tourist industry has always sponsored a very particular mode of engagement with the world. Thomas Cook, an early innovator of modern tourism, set a precedent for a romantic sensibility that tourists were asked to adopt prior to their journey. As mental preparation for his so-called 'Tartan Tours' of Scotland in the 1850s, for instance, Cook asked his clients to read Walter Scott's historical novels. To fully appreciate the scenery, architecture, ruins, and nature of a tour, tourists were strongly advised to first invoke their beauty through language, poetry, and their imagination. They were urged to first *desire* what they were going to experience, which was considered to be an integral element of the touristic experience itself.[38] Referring to Colin Campbell's *The Romantic Ethic and the Spirit of Consumerism*, Adrian Franklin writes that this psychological preliminary was eventually extended to other forms of consumption as well. '[T]he romantic sensibility', he points out, 'gave rise to the pleasures of anticipation and desire ahead of [the product's] physical consumption'.[39]

What Cook was preparing his clients for was a distinct kind of perception that Bauman denotes as the *'aesthetic space'*. For its sales, the tourist industry, capitalizes on an aesthetic interaction with the world. What it conjures through its goods, services, advertising, and television programs is an environment that is mapped on the different types and degrees of amusement value it can hold in store for us. No other value is to be given any consideration in this emplotment. A spirit of self-indulgent fun is endorsed that is drawn only to the enjoyment potential of anything around us. We are encouraged to imagine whatever we like about anything – place, person, object, event – that happens to spark our curiosity or desire. From this bystander perspective, the world appears as gentle, receptive, and malleable, full of options that are ready to oblige our whims or wishes. It offers itself up for our arousal. Life assumes the status of an aesthetic adventure, an exhibitionist drama staged by us as its only director, scriptwriter, audience, and critic.[40] What would otherwise be a routine working day for the natives of a certain town, it can transform into 'a collection of exotic thrills'.[41]

The aesthetic space is appealing and addictive because of its inconsequentiality. Our imagination can manipulate and spin its own meanings on just about anything we encounter in the knowledge that our private spectacle will not intrude into the realities observed. Our fantasies and the conduct they inspire are granted free license since they operate at a remove from the seriousness of actuality with its actions. The aesthetic space we inhabit is safely severed from the life of work, relationships, and responsibilities. It can be indulged without limits because it is 'unspoiled by the fear of danger, guilty conscience, or apprehension of shame'.[42] As tourists we pay to have this very freedom. We assume the persona of a tourist to *legitimate* this unfettered gaze.

In our times, however, the aesthetic space is no longer delimited to vacations only. Since the 1990s, scholars who introduced the perspective of postmodern tourism in tourist studies have diagnosed what appears to be a gradual dedifferentiation between tourism and everyday life. Adrian Franklin in *Tourism: An Introduction* (2003), for instance, remarks on the growing number of places that are being reconstructed as tourist attractions: reidentified for the aesthetic consumption of others. We are consequently inclined to perceive formerly 'typical' buildings, streets, and squares with the same aesthetic eye as tourists, a practice which is becoming more common. The mundane and functional is slowly being transformed into a spectacle.[43]

Contributing to the blurring of the boundaries between tourism and quotidian life is the plurality of leisure activities available for tourists to pursue alongside equally enthusiastic locals. Options can include sports, such as tennis, skiing, abseiling, climbing, diving, horse riding, golf, etcetera, the acquisition or practice of knowledge and skills, such as learning a foreign language, painting, dancing, etcetera, or nature-oriented practices, such as hunting, trekking, or fishing. The activities themselves can also take place in sightseeing destinations that can range from museums, galleries, and local theme parks to bars, sports facilities, and cycling routes.[44]

Moreover, as Mauro Dujmović and Aljoša Vitasović point out in 'Postmodern Society and Tourism' (2015), in today's society 'We do not have to travel to other cultures, they travel to us in multiple forms, through objects themselves, through media and advertising, through television images, internet and print media, through foods, aromas, and technologies […]'.[45] This leads Dujmovi and Vitasovi to conclude that 'Difference and multi-ethnicity of big cities in the world in combination with cultural variety of restaurants, bars, shops, and shopping centers speak in favor of the fact that people consciously or unconsciously spend the majority of their time as tourists'.[46]

The inevitable question must then be asked as to whether the aesthetic space is assuming a more prevalent motive in our standard behaviour. Is it increasingly becoming a predominant way how we live our life and interact with others? And does this psychological reorientation come at the expense of other mindframes, namely, the moral mindframe? Insofar as the tourist experience is owned and fabricated by the consumer industry, Bauman seems to think so. The self-profiting agenda of business corporations impose upon tourism goals that are far from fulfilling 'the nineteenth century ambition to travel to learn, travel to understand, travel to get in touch with alien people and to embrace and imbibe and assimilate the untold riches stored in their heads, in their timeless cultural lore . . .'[47]

The self-spiritualist

Thomas Luckmann was the first to identify a shift in Western religiosity in the mid-twentieth century, coterminous with the decline of Christian culture and a rise in the popularity of the theory and methods of psychotherapy. What various social thinkers call 'new age spirituality', 'new spirituality', or 'self-spirituality', emerged in the context of the 1960s countercultural movements and is nowadays used to describe a variety of discourses and practices that are still predicated on a criticism and resistance to neoliberal and capitalistic principles, in promoting alternative mindsets and ways of living.[48]

Jennifer Rindfleish in 'Consuming the Self: New Age Spirituality as "Social Product" in Consumer Society' (2005) explains that self-spiritual systems of thought constitute eclectic assimilations of isolated segments from traditional religions, esoteric, philosophical, and scientific theories, all appropriated and reenvisioned to fit particular meta-theories.[49] Despite their apparent differences, most systems of thought are grounded in pantheist and panentheist theologies of a divine spirit that is both the creator and a life-sustaining, underlying force of the cosmos, evolving as it unfolds.

Gordon Lynch in *The New Spirituality: An Introduction to Progressive Belief in the Twenty-First Century* (2007) writes that the gurus of self-spirituality view the divine as 'an ineffable unity' that is both 'the guiding intelligence behind the evolutionary processes of the universe, and (within) the material form and energy of the universe itself'.[50] Nature becomes the dwelling-place of the divine while the self becomes the conduit of divine agency.[51]

Self-spiritualists hold that we are all hosts to a spark of the divine or what they describe as a unitive self that is a point of convergence between the mind, body, and cosmos. An immanentist vision is presented whereby the material and corporal domains are seen to embody and express the sacred just as the sacred depends on them to embody and express its processes. The relationship is thus established on a necessary reciprocity that sacralizes the material and materializes the sacred.[52]

Much unlike the theistic traditions, new spirituality does not attach too much importance on theories, doctrines, and ethical precepts in its realization of the spiritual self. It relies instead on *practice* and *experience*. The way to emancipation from the egotistic self can be facilitated through a variety of activities, most of them extracted from the spiritual traditions of the East that range from yoga and reiki to spiritual massage and forms of the Alexander Technique.[53] Because the divine is believed to be immanent in the body and the physical world, spiritual experience is also believed to be found in what we usually consider to be 'profane' physical activities, such as martial arts, healthy eating and exercising, sport, and even gardening. As a result, Andrew Dawson points out, 'the material aspects of life which nurture and allow the body to flourish become significant means of spiritual expression'.[54] Worldly accomplishments such as material success and psychological well-being assume the status of a gateway as well as a reflection of our level of spirituality, a means toward and an indication of how close we are to enlightenment.

In self-spirituality, we are also encouraged to find our divine self through our own personal experiences. Through the power of positive thinking, we are asked to reassess our life not as a series of limitations but as a series of *potentials*. We are told that we have the capacity to shape our own destiny in life. The path to enlightenment is to be found *in our own way*, according to *our* unique personality. A form of 'religious' individualism is thus emphasized, elevating the subject as the free arbiter of spiritual authority and therefore the primary agent of spiritual transformation. Social thinkers such as Guy Redden and Paul Heelas in fact define self-spiritualists as 'seekers', ceaselessly searching for any available means and opportunity that can help them come closer to their objective.[55]

Despite new spirituality's professed opposition to neoliberal and capitalistic values, its beliefs, techniques, and practices are also commodified. Their access comes at a fee. As with all the other mainstream identity-types, the infrastructure of new spirituality is the market. Several thinkers such as Neville Drury, Jeremy R. Carrette, and Richard King in fact define the life-strategy's setting as a 'spiritual supermarket', where various updating and innovating goods and services along with their guru-entrepreneurs engage in a competition of promises of who can best deliver enlightenment in the quickest and easiest way at the most decent price. All we have to do is perpetually choose from among the array of offers for the unending and ever-changing development of our spiritual welfare.[56]

Identity as a life-story and a dwelling

If the five life-strategies illustrated are often deployed as identities, we need to consider the issue of their efficacy in stimulating the expression of our unique personalities and vision of the world. We also need to ensure ourselves of their capacity to help us grow into 'better' people, providing us with guidelines and values that help us navigate the diverse hurdles of life in a manner that is ethical and rational.

Various recent thinkers on identity agree above all on its *narrative* structure. For narrative identity psychologists such as Erik Erikson, Dan P. McAdams, Lynne Angus, Arnold Bruhn, Jane Kroger, and Abigail Stewart, as well as sociologists and philosophers like Anthony Giddens, Alasdair MacIntyre, Paul Ricoeur, and Richard Kearney, identity is formed by creating a developing self-story. Through this personal narrative we can convey to ourselves and to others who we are now, how we came to be, and where we think our life is heading in the future. 'Life stories', McAdams writes, 'are based on biographical facts, but they go considerably beyond the facts as people selectively appropriate aspects of their experience and imaginatively construe both past and future to construct stories that make sense to them and to their audiences, that vivify and integrate life and make it more or less meaningful'.[57]

The narrative that defines our identity meaningfully configures our past, present, and future experiences through a commitment to certain values and beliefs that emplot and direct it. Their constancy would give all the different self-elements in our life – our roles, talents, relationships – a psychological and social coherence and purpose. They can, for instance, integrate our sullen and bored feelings at the workplace with the great surge of optimism and love we feel when we are talking with certain friends; or connect the time we used to love playing baseball with our current ambition to be a great social psychologist. Our behaviour's relative consistency and motivation depend on these underlying themes in our self-story. They constitute the propelling force to how we think and decide.

Two common overarching themes are agency and communion. Agency is characterized by qualities associated with self-mastery and empowerment while communion embodies associated with intimacy, caring, and a sense of belonging to a certain group and/or person. The following are two representative extracts that are based on the two themes respectively:

(1) 'I challenge myself to the limit academically, physically, and on my job. Since the time of my divorce, I have accomplished virtually any goal I set for myself.'
(2) 'I was warm, surrounded by friends and positive regard that night. I felt unconditionally loved.'[58]

The storyline and its thematic premise forming an identity have a crucial function. They supply us with an affective-cognitive *identification with* a worldview. They are tools that furnish us with a vision of how we can dwell and participate in existence. Through them, we *belong* to a comprehensive perspective that we can fall back on in times of insecurity and doubt. To a large extent, identity is concerned with the process of embedding our self in an ontological mindset, whose affirmation in turn serves to affirm that self and assist in a re-cognition of the world around us. It entails the construction of foundational convictions that enframe raw existence. In the beginning of his essay, 'A Short History of Identity',

Bauman draws attention to the ontological need to belong. He argues that it is no coincidence that the modern societal consciousness of identity occurred precisely at a time when the need to associate ourselves with a higher purpose had never been greater. It is our estrangement from all grand narratives and its symptomatic isolation that has caused us to conceive the very idea of identity in the first place. Its phenomenon is to be seen as a mirror to our troubled times: an urgent aspiration or 'a name given to the escape sought from that uncertainty'.[59]

In *Ethics of Authenticity* (1991), Charles Taylor discloses another form of belonging that is intrinsic to an identity representative of our authentic self. The principles that structure it, he claims, cannot be self-made: we cannot invent them ex nihilo. They are chosen in relation to settings and demands that are beyond us.[60] Our self-definition can only be constructed by interacting with principles invoked by what George Herbert Mead calls 'significant others'[61] – parents, friends, partners, teachers . . . – who induct us into societal standards that are derived from our culture, history, biology, the ties we have with other people, their needs, the duties of citizenship, etcetera. Altogether these form a fundamental background that educates us into what is important and what is less so, how we can choose to do the right thing, the various ways we can excel in life. Our values and ideals can only be so precisely because they are valued and idealized already by others. Our self-expression can therefore only be fulfilled through a dialogic relationship with a pregiven setting: what Taylor calls 'horizons of significance'. Our beliefs take on significance in dialogue, sometimes in a conflict, with these horizons.[62] If our identity articulates who we are as unique individuals, Taylor argues, 'then perhaps we can only achieve it integrally if we recognize that this sentiment connects us to a wider whole.'[63] We can only interpret ourselves in relation to bonds that transcend us. Identity 'is "who" we are, "where we are coming from". As such it is the background against which our tastes and desires and opinions and aspirations make sense'. 'I can define my identity only against the background of things that matter'.[64]

Assessing the concept of identity with consumerist life-strategies

Eminent thinkers of identity seem to generally agree on the task of identity to emplot our past, present, and future into a biography that is held together by themes that articulate our personal values and ideals. Biography and themes in turn construe a worldview to which we feel we belong, along with the indissociable relationship of such themes with the greater whole of society or the 'horizons of significance'. It is after all the embeddedness of those themes in the horizons of significance that precisely *validates* them as a foundation to our worldview.

Upon careful assessment, the readymade popular life-strategies that many people today take as identity-types seem to lack the criteria that have been established as constituting a successful identity. To an extent, their comparative shortcomings are the result of their incorporation in the market infrastructure. It is also, however, perhaps due to their inherent design, which cannot be extricated from the prevalent influence of the consumer culture of our times, whose logic they have absorbed regardless of whether or not they have been co-opted by corporate companies. When they are, and all five life-strategies have been, the inevitable result is an amplification of their consumerist logic, which devalues and diminishes in turn other (nonconsumerist) characteristics they might have comprised beforehand, including those that relate to ethics.

What is evidently different in the life-strategies in contrast to the operative identity is their *type of narrative*. On all accounts, they present a narrative that is *strictly* targeted toward an objective, from which they derive all their standards and principles. In their rigid focus, they are indifferent to our particular personality and its needs, our own ideals and values, our personal life with its past and present factualities, its unresolved issues and achievements. What makes me, *me*, and not another is ignored. Substituting it is a storyline that is single-mindedly dedicated to accomplish a fixed goal, which establishes it as one-dimensional and functionalist in character. In the service of its goal, a set of prepackaged values and ideals are imposed on us regardless of the differences of our individuality.

In their assimilation in the consumer culture, commercial life-strategies designate targets that are forms of exclusive self-gratification. The life they seek to explain is defined as a linear quest beset by difficulties that we need to overcome for our self-gratifying rewards. The principles we are to follow for our achievements are therefore not designed from a dialogue with the standards of a societal background. The narratives offered are severed from beliefs and customs that transcend them and me. They are unconcerned with any knowledge pertaining to others and their regional cultural, historical, and political environment. The element of belongingness as found in the concept of identity is disregarded. The consumer culture entertains a hyperindividualist rationality that suggests a vision of society that is atomised rather than bonded by mores of any kind.

The perspectives extolled by the five life-strategies are also not primarily intended to be inhabited as a dwelling-place we can always return to in order to reaffirm ourselves and reorganize our world, especially in the face of opposition. If they are precisely strategies oriented toward the achievement of an objective, then, the mindsets they provide for us are not focused on a dwelling but a *seeking*. Every one of their narratives can in fact be reduced to a version of a statement that expresses a species of strong desire for an object: 'I want to acquire the high-status body', 'I want my business to thrive', 'I want to reach self-realization', 'I want to be a leading model in fashion and beauty', 'I want to have innumerable exotic adventures in my life'.

Therefore, on the one hand, consumerist self-narratives seem to be constructed only in terms of their goals, as a search for those goals. They are indissociable from a movement toward a futural point. In an operative identity, on the other hand, any goal and its attendant search seem to be *expressive of* and therefore *subordinate to* the overarching themes predicating its narrative. They articulate the preceding values and ideals that make our worldview possible. If our actions do on occasion contradict the themes of our self-story, they are still seen as fundamentally *interacting* with them, whether in the form of a transgression or with the intent of modifying or developing them. In this way, our aspiration for an objective is always to be configured in the overall story we are recounting. Conversely, the consumerist self-stories' aspiration for an objective *is* the configuration of their story. It determines all that they endorse.

Consumerist life-strategies as lifestyles

If fashion, entrepreneurship, travel, fitness, and self-spirituality are predominantly designed to be enterprises, then it follows that they are heavily reliant on the *practices* and *experiences* required to fulfil the enterprises they set in motion. Rather than focusing on values and beliefs that can lay the foundations for a biographical narrative, they focus on 'ideal' ways *we can live*. In centring themselves on *methods* of how we can be happy, they are qualified more as *lifestyles* than as identities.

In his major work, *Modernity and Self-Identity* (1991), Giddens designates a lifestyle as follows:

> A lifestyle can be defined as a more or less integrated set of practices which an individual embraces, not only because such practices fulfil utilitarian needs, but because they give material form to a particular narrative of self-identity [...].
>
> Lifestyles are routinized practices, the routines incorporated into habits of dress, eating, modes of eating, and favoured milieu for encountering others but the routines followed are reflexively open to change in the light of the mobile nature of self-identity. All such choices of action are decisions not only about how to act but who to be.[65]

Mike Featherstone in *Consumer Culture and Postmodernism* (2007) connects 'lifestyle' with the manner we express ourselves especially through our purchase choice of products. Changes in production techniques, market segmentation, and general demands for a broader range of products now provide us with an unprecedented range of options for sale on how we can display our individuality. In the consumer culture, our commodity tastes are crucial in exhibiting who we would like to be. The style of the goods we own comes to represent our unique personality. As Featherstone remarks:

> Rather than unreflexively adopting a lifestyle, through tradition or habit, the new heroes of consumer culture make lifestyle a life project and display their individuality and sense of style in the particularity of the assemblage of goods, clothes, practices experiences, appearance and bodily dispositions they design together into

a lifestyle. The modern individual within consumer culture is made conscious that he speaks not only with his clothes, but with his home, furnishings, interior decoration, car and other activities which are to be read and classified in terms of the presence and absence of taste.[66]

What Giddens and Featherstone seem to infer is that a lifestyle entails the *practical articulation* of an identity (with its underlying principles) through the pursuit of several distinct techniques. If we intend to capture our singular self through our lifestyle, then we do so only in connection to an eclecticism of material practices. A lifestyle does not seek to define or redefine who we believe ourselves to be though in many ways it can influence this knowledge. It is rather the other way round. It consists of a strategy on how we are to manifest our self-conception. We choose it to outwardly express our identity. It is its routine exteriorization.

The five life-strategies of fashion, entrepreneurship, travel, fitness, and self-spirituality are therefore closer in characterization to the general definition of a lifestyle. Bauman as well attaches this label to them in 'A Short History of Identity', as well as describing them as 'styles' and 'types'.[67] Contemporary society, however, tends to celebrate them as if they are identities. It misperceives and elevates their scripts to *life* scripts: comprehensive explanations of how we can interpret our self and existence. The consumerist procedures they advocate are thereby (mis)interpreted as procedures that formulate a worldview that we are told will lead to our self-discovery. If such procedures mostly revolve around what goods and services we should pay for, then it follows that what we pick becomes crucial for the very formation of our interiority. What we acquire – as per the dictates of the five lifestyles – becomes who we are. A reverse process is here in effect where the objects that are usually used to express our interiority come to *create* our interiority. As Rindfleish argues in agreement with Giddens, 'The context of post-modern social life is segmented and diverse leading to "lifestyle sectors" that tend to dictate our actions'.[68]

To confuse consumerist lifestyles with identities is to expand their aspirational narratives to signify a worldview in which we can dwell. Identity becomes the product of a lifestyle. What results is the wholesale adoption of prepackaged personalities that are not ours and which are ultimately incapable in many ways of satisfying our particular needs. We are told that this adoption will realize our 'true' self when it is nothing short of a rigorous *standardization* that suppresses our singular personality with its history, values, passions, strengths, and insecurities. We are paradoxically convinced to roleplay a stock character in the belief that this character will deliver us to our singularity.

▋▋

The Refiguring Identity's Narrative Model

Consumer personalization (Baudrillard)

The commodities we need to use to successfully perform any of today's mainstream lifestyles come equipped, we are told, with the special feature of *personalizing us*. In their diverse ways, all the lifestyles call on us through their discourses and virtually limitless offers to 'Personalize Ourselves!': a proposition whose urgent undertones makes it sound more like a duty than a rare option. We are told that to apply or experience a holiday package deal, an outfit, a car, a hairdye and shampoo, a fitness regime, or a spiritual retreat or workshop will reveal our true self in an unprecedented way. It will unlock aspects of who we are previously hidden from us. Each commodity presented is often characterized as a lifetime opportunity in its promise of bringing out our individuality in a way that has been unachieved so far by other commodities.

Jean Baudrillard in *The Consumer Society* (1970) shows what the '"over-reflexive" expression', 'personalizing ourselves', is actually saying without saying it. If the action of personalizing ourselves references the application of commodities as a means to discover our singular self, then by implication, there can be *no singular self* that will do the personalizing. We are a *nobody* until we consume the right products. As Baudrillard stresses, it is an 'absent person, this lost instance which is going to "personalize" itself'.[1] What this inevitably suggests, in my view, is that we are in no position to find who we are by ourselves, by our own freely taken decisions; we are as yet 'lost' so we are in no position to know what can deliver us to our interiority. The implicit conclusion that follows is that it is the market and its corporate companies that are to assume the role of leading us to our self-discovery through the 'transfiguring' wares they provide for us.

We are to follow their recommendations in order to gain the identity 'we always wanted and deserved'.

Baudrillard in fact argues that our shopping choices are never strictly self-determined. They follow the market's dictates through the *rounds of fashion*. Our motivation to pick and combine our purchases is stimulated by certain trending codes of the season. We are exhorted to find our individuality from items and services that we are told we *should* desire at the moment. To be ourselves we are told *how* to be ourselves. 'The narcissism of the individual in consumer society', Baudrillard states, 'is not an enjoyment of singularity; it is a refraction of collective features'. 'It is by coming close to your *reference* ideal, by being "truly yourself", that you most fully obey the collective imperative and most closely coincide with a particular "imposed" model'.[2] Our personalization is anything but personality-conferring. It belongs to the musts-and-don'ts of the current style and taste whose perpetual recycling ensures a fresh supply of demand.

The market capitalizes heavily on the current predicament of identity-crisis. It abets it and relies on it for its raison d'être. In claiming to provide us with the gift of identity, it also alters its *definition* in the same move. As Baudrillard writes, the concept of identity as 'based on autonomy, character, the inherent value of the self [...]',[3] is replaced with one based on *commodity choice* (which is hardly ever really our choice). The consumer market feeds on the abolishment of 'the real differences between human beings, homogenizing persons and products [...]'.[4] To differentiate ourselves therefore comes to signify in great part our conformation to what happens to be in vogue. We become what we acquire.

Authenticity as the call of conscience

Given the contemporary predominance of the consumer market in identity-formation, it is ironic that the ideal of 'being authentic' has never gained a wider currency than in our times. What we have come to understand by 'authenticity', however, is a degraded and distorted version of its original significance. To trace out what the ideal actually stands for, we need what Charles Taylor would call a 'work of retrieval'[5] to help us restore its practice. Taylor undertakes the task in *Ethics of Authenticity* (1991), where he introduces one of the first proponents of authenticity as Johan Gottfried Herder.[6]

Herder declares that each one of us has an inner 'voice' that we are ethically obliged to endorse. It calls on us to be who we really are as singular individuals and to *derive* our life and values from this singularity. The key to a fulfilling life is to answer the summons by pursuing it in our thoughts and deeds. Herder acknowledges that what is asked of us is no easy feat since we cannot depend on external standards to guide us in our journey of self-discovery. He is convinced that we are at heart inimitable and the answer to finding our own purpose in life can never be reduced or compared to the path of others. The expression of our singularity necessitates a self-reflexive originality. Taylor formulates the argument as follows:

> There is a certain way of being human that is my way. I am called upon to live my life in this way, and not in imitation of anyone else's. But this gives a new importance to being true to myself. If I am not, I miss the point of my life, I miss what being human is for *me*.
>
> This is the powerful moral ideal that has come down to us. It accords crucial moral importance to a kind of contact with myself, with my own inner nature [...]. And then it greatly increases the importance of this self-contact by introducing the principle of originality: each of our voices has something of its own to say. Not only should I not fit my life to the demands of external conformity; I can't even find the model to live by outside myself. I can find it only within.
>
> Being true to myself means being true to my own originality, and that is something only I can articulate and discover. In articulating it, I am also defining myself. I am realizing a potentiality that is properly my own.[7]

The 'refiguring identity', the identity model at the centre of this work, is precisely purposed toward the realization of a form of this authenticity. It lays out the basic framework of a plot that can stimulate and structure our respective life narrations in a way that articulates our ownmost sense of self. The primary motivation of its plot scheme is to steer us toward a knowledge and practice of a self that incorporates dimensions other than the hedonistic and narcissistic dimension that is usually the focus of consumer culture. Its structure is there to ensure that we do not confuse self-absorption with self-authenticity. It reminds us that there is a world out there that is also intrinsically implicated in the idea of being who we really are. The premise of the refiguring story is designed to help expand our horizon of concerns beyond our need for feelgood sensations and in doing so help augment awareness of our original self or our definition of it. That way the biographies we compose will be predicated on a fuller and more self-responsible way of life that could be more fulfilling for us.

Much alike Herder's and Taylor's ideal of authenticity, the plot of the identity model under study is hinged upon the call to be true to ourselves. What defines the call in this model, however, is *conscience*. The enjoinment to be true to ourselves is the enjoinment of conscience. The refiguring identity does not just interpret authenticity as an ethical phenomenon but arguably as *the* ethical phenomenon. The self we are summoned to be, then, is above all else a self that is good, a self that does good. To formulate its idea of conscience, the refiguring narrative takes recourse to Paul Ricoeur's own hermeneutic-phenomenology of conscience as explored in *Oneself as Another* (1992).

Conscience, for Ricoeur, signals toward an *original ontology* that preexists our separation as thinking subjects acting upon a world of objects. Conscience is 'older' and outside the experience of ourselves as separate from our environment, appropriating it with our intentions. What it reveals is that before the I coincides with itself in autonomy, I am indissociably bonded with an interior presence or Other that calls me. Anterior to my self-reflexivity lies a selfhood that is inextricably involved in a summoning. More than any other idea and image of an independent self or selves that I think I am, this self-that-is-called is ineffably 'deeper' and 'truer' to myself. It constitutes what Simon Critchley, in *Infinitely Demanding:* Ethics of Commitment, Politics of Resistance (2012), calls 'ethical subjectivity' whereby I am me *inasmuch* as I am an affirmation of a call. I am me as given unconditionally to a call. By implication, myself as affirmation would not exist were I not called. Equivalently, the call would not exist were I to refuse it. In ethical subjectivity, as Critchley states, 'demand and approval arise at the same time and [...] the demand is only felt as a demand by a subject who approves of it [...]. [E]thical experience begins with the approval of a demand, a demand that demands approval'.[8] In the necessary co-originality of its two components, the subjectivity at issue is thereby *circular* in structure. And the good toward which it aspires renders its circularity *virtuous* rather than vicious.

For the refiguring identity model, it is in this selfhood, which is the phenomenological selfhood of conscience, that I can find my authenticity. The Other that speaks to me here, that *speaks me*, is unknown. As Ricoeur remarks:

> Perhaps the philosopher as philosopher has to admit that one does not know and cannot say whether this Other, the source of the injunction, is another person whom I can look in the face or who can stare at me, or my ancestors for whom there is no representation, to so great an extent does my debt to them constitute my very self, or God – living God, absent God – or an empty place. With this aporia of the Other, philosophical discourse comes to an end.[9]

The voice of conscience entails a self-proximity that can verge on the unbearable. Its intimacy can be inordinately intimate to the point that I cannot reveal its nature to myself. It is in this inordinateness wherein its strangeness lies. Steven Shaviro in *Passion and Excess* (1990) remarks that it is 'the most intensely personal experiences [that] are also the most inaccessible, the most rigorously impersonal'.[10] Because the presence of the voice is the most interior to my interiority, it is exterior to me. Despite its occasional articulacy, it is too personal or immediate to distance myself from it in order to understand it in any way. Too familiar and yet too unknown, it dwells in the paradoxical event of an 'intimate foreignness'. If the voice calls my inmost self, of which it is a constituent, then it addresses me in the second person. I am therefore reciprocally compelled to address it as well in that mode but as a Thou. The authority its voice holds inspires such respect.[11]

Ricoeur emphasizes that the call of conscience is by no means a command. It arrives as an optative mood, a wish. It desires that I live a good life. If the self of conscience is my most interior self, then how I evaluate myself ultimately depends on how well I execute the wish of its call. Its self-foundational nature is such that were I not to heed it, I know that I would be betraying who I really am with all the devastating guilt and remorse that would follow. My sense of worth is fundamentally premised on the extent I pursue the kind of life it summons me to follow. It is in this sense that Ricoeur defines 'self-esteem'. I esteem myself insofar as I act as an agent to the enjoinment to live the good life.[12]

My dedication to conscience can offer me counsel, reassurance, peace. Just as often, however, it can result in profound doubt and scepticism. There is a weakness that is intrinsic to the call in its lack of a foundational claim. Its motivation is not secured by known certitudes of any kind. It refers itself to no clear and irrefutable cognitive knowledge for its support. I never know who or what is calling me . . . if anything *is* calling me. Ricoeur recognizes that my testimony to the voice is often haunted by the 'who?' of that voice and therefore can lead to suspicion.[13] Because the call comes from the unknown, if it comes from anywhere, I suspect its nature and therefore suspect what I believe it is asking me to do. I may even distrust myself on whether I know what it is actually asking of me. Despite the frequent ambivalence of the call, I may yet still persist in the decision to listen to it as best as I can on account of an *intuitive faith* I have in it. If my faith has no guarantees, no show of proof, it may yet sense that on some ineffable and inevitable level my decision is the right one. Inherent to this conviction is an instinct that antedates and thus exceeds the conditions of reason and doubt. My approval of the voice derives from an understanding that 'surpasses all understanding'.

The three constituents of the good life schema

The faith in our conscience defining the narrative model under study is intended to orient us toward an ideal life we are to strive for. The identity-type we are considering is therefore teleological in character. It explores this futural state of affairs by borrowing again from Ricoeur who by way of Aristotle describes it as '*aiming at the "good life" with and for others, in just institutions*'.[14] The telos comprises three components: 'the good life', 'with and for others', and 'in just institutions', which develop innately from one another. I will illustrate the triad separately while also indicating how each one can grow into the other.

The 'good' in 'the good life' is not a universalizing notion but rather a question of the good for me as an individual: an objective that exists relative to me and no one else. It refers to those personal goals whose achievement will bring my satisfaction. John Stuart

Mill in his classic work, *On Liberty* (1859), in fact argues that 'The only freedom which deserves the name, is that of pursuing our own good, so long as we do not attempt to deprive others of theirs, or impede their efforts to obtain it. Each is the proper guardian of his own health, whether bodily, or mental or spiritual. Mankind are greater gainers by suffering each other to live as seems good to themselves, than by compelling each to live as seems good to the rest'.[15] With Aristotle in *Nichomachean Ethics* (340 BCE) we can say moreover that the good is oriented toward what is lacking in my life and what I am constantly aspiring for through my practices. It therefore concerns objectives toward which I am currently progressing: desired circumstances that have not yet been reached. Most if not all of our actions are motivated with some form of the good in mind.[16]

'Life', as Aristotle explains, refers to all those empirically essential elements that comprise my being as a whole. It addresses all those aspects that make me an individual: the biologic, cognitive, emotional, and spiritual. The phrase, the 'good life', hence captures the sum of those objectives wherein lies the purpose and satisfaction of my whole person. It involves all those goals whose totality assesses my conduct. They are therefore what constitute the directedness and meaningfulness of my life. They perform the role of its subjective interpretation. Ricoeur identifies the phrase as 'the nebulous of ideals and dreams of achievements with regard to which a life is held to be more or less fulfilled or unfulfilled'.[17] 'Self-esteem' on this level is contingent on the extent of my pursuit and accomplishment of my personal ideals.

If many of our actions have an immediate finality to them, most of them also aim for the higher finality of the good life. The good life, Ricoeur confirms, 'would never cease to be internal to human action'.[18] We do not only act for the short-term but also just as often and at the same time we act for that long-term which gives an overarching destination to our existence. Decisions we consider important, such as those that have to do with our career, relationships, leisure activities, and so on, especially apply to this intentionality. They are usually motivated by our definition of the good life. As Ricoeur makes clear, however, the obverse is equally true. We also tend to redefine and readjust our understanding of the good life according to the type of important decisions we make. A reciprocal interpretation is often enacted between the integrating ideal and the particular choices it integrates. A type of hermeneutic circle is brought to light 'in which the whole and the part are to be understood each in terms of each other'.[19]

Certain experiences can also contribute to the revision of our life plans. They can reorient our self-understanding to such an extent that our dreams and ideals would undergo a fundamental modification. Much as it can provide us with a stable and coherent view of who we are and why we do what do, our conception of the good life cannot remain constant. It has to evolve in response to changes within and outside ourselves. Otherwise it will risk severing its ties with reality and edge itself toward a delusion.

'With and for others' constitutes the second constituent of the good life as defined by Ricoeur. It emerges with the realization that other people also possess their own ideals, that they too can have their own life plans. I recognize that others are also capable of self-esteem insofar as it is directed toward their own sum of ideals. To this end, I realize that my own self-esteem needs to factor in its aims their aims as well. It is therefore required to expand its horizon in order to include those who require assistance in the exercise of their own self-esteem. To deny this dimension is to categorically close myself off from the implacable actuality that I am not and cannot be alone, that I need the help of those around me to pursue my own life-projects just as they need mine. No one can fulfil the good life on one's own. What results is a deep sense of respect, concern, and appreciation for the people around me that stimulates a mode of practice that incorporates both my own interests and theirs. A dialogic relationship is opened between activities geared toward my own ends and those geared toward the ends of others.[20]

Friendship, for Aristotle, is *the* relationship that is premised on the esteem of another's self-esteem. Ricoeur emphasizes that friendship does not pertain primarily to emotions of affection and attachment but to an ethics.[21] In my friend I recognize myself as someone who values themselves as I value myself. I therefore love them as the person they are, and if they are true friends they would return this love. Expressing our mutual recognition and appreciation leads to a life characterized by reciprocity and sharing.

Beyond friendship, the concept of 'solicitude' as explored by Ricoeur inaugurates a more fundamental care to the you of the suffering stranger. Your powerlessness reveals to me what could not have been revealed had you been empowered to decide and act.

The vulnerability you show me mirrors my own potential vulnerability, my own subjection to mortality. I am reminded that I too can fall prey to suffering. Out of a consciousness of our joint finitude, a sense of kinship is thus exchanged that arouses in me feelings of compassion toward you. Solicitude, Ricoeur tells us, comes from a *'benevolent spontaneity'*.[22] From our underlying kinship evolves also the recognition that you too are capable of finding purpose in the world, constructing your own projects, prioritizing some aspirations over others, assessing the goals of your actions, *and thus* valuing yourself the way I value myself.[23] The raw bond between my self-esteem and my solicitude for you provokes what Ricoeur calls an awareness of 'similitude'. It exposes me to the actuality of another as myself, and therefore, myself as that other. What similitude teaches me is that I cannot henceforth esteem myself if I do not esteem you as myself. My praxis is to be derived from this indelible reality.[24]

My solicitude toward you as a vulnerable stranger in turn implies that *all other* others require the same attention as I am giving you. Each and every you around me, Ricoeur explains, is also disposed toward self-esteem and should thereby be treated in exactly the same manner as I am treating you. It is here that the dialogic dimension of the good life unfolds into the societal dimension as indexed in its third constituent: 'in just institutions'. The recognition solicitude inspires has to inherently expand beyond face-to-face encounters to invisible third parties that are also in need of my care. Justice to you presupposes a justice to everyone else. From this principle of fairness is derived the notion of *equality*. The motivation for a universalizing justice originates from the wish to live by according everyone the same dignity as anyone else (including myself). If the you in solicitude was regarded and cared for in all their exceptionality, they must now become *unexceptional* in the requirement to treat every other person as having the same rights and duties as that you.[25] The task toward this vision demands yet a new way of conceiving the self. As Ricoeur makes clear, 'Solicitude provides to the self another who is a face [...]. Equality provides to the self another who is an *each*'.[26]

Political institutions are required to legislate and enforce our commitment to equality. 'By "institution"', Ricoeur explains, 'we are to understand here the structure of *living together* as this belongs to a historical community – people, nation, region, and so forth –

a structure irreducible to interpersonal relations and yet bound up with these in a remarkable sense […]'.[27] In their aspiration to extend the interpersonal relation to third parties, institutional policies have to treat the third party as the standard in any exchange. An *'inclusive middle term'* has to be postulated if the you is to be treated like any other you. If every you is to become an each, limits and conditions to how much I am obliged to help you have to be implemented. To help beyond these stipulations would be officially considered as optional.[28]

Social justice is what ascertains that the standards of care for everyone are met and constantly reassessed. Justice, Ricoeur tells us, has a twofold aim. On the one hand, its distributive aspect seeks to extend the dyadic relationship of solicitude to everyone as much as possible through institutional policies (despite the inevitable restrictions to care that they entail). To accomplish this, justice has to time and again 'touch base' with the personal experience of solicitude, as its original stimulus, in order to disseminate it among the citizens in the fullest and most authentic way possible. By constantly referring itself to its ideal, it can recurrently review and develop its programs and their management in order to revitalize and hence improve its commitment and cultivation of the good. On the other hand, the reparative aspect of justice aspires toward the legal by seeking to enforce equality through the judicial system with its laws and their coherence, along with the right of constraint if the laws are broken. The second facet of justice adjudicates on laws; it believes and depends on their authority. They are its offence and defence to maintain equality or reinstitute it if it has been transgressed. Should the laws expose an inadequacy or contradiction with one another in certain exceptional situations – which admittedly happens quite frequently – justice would then have to turn once more to the ideal of solicitude whence it can procure the wisdom needed to modify the rules in a way that can resolve its dilemmas.[29]

The refiguring identity's schema of the good life just illustrated aims to present us on a fundamental level an integral picture of how to construct our life plans. It provides the ideal *structuration* of what are to be our higher finalities by emphasizing the three dimensions through which we are to enframe our ambitions. The schema proves to be crucial as a standard of reference especially when the validity of those ambitions is questioned, whereby it encourages us to revise and possibly alter them in accordance to its triadic model. It acts as reminder and staunch guide.

By basing its content on the most minimal essentials, the good life schema also ensures the freedom to construct *our own subjective* vision of the good life. It allows us to devise ideals derived from our own particular personality, history, culture, as well as our own needs and interests. The leeway its open-endedness provides means that we can define it through our own personally fulfilling goals while defining those that transcend us *in our own way*. Its indeterminateness is pivotal for the authentic formulation of a future that involves our wellbeing and the wellbeing of others and their environment.

A primary component that enables the refiguring identity to express our differences as individuals is to be sought therefore in the flexible and adaptable features of its objective. The good life ideal constitutes a way of forming our own unique plans without neglecting what transcends our self, namely, other people and social institutions. In modelling what is authentic in us on the inextricable relations of the self, the other, and justice, it stresses a fundamental commitment to ourselves and the world around us that we can nonetheless articulate in a way that is most suited to our peculiar character.

▮ ▮ ▮

The Five Virtues of the Refiguring Identity

The virtues can deliver the good life from self-centred interpretations

It can be argued that the good life schema is not sufficient as an ethical guide to decisions responding to the call of conscience. In the absence of any further ethical parameters, we can easily factor other people and their institutions as part of a personal interpretation of a self-serving type that is precisely inattentive to the actual world around us. Our definition would here include the structural elements of the good life *as a means* to affirm and benefit ourselves. In such cases, we are also not so far off from the inclination to use the schema to reinforce an oppressive or ultraconservative ideology that can include religious fundamentalism, certain forms of socialism, ultranationalism, and even turbocapitalism. What inevitably accounts for the possibility of such self-centred and highly conservatist representations of the good life is the same quality that enables us to explain it in our own authentic mode: the indeterminateness that underlies its minimal schema. We can interpret 'with and for others' and 'just institutions' in virtually any way we wish.

To orient us toward a telos that transcends self-interests, whether conscious or unconscious, the refiguring identity model upholds the practice of several virtues. The concept of virtue designates an excellence of mind and character that is intimately related to ethical behaviour. As a cognitive-affective disposition, a virtue is deeply entrenched in our conduct, characterizing a particular *mindset*. Every virtue in the refiguring identity is in fact committed to a distinctive way of seeing life that acts as a motivator for our decisions. The mindset of every virtue is nonetheless compatible with the rest in such a way that each expands on the other or develops it further. In this sense, they complete each other. The ability to exercise them to their full capacity, however, is difficult to achieve. It is rare for our actions to fulfil the complete potential of any of the virtues, let alone their sum total. Our virtuous decisions are always to some extent preconditioned or at some point swayed by subjective desires that prohibit us from attending sufficiently enough to the situation at hand.

Five virtues inform our action in the refiguring identity model. These it calls 'exposure', 'imagination', 'practical wisdom', 'acceptance', and 'hope'. Their shared mission is to provide a hermeneutic framework that can direct our decisions toward a more altruistic and inclusive vision of the good life on which we can base our praxis. This directedness is offered primarily through their common character of *affirming the foreign in experience*. The mindset of every virtue extols a type of susceptibility to what is other to us in the outside world. In their distinct modes, the virtues train us to engage with what at any point in time can differ from the 'normality' we have established for ourselves with its circumscribed knowledge. In doing so, they let other 'realities' reveal and impress themselves upon our self-enclosed 'reality', revising it for development if needed. Included especially in this reassessment is our personal vision of the good life, whose contact with ideas and facts that it might have misinterpreted or neglected can further its growth. Only by acknowledging and registering perspectives that are foreign to ours can we avoid the pitfalls of self-absorbed ideologies and ensure that we are on the way toward a knowledge of a better future that is integral and authentic. Herein lies the conviction of all of the five virtues.

Consumerist life-strategies as simulations of the virtues

The lifestyles disseminated by the consumer culture tend to promote their own personality values, which are perhaps in part a symptom of the postmodern Western predicament of a general absence of metanarratives and traditions. Social thinkers like Christopher Lasch, Anthony Giddens, and Zygmunt Bauman hold that in consequence of this loss, a new normality seems to have arrived where our exposure to situations in life that are uncertain, ambiguous, and contradictory to our worldview has reached an unprecedented regularity.[1] What has therefore necessarily grown in demand, in my view, is a certain model outlook that can defuse and successfully engage with this kind of circumstances. The lifestyles advertised by the market in fact all come prepackaged with similar attributes capable of turning the pervasive presence of the unknown in everyday life into a productive force. Rather than inclining us to fear, suppress, or escape from the disorienting unfamiliar, they all seek in some manner to redefine them from a source of disruption and potential disempowerment to a source of potential happiness, personal growth, and self-fulfilment. Not only so, but they even anticipate and actively search for them in the belief that they can genuinely sublimate our life into a more satisfying and exciting version. The five most prominent personality traits that claim to accomplish the task, I will term, 'open-mindedness' or 'openness', 'creativity', 'instrumental reason', 'surrender', and 'desire'.

In many respects, the values displayed by today's commercial life-strategies seem to bear an uncanny affinity with the five refiguring identity virtues, each one operating as a counterpart to the other. Given their consumerist framework, however, they evidently differ from them at the same time – evincing a resemblance to them that seems to be distorted and incomplete. We can perhaps best capture their peculiar association through the mode of organization that Jean Baudrillard in *The Consumer Society* (1970) calls 'simulating'. To 'simulate' or to 'recycle' for Baudrillard entails a predominantly industrial trend that is increasingly being applied to every aspect of our culture and society. Corporal, medical, fashion, mass culture, and cultural creativity simulation are explored but it is in his illustration of Nature's simulation that a revealing analogy can be drawn.

Like so many other facets of everyday life, Nature, Baudrillard explains, has today undergone a process of 'rediscovery' but:

> in the form of countryside trimmed down to the dimensions of a mere sample, surrounded on all sides by the vast fabric of the city, carefully policed, and served up 'at room temperature' as parkland, nature reserve or background scenery for second homes […]. [I]t is no longer an original, specific presence at all, standing in symbolic opposition to culture, but a simulation, a 'consommé' of the signs of nature set back in circulation […].[2]

The Nature that we now propagate has nothing to do with our conception of Nature in the past as a wild and foreign force. Previous generations saw in Nature a world that is alien to civilization: an incontinent, measureless, and mysterious presence that abides outside our organized and coherent reality, occasionally resisting and even destroying our self-profiting projects. What has popularly emerged instead in our times is an idea of Nature that is *managed for us*: manipulable in accordance to our current tastes of what looks beautiful. The simulated Nature that is being disseminated does not refer to what is other to us, what transcends us, but is of an order that is designed to satisfy our aesthetical styles.[3] It has come to reflect the ubiquity of our ego, whose archetypal process has appropriated the alterity of Nature into an object for its self-affirming consumption. As Teresa Brennan points out in *History After Lacan* (1993), 'The ego [...] is opposed to the history of anything different from itself. It is interested in difference only in so far as everything different from it provides it with a mirror for itself. In this respect, it will reduce all difference to sameness'.[4] What has been really rediscovered therefore is a Nature that has been packaged as a product for our enjoyment.

It can be argued that another simulation procedure has taken place in the production of the five lifestyle values on account of their separation from an essential part of what might have constituted their originary significance. Analogous to the contemporary simulation of Nature, 'open-mindedness', 'creativity', 'instrumental reason', 'surrender', and 'desire' express attributes that have been *processed* in the manner of all other commodities so that their definition now converges on our subjective wellbeing while excluding all reference to an external environment. Their simulation can be explained as the result of their embeddedness in the lifestyles' flat linear narratives fixated on self-enjoyment. If they pose as dispositions capable of turning unfamiliar situations to a productive process, they do so by ironically narrowing down our view of them to mere opportunities for our personal gain. This conforms to their common fundamental vision of an insatiable exploitation of anything for the satisfaction that can be extracted from it. An acquisitive perception unifies the behaviour they encourage whereby our environment becomes a map of potential resources for our egotistic use. The values they offer us are thereby served up solely for our comfort, at 'room temperature' as it were. For this reason, they are anything but 'virtues', which typically refer to standards of behaviour that are founded on responsibilities that transcend self-care in involving other people and social institutions.

Nonetheless, the refiguring identity model sees in the lifestyle values the *potentiality* of five modes of relating meaningfully with events that are outside our self-jurisdiction. It too holds that to be able to engage effectively with what is foreign to us is crucial for the times we live in and were it not for their narcissistic underpinnings, the lifestyle values would provide inspiring directives on how we can make sense of what often does not seem to. To this end, the identity seeks to *retrieve* what it broadly considers to be the values' authentic significance by drawing on a few select philosophical writings that explore faculties, values, and virtues that bear a respective similarity to them. In its perusal of these texts, it draws attention to the particular modes of affirmation that these qualities all demonstrate in relation to the outside (rather than exploitations), which it then seeks to recapture in the corresponding virtues it introduces us to. The virtues are given different names from their lifestyle 'equivalents' predominantly in order to highlight their inherent reference to the foreign component.

By directing the five virtues toward the objective of the good life, the refiguring identity model also opens them to an ethical dimension. Their interaction with the outside comes to be regarded as a possible means to develop our ethical vision and its praxis with their focus on our solicitude toward others and society. 'Exposure', 'imagination', 'practical wisdom', 'acceptance', and 'hope' can indeed be said to represent a more complete and fundamental version of the lifestyle values in augmenting their horizons of care to include not just ourselves as individuals but the world around us with its diverse experiences. If the values guide us on how to affirm ourselves through alterity, the virtues, along with the refiguring narrative in which they are embedded, guide us on how to affirm that alterity in view of how to make the world with its people and customs a better place. The virtues thus instruct us on how to affirm alterity in the most ethical way possible. They provide a general ethics of alterity.

The virtues as gifts of the call

The significance of the five virtues is also expanded on account of their integration in the overall narrative of conscience. The narrative attributes to them a particular nature that distinguishes them as well from the corresponding qualities in most of the philosophical texts referenced for comparison. The closest definition to their distinctive nature is captured by Gabriel Marcel's own concept of a virtue in his essay, 'Sketch of a Phenomenology and Metaphysic of Hope' (1951). Marcel writes the following in connection to hope as a virtue among others:

> [T]he truth is that all virtue is the particularisation of a certain interior force, and that to live in hope is to obtain from oneself that one should remain faithful in the hour of darkness to that which in its origin was perhaps only an inspiration, an exaltation, a transport. But there is no doubt that this faithfulness cannot be put into practice except by virtue of a co-operation, whose principle will always remain a mystery, between the goodwill which is after all the only positive contribution of which we are capable and certain promptings whose centre remains beyond our reach, in those realms where values are divine gifts.[5]

In contrast to character values, virtues, we are told, are not dispositions that we can acquire with full intent for ourselves. They are always already *given to us* before we have ever chosen them. They are received from a transcendental force that yet speaks to our interiority. In expressing this force in particular ways, in enabling *us* to express it – through their performance, they are described as 'divine gifts'. Virtues are capacities to manifest the divine offered us by the divine.

In a similar fashion, the refiguring narrative enjoins us to receive the virtues through the call of conscience. They are not our active response to the call inasmuch as they are ways through which we can embody it. We express the call when we affirm them in our conduct. To welcome them is to welcome the invitation to aspire for the good life. The call offers them to us so we can live well. In different ways, their performance heralds a path toward a better world for us and everyone. 'Exposure', 'imagination', 'practical wisdom', 'acceptance', and 'hope' respectively express the five indissociable frames of mind required for such a future to be conceived and constructed. As such, they are the call's 'gifts' to us. In arriving from the call, they share in its anteriority to our self-constitution and the ontotheology of being and beings. They are, for the refiguring identity, *innate* to us all regardless of whether we subscribe to its story or the extent of our susceptibility to what we believe is conscience. The refiguring identity instead sees its commitment as drawing our attention to what are already our inmost dispositions despite the fact that we are more than often diverted by individualistic desires.

To practice the refiguring virtues is to have given our consent to them. It is to have made ourselves available for them to work through us. We make the decision to accept an invitation that has always already taken place. This is perhaps what Marcel means when he speaks of our 'co-operation' and 'goodwill' toward the 'mysterious principle'. Being virtuous is therefore to have our thoughts and deeds stimulated, sometimes even inspired, by our willingness to receive the call.

The virtues as aspects of the refiguring decision and their difficulty in practice

Each chapter that follows will treat a virtue separately to study it in some detail. This should not, however, mislead us from seeing all virtues as *aspects* of *one* single decision that is focused on what is other to us in any experience. As the underlying components of any crucial decision issued by the refiguring identity, they can be compared to the Kantian apriori categories in the cognition of objects. In its endeavour to understand an experience as much as is possible on its own terms, the decision they configure is essentially hermeneutical. It seeks to put all our judgements and assumptions at risk in order to bear witness to what the event in itself, as itself, could be disclosing to us.

In reevaluating and possibly renewing our ethical vision, the decision undertaken can be described as 'refiguring' us, whence the identity model it is derived from also draws its name. The efficacy of this decision especially relies on the dialogue that all five virtues conduct with one another as it is being deliberated. If the virtues are to be practiced in synchrony, the same synchronicity has to produce at the same time a *reciprocity of influence*. The exercise of each virtue impacts upon the others in such a way that each is assessed and motivated in its performance by the rest. A network of mutual impression and empowerment is brought into play that also helps to contain and rectify the possible wayward behaviour of any virtue by reason of our fallibilities. In their interactions, the virtues can thus also regulate one another. If the refiguring decision is to be successful, none of them is to be given autonomous license. Only as a symbiotic group are they capable of aspiring toward the life we are called upon to desire. A narrative statement that captures the refiguring decision can chart out the role of every virtue as follows:

> Because I *hope* for a better life, I *expose* myself to the foreign in experience, and yet I *imaginatively* reconcile myself with it as well as discover through *practical wisdom* what moral projects need to be done at its behest, while all along *accepting* it as always foreign to me.

The refiguring decision is taken in times when we are called by conscience to respond ethically to a certain event. Its assumption issues from a prereflective drive to act according to certain circumstances for the good life to be eventually realized.

It is no easy feat to surrender ourselves completely to what the virtues ask of us. Our main obstacle would always remain some aspect of our ego-cogito and its possessive compulsion of turning anything it sets its gaze on into an object it can determine and control. Likewise, the virtues along with their telos can easily attach themselves to its own criteria and agenda, subjecting them to its manipulation. Our ethical conduct is never so far from its appropriation. To give in to the ego is often to *forget* our faithfulness in the call. As a result, the virtues it expresses itself with are misidentified for character values of the kind promoted by the consumer culture lifestyles, in their degradation into features of ourselves we can direct and modify at will.

The practice of the virtues is therefore a project in the making in its own right. It inaugurates a journey of development whereby our receptivity to the five dispositions is constantly assessed and reassessed through the memory of how we engaged with the outside world in the past and the knowledge it has provided us. With the refiguring narrative schema as point of reference, we improve the exercise of the virtues by reviewing the ways we have formerly interacted with experience and the sort of hermeneutics elicited. Improvement also entails vigilance *as* we exercise the virtues in order to prevent our preflective criteria, including especially our own idea of the good life, from dictating our hermeneutical decisions. To disown our biases as much as possible, our virtuous practice often requires us to concentrate on the originary enjoinment of conscience. To act 'rightly' we often have to *renew* our attentiveness, our complete faith in the call.

IV

From Openness to Exposure

Openness for arousal and status

Highly esteemed for all consumer culture lifestyles is the ability to be open or open-minded to the non-routine in life, to be a risk-taker. They emphasize that a key factor in our growth is the ability to break out of our comfortzone and seize any unusual opportunity that the moment has to offer. We should be ready, they tell us, to embrace difference and change. We must be able to adapt to them and let them transform us. Our times, Zygmunt Bauman claims in *Liquid Modernity* (1999), promote a mindset based on the three characteristics of flexibility, absorptiveness, and adjustability to the novel and surprising.[1] We are required to develop 'the capacity to move swiftly where the action is and be ready to take in experiences as they come [...]'.[2] To be open in this sense is 'to live through sensations not yet tried and impossible to specify in advance'.[3]

In the consumer culture, we are urged to take on the unprecedented above all *insofar* as it evokes the allure of *prestige*. Product and service updates, novelty, brands, high prices, general popularity as well as the luxurious and/or exotic connotations of their look and their endorsement by influencer or lifestyle expert or celebrity, all factor in varying degrees in constructing an aura of status around them. These *signs* collude in the organization of a status system wherein commodities are often unconsciously placed and interpreted. Jean Baudrillard in *The Consumer Society* (1970) clearly marks out status and enjoyment as the two criteria that determine our choice of commodified experiences when he explains that 'rather than matching up "aspirations, needs and satisfactions" as it claims to do, this society creates ever greater disparities both among individuals and among social groups who are wrestling, on the one hand, with the imperative of competition and upward social mobility and, on the other, with the – now highly internalized imperative to maximalize their pleasures'.[4]

Commodity-status has been termed by various sociological and philosophical thinkers as 'cultural capital'. The concept has been developed by Pierre Bourdieu in *Distinction* (1979) and 'The Forms of Capital' (1986) as well as by Michele Lamont and Annette Lareau in 'Cultural Capital' (1988). Contrary to economic capital, which is instantly calculable, realizable, and exchangeable, cultural capital is a more abstract form of wealth that derives its power and investment from cultural beliefs. It is based on the accumulation of materials that society deems valuable for their own sake, as separate from their functional value. To possess a high level of cultural capital is to follow the dictates of the current fashion, to be in the know. Mike Featherstone discloses that the worth of such an investment, though often hidden and misrecognized, 'may nonetheless be redeemable and reconvertible back into economic value through a whole series of direct and indirect routes'.[5] Cultural capital, he explains, referencing Bourdieu's essay, 'The Forms of Capital', 'can exist in the *embodied* state (style of presentation, mode of speech, beauty, etc.), *objectified* state (cultural goods like pictures, books, machines, buildings, etc.), and in the *institutionalized* state (such as educational qualifications)'.[6]

The prominence of cultural capital in consumer culture can be seen for instance in tourism, which defines the idea of travel as the search for the *authentic experience*. The search, as Ian Munt makes clear in his essay 'The "Other" Postmodern Tourism' (1994), is often motivated to increase our social standing, to distinguish us from the rest. The accumulation of 'real' experiences in the repertory of our life – the more exotic, the more real they are often considered to be – is here an investment in social recognition.[7] Evidence of our 'worth' is seen especially through the pictures and videos we take of our vacations, usually filtered in order to enhance their 'foreign' element and thereby their value as consumed objects.

The promise of *arousal* constitutes the other indicator for our choice of novelty in a consumer culture. We are urged to try different commodities on account of the new and better feelgood emotions they are supposed to deliver. In this sense we are to shop for positive feelings – previously unfelt and enhanced. Bauman highlights that 'excitement of a new and unprecedented sensation is the name of the consumer game. Consumers are first and foremost gatherers of sensations [...]'.[8] The experiences we are urged to buy and pursue often come with the guarantee of being affectively intense. It is above all their capacity to make us 'feel alive', to 'revitalize' us that is made to justify their marketability as 'breakthroughs' to our mundane existence. We are therefore often told that to go for these experiences requires an act of courage and sheer determination. It would take a leap from our less-than-real quotidianity, governed by work, responsibility, and routine, to their more-than-real or hyperreal world where enlightenment surely awaits. Typical lifestyle motivational slogans advertising the decision to take up the adventures their products offer us include: 'Let your spirit run free'; 'Go where the guides don't'; 'Leave ordinary behind'; 'Dare to be great'; 'Be fearless in the pursuit of what sets your soul on fire'; 'Let your faith be bigger than your fears, have faith success will be near'; 'No dream is too big when you realize abundance is your birthright'; 'Open yourself to new and wonderful changes'; 'Today create a wonderful new day and a wonderful new future'; 'Be unique, be brave, be divine'; 'Find your inner diva'; 'It's hard to be nice if you don't feel comfortable'; 'Life begins at the end of your comfortzone'; and so on and so forth.

In her work, Melanie K. Smith shows that the attraction toward the unexpected intense is nowadays prevalent in the popularity of new leisure tourism, which is focused exclusively on escapism, entertainment, and fun. The difference of these tourists from the traditional ones lies in their unabashed disinterest in local societies and cultures, which are substituted in their itineraries for activities oriented around the pursuit of excitement and thrills usually from the secure confines of a hotel, resort, or themed attraction.[9]

Leisure tourists are perhaps one of the most immoderate representatives of that mindset Bauman calls the 'aesthetic space', which captures in different measures the mode of conduct of most types of travellers. For Bauman, tourists navigate a world that is mapped on what is 'novel and surprising (the mysterious, simultaneously dazzling and vaguely frightening – the sublime) [...]'.[10] The moment a site, an activity, or an encounter loses its potential to amuse, they move on to the next one, exhibiting what Bauman in 'The Tourist Syndrome' (2003) calls 'grazing behaviour'. Tourists' journeys are thus directed by the search for 'experiences – unlike the experiences they lived through before, unlike everything else they knew [...]. But sensations are un-experienced and tastes are untried only once'.[11] Once they grow familiar, their appeal is lost, they grow dull, and so the tourists will move on to another field of unsampled adventures to graze on.

> Tourists have by definition 'pure relationship' to the place they visit – 'pure' meaning that it has no other purpose than the consumption of pleasurable sensation and that once the satisfaction wanes, it wilts and fades as well – and so [they] to another relationship, hopefully as 'pure' as the last one. The world of pure relationships is a huge collection of grazing grounds, and living in such a world is shaped after the pattern of wandering from one succulent and fragrant meadow to another.[12]

It is against the tourist protocol to commit to anything. In their insatiable search for what is fresh and vivid, tourists cannot afford to settle or belong anywhere they go to. The aesthetic space they are expected to inhabit, that they pay for in fact, precisely licenses their free-floating psychology. As a result, the connections they build on their way are often loose enough to be easily abandoned when the time comes to move on to the next adventure. By living from one moment to the next, living for the moment, travellers often hardly worry about the far-reaching consequences of their decisions.[13]

In equal measure, the kingdom of fashion, as Japanese designer Rei Kawakubo announces, 'has no reality except in stimulation'.[14] Thrills in the world of fashion are not only contingent on achieving originality within the bounds of conformity as Georg Simmel explains.[15] Gilles Lipovetsky remarks that it is also aspired for in the adoption of looks to evoke specific emotions, personalities, and character traits. Changing wardrobes is regarded as a renewal of our psychological makeup. Intense pleasure is derived from 'transforming oneself in one's own eyes and those of others, of "changing one's skin," feeling like – and becoming – someone else, by changing the way one dresses'.[16] It was haute couture that first diversified style in an attempt to capture through wear a spectrum of personalities.[17]

If the arousal so promoted by the travel and fashion lifestyles (along with fitness) is usually defined in relation to the physical, self-spirituality transposes it into a spiritual domain, variously calling it 'peak experience', 'enlightenment', and 'self-realization', among other terms. In its belief that the transcendental reality is immanent in the material reality, however, several of its theories prescribe the pursuit of our psychological and physical wellbeing as well as material success as crucial, even indissociable for our spiritual evolution. If our body and physical environment are expressive manifestations of the 'cosmic force', then, their enjoyment is seen to be an indispensable means toward reaching the spiritual realm. In assuming a dominant role as a locus of enlightenment, material enjoyment thus becomes almost or as important as nonmaterial enjoyment. Indeed, the close proximity in nature of these two separate types of experiences in self-spiritual discourses can some-times result in their professed mergence. As Russell W. Belk, Melanie Wallendorf, and John F. Sherry Jr. claim in 'The Sacred and the Profane in Consumer Behavior' (1989), 'the rise of individu-alism has made it possible to define the sacred as that which brings secular ecstasy to the individual',[18] as happiness becomes intrinsi-cally implicated with the fulfilment of the self. And to be fulfilled for self-spiritualists, as Andrew Dawson makes clear, is to attain a deep knowledge of existence that gives rise to cosmic mastery.[19]

If arousal is seen to constitute a decisive criterion for our choice of experience in the consumerist life-strategies, then, it is also often regarded as having a coterminous relationship with the other crite-rion of status. The life-strategy discourses often presuppose a reciprocity of effect between the two whereby the object that arouses is given status while status itself is seen to arouse. One is believed to mirror the other in a single package.

The value of openness in the entrepreneurship lifestyle is also provided with a central role though its appraisal is here intrinsically connected with a firm's survival, growth, and profitability. The demand to keep pace, or better, to outpace, the endless economic fluctuations of the market with its constantly evolving technology calls for a readiness to see a potential for creative change in what might otherwise be seen as an intimidating complication or diffi-culty. The ideal entrepreneurs must have the instinct to recognize and embrace unprecedented situations and utilize them to imple-ment innovation by altering their business strategy or formulate untried ideas to cut costs, accumulate profits, and/or improve the bottom lines. Wright Schermerhorn Jr. in *Management* (2014) writes that 'A classic entrepreneur is someone who takes risks to pursue opportunities in situations that others may view as problems or threats'.[20] In *Personality Traits of Entrepreneurs: A Review of*

Recent Literature (2018), Sari Pekkala Kerr, William R. Kerr, and Tina Xu likewise emphasize the significance of welcoming changing environments and new challenges in order to design creative solutions and business models and products through such situations.[21] On a similar trend, Thomas Grebel and Christopher Freeman indicate that entrepreneurship theories have often focused on the entrepreneurs' motivation to alter the products they produce and create new investment, growth, and employment in their firm by drawing upon the discoveries of scientists and inventors as well as the ideas of philosophers that have not yet been applied to economic processes.[22]

Exposure is the readiness to see the foreign in experience

All of the mainstream lifestyle discourses usually present risk-taking or open-mindedness or openness to the unexpected and unordinary in an overwhelmingly positive light. Their language, aimed for instant engagement, confers above all an exciting grandeur to our journeys into the unknown. Ignored is the much less appealing side to such decisions.

In his major work, *Truth and Method* (1960), Hans-Georg Gadamer draws attention to the indispensable 'negative' aspect of openness when he explores the mindframe of what we typically call the 'experienced person'. For Gadamer, we often misperceive what it means to be experienced on account of our disregard of the importance of an experience's *'negativity'*. The quality at issue, he claims, does not amount to a sum total of knowledge that has been amassed from a large number of past events. To think this is to imply that there is a finality to our knowledge, that there can come a point at which we can say that our understanding about life is now complete, our learning process concluded. Consequently, what-ever else can come to pass would no longer contradict us. It would only serve to confirm our omniscience and would be made redundant. Novelty of any sort would be obsolete.[23]

To be experienced is rather to understand *through* experiences what Gadamer calls 'the *process* of experience'.[24] This process 'stands in an ineluctable opposition to knowledge and to the kind of instruction that follows from general theoretical or technical knowledge'.[25] It entails the revelation of insights whose anomalousness *undermines* everything we already know. To be experienced is to have gone through times that have violently shaken and altered, what Gadamer would call, our 'horizon of understanding'[26] over and over again. A predisposition is subsequently developed to accept our submission to change once more when the unprecedented happens again. We grow in our willingness to be deeply instructed once more, always once more, by what life throws at us. The experienced person, Gadamer claims, is 'someone who is radically undogmatic; who, because of the many experiences he has had and the knowledge he has drawn from them, is particularly well equipped to have new experiences and to learn from them'.[27] The cultivation of an affirming orientation toward the unknown therefore signifies the prospect of having our expectations questioned and disappointed, our worldview uprooted to dispose ourselves to a new understanding of life. The consumer culture lifestyles, and for Gadamer, our everyday conception of experience, precisely dismiss and suppress this negativity.

'Exposure' is that virtue in the refiguring identity that expresses our consent to be open to experience. As a term, 'exposure' means placing ourselves at risk or the state of having no protection. As a virtue enabling the refiguring decision, it enjoins us to be vulnerable to the outside world. It motivates us to be psychosomatically prepared to suspend and jeopardize all our prejudices and judgements for whatever may arrive in the near future. We do not know what is to arrive but we need to be willing to unlearn all that we have learnt when it does. 'Exposure' signifies a preemptive yes to our negativity. It is a yes that must be constantly re-confirmed.

What the virtue asks us to ratify is the not-us in the outside world. On such occasions, the call of conscience asks us to give ourselves to the potential *otherness* of an experience – which can be *any* experience – in order to let it act upon us as it will. We are to revert to a mode of seeing that provokes the foreign from a familiar or unfamiliar episode for its disclosure in all its unmediated foreignness. Exposure seeks *to expose* what can usually be hidden in the guise of ordinariness, sameness: that moment's singular difference from us. When enjoined, exposure motivates and continuously revives an uncompromised susceptibility to the unknown principle in existence. It expands on the meaning of the consumer culture's value of openness to account not only for that otherness that is intrinsic to the new experience but also for that latent otherness that can be found anywhere in our surroundings and encounters in any single moment of our life.

By embracing the prospect of self-uprootedness, exposure embraces the prospect of our *self-transformation*. It testifies to the admission that our worldview with its own representation of the good life is far from omniscient – that it will always be inherently incapable of fully comprehending the world *as it is*. In its coherence, our vision of an ideal future will always inevitably exclude other worldviews, other visions, as well as certain aspects of existence. Our portrayal of a better future for everyone will always be limited in some manner. Consequently, it must always remain open to further revision and change. As with the rest of the virtues, exposure is thus characterized by a deep humility. The decision to take the leap out of the known and into the unknown also takes courage, which is another attribute that is present in all five virtues. The statement expressing the refiguring decision positions the virtue in the second clause: 'Because I hope for a better life, I *expose* myself to the foreign in experience . . . '[28]

Consumer culture experiences as images (Baudrillard)

Mainstream lifestyle discourses tend to deemphasize or disregard completely the negative side to openness in their attempt to turn the character trait into a selling-point. The idea of celebrating what is outside our familiar horizons is here presented in connection to the experience delivered by commodities whose only intent is to be sold. In a commercial system, the idea of openness is *meant* to be instantly appealing. Any connotations that might suggest it to be an arduous process have no place in the sensational, hyper-optimistic visuals and language that are usually affixed to market wares.

In a consumer culture, it is above all the *image* of the experience that the commodity evokes that convinces us to choose it over others. Openness is encouraged by the *glamorous looks* of any purchasable object and scenario that is advertised in the media. The predominating influence of the image in the late twentieth and twenty-first century Western society has in fact been a focal subject for several sociologists, cultural theorists, and philosophers. The general consensus is that everyday life has become saturated with the rapid flow of titillating images capturing product experiences that promise bliss if tasted. The theorization of this essentially post-modern culture has drawn much from Karl Marx's extensive observations on the fetishism of commodities, which have been developed in variant ways by György Lukács, Henri Lefebvre, the Frankfurt School, Wolfgang Fritz Haug, Frederic Jameson, and Jean Baudrillard.

Under late-capitalism, Baudrillard claims, our consumerist choice of novelty is not determined by the inherent character of what it refers to. Our purchases do not consider the material utility or use-value of products and services. It is their appearances that have assumed primary importance insofar as they have become *markers* of certain values. What commodities taste like has been externalized into signs that allude to different levels of status and stimulation. An abstract system of emotive meaning is thereby created out of the sign-values allotted to commodities, which we come to read fluently through our overexposure to their displays. This system is a language in the Sausserean sense of the term in that the signified of any of its signifiers is determined by its position or difference from the others. The signified is here decoded exclusively through the comparative looks of commodities and any allusion to an outside reality or standard of truth is absent. In signifying only in relation to one another, commodity images therefore operate through a self-referential system of meaning. This signification is also constantly shifting as new images are introduced while others are enhanced, degraded, outdated, or recycled in value.[29]

Commercial lifestyles are fully embedded in the same coded system in their prioritization of the manicured display of their product experiences over their interior character. The 'actuality' of the experience is here substituted in value by its glossy image, whose aesthetic by degrees evokes the prestige of luxury, exotica, beauty, romance, and other 'aristocratic' and feelgood emotions. What the prolific outpour of lifestyle pictures and videos on Instagram, Facebook, YouTube, and TikTok, for instance, often demonstrates is how far their interpretation has become dominated by their pervasive aesthetics. Generic images on the social media that in many ways have come to define fashion, fitness, self-spiri-tuality, travel, and to an extent even entrepreneurship, include complicated healthy dishes that are often vegetarian, vegan, and/or foreign; exotic regions in remote countries (ideally Asian) that are touristic landmarks or refer to some local customs; sporting the chic outfits of the season; the practice of adventure sports (abseiling, climbing, kayaking, snorkelling, trekking, etcetera); postures in the countryside to suggest some sort of oneness with nature; spiritual exercises preferably involving a nature setting (beach and rocky sunsets are a favourite) and physical gestures suggesting harmony, balance, and peace (yoga practice is always effective at portraying this), and so on and so forth.

What the proliferation of lifestyle images testifies to above all is the prevalence of a media-generated aestheticized world that precisely constitutes the general nature of consumer culture. The sensational, spectacular, and idealistic qualities of these images stimulate a fascination that encourages their imitation in our life. Their all-encompassing spectrum of intensity and status often tends to stimulate us to comprehend our life in accordance to their standard. Life becomes a tirelessly active venture to model itself on the media fantasy. What we had formerly considered as real is emptied out, its point of reference supplanted by the media-conjured world that has become in turn the new 'real'.

Bauman stresses on the mediation of society by consumer culture in 'Identity – Then, Now, What For?' (1998) where he notes that social relationships have been subjected to 'the powerful images on ubiquitous screens that set the standard for reality, for its evaluation, for the urge to do something to make it more palat-able'.[30] In his later work, *Simulacra and Simulations* (1981), Baudrillard likewise argues that the density and overwhelming production of images in our society heralds a qualitatively new society where 'TV is the world', where the distinction between reality and image ceases to exist. It is replaced instead by a perpetual aesthetic absorption.[31] Art is no longer its own autonomous world but has impregnated the production and repro-duction of all goods so that everything 'even if it be the everyday and banal reality, falls by this token under the sign of art, and becomes aesthetic'.[32] The end of the dichotomy between the real and art leads to a *hyperreality* or *simulation world* whose idealistic images are not anchored in any sense of reality as this has been effaced. The meaning of hyperreal images refers only to themselves. We find ourselves, Featherstone remarks, in 'a world in which the piling up of signs, images and simulations through consumerism and television results in a destabilized, aestheticized hallucination of reality'.[33] For Baudrillard, 'it is quotidian reality in its entirety – political, social, historical and economic – that from now on incorporates the simulating dimension of hyperrealism'.[34]

What the consumer culture lifestyles count as experience thus often comes to be *misrecognized* for its hyperreal images. Experience is chosen, assessed, and altered in accordance to the media aesthetic. It is not enjoyed for itself but for its signs. Our lifestyle becomes a pursuit that is more makebelieve than authentic. It verges closer to a fantasy of prestige than an honest expression of our subjectivity.[35]

The worlds of fashion and fitness especially are defined by a hyperreal standard of beauty that prescribes our behaviour. Baudrillard confirms that a manipulation of our looks is here continuously in the works as we seek to conform to the ever-updating images prefabricated and disseminated by the industry as *the* standard of every comparison. To be paragons of what we are shown as beauty is to single ourselves out as members of the elite and emancipated. We take endless and inordinate care of our faces and figures to turn them into markers of our 'election and salvation [...]'.[36]

The achievement of the hyperreal look in fitness and fashion is believed to be the gateway to a transfiguration of our selfhood. In fashion, the permutations of clothes, accessories, and cosmetic products that are to be imitatively applied are seen to be so many seductive personalities we can try on and become. In a very literal sense, fashion presumes that it can grant us the gift of changing or upgrading our self to any self we desire if we follow its media-produced and reproduced visual dictates.

In fitness, the aspiration for the high-status body is also the aspiration for a new inner self. The sole purpose of the 'incomplete' self we currently possess is to work on the body. It is conceived strictly as *the will* to possess the idealized look. The physical improvements that result are seen to reflect the extent of our capacity to reveal who we really are. Our true inner self is seen to emerge through the enhancement of our outer self. The closer we are to reaching the high-status body, the more authentic, the more 'actual' we believe we have become. Success and contentment thus depend on our distance from this destination. As Barry Glassner emphasizes in 'Fitness and the Postmodern Self' (1989), the physique is here 'a cardinal sign of the self'.[37] It is the body and its futural possibilities that makes me *me*. By this logic, the outer and inner self become indistinguishable from one another.

Also absorbed by the simulational reality of consumer culture is tourism, which in many cases has gone beyond the influence of adverts, reality shows, documentaries, virtual tour guides, etcetera, on our travels. The simulational has become a form of tourism in itself. Social thinkers like Scott Lasch, John Urry, Chris Rojek, and George Ritzer draw attention to the contemporary decline in the belief that physical travel can offer an unparalleled and authentic experience. This is replaced instead by the conviction that the history and culture of a destination can be experienced as intensely (and perhaps even more so) through onscreen media and their multiplicity of interpretations.[38] Representations of tourist sites have become just as significant in value as the sites themselves. In *Ways of Escape* (1993), Rojek indicates that there is an increasing indifference in drawing any distinction between an original and its hyped-up images, which is exhibited in the popularity of holidays that are designed specifically to be entertained by various simulational environments. The itinerary of such tourists hardly features events that revolve around a country's actual culture and history but is rather focused on visits to shopping centres, department stores, theme parks, and other sites that inspire fascination by hyperreal images.[39]

To expose ourselves is to suffer

While the virtue of exposure refers us to actuality and its irreducible difference from us, the value of openness exploited by the commercial life-strategies refers actuality to an aesthetic hallucination of signs that has itself usurped the originary role of actuality. It is the hyperreal that now comes to determine *which* new experiences we are to pick and *how* we should experience them. The criteria it sets for our conduct are expressed especially in visual codes that signify various levels of arousal and status.

If the mode of engagement with the outside world prescribed for us by consumer culture is principally concerned with narcissistic investment, then it categorically devalues and often dismisses what cannot be utilized for our self-aggrandisement. Circumstances grounded in issues that transcend the self are abandoned. Virtually excluded from the fashionable moments the consumer culture puts on display are situations that are *ethical* and *political* by nature. In the lifestyles' hyperreal there is no place, for instance, for care toward a suffering stranger or a poor family's squalid existence. Nor is it 'cool' to exhibit any affiliation with an NGO in protest against our government's corruption or the greed of corporate CEOs, or any active commitment against saving natural attractions from development. It is rare to find any activities of the kind featured in the lifestyles' glossy vision as propagated by the media. What the vision tends to tell us instead, in the hyper-optimistic manner that characterizes its hyperreal character, is that our happiness *means* that everything else is or will be just fine. 'Stay positive and good things and good people will be drawn to you.' 'Smile and the world will smile with you.'

The virtue of exposure does not seek to subordinate our environment to preset criteria. Quite the contrary, it seeks to let it reveal itself *as itself*. An experience, familiar or new, is approached insofar as it is unconcealed as irreducibly other to us. While the openness mindset in consumer culture reveals experience by enabling a self-centred system of meaning, exposure reveals it *as a disabling* of our systems of meaning. In different degrees, our exposure becomes a *suffering*, where 'suffering' refers to a process of dispossession brought about by a ceding all control to a foreign outside. The subject becomes the subjected. We abdicate our status as interpretative master to a hostage to the outside's emergence.

Suffering can thus be seen as an endurance characterized by a process of *negative* or *negating infinity*. This conception of forbearance is not so far removed from Emmanuel Levinas's own phenomenological idea of infinity, which is explored at some length in *Totality and Infinity* (1961) in connection to the ethical scene. Our subjection to the event of the vulnerable other introduces an incessant failure in our recursive efforts at representing it. An interminable nonadequation is perpetuated between our appropriating impulses and the other's radical unfolding. 'Infinition' is the more proper term that Levinas uses to capture the active endlessness of the event, whereby the limits imposed by our ego, the limits of our ego are incessantly breaking down 'as revelation, as a positing of [the event's] idea in *me*'.[40]

The infinity endemic to suffering is also analyzed by Maurice Blanchot, who similarly describes it as an endless and increasing incapacity to do or be anything. The suffering of what is variously termed 'passivity', 'neuter', 'outside', and 'passion' among other names, entails the absence of reprieve or finality in a disempowering that is continuously exceeding itself in its disempowering, a passivity that is recurrently surpassing itself. This passivity, Blanchot remarks in *The Writing of the Disaster* (1980), 'is never passive enough. It is in this respect that one can speak of infinite passivity: perhaps only because passivity evades all formulations – yet it seems that there is in passivity something like a demand that would require it to fall always short of itself'.[41]

What Blanchot's and Levinas's portrayals of suffering further illuminate is its *singular violation*. Regardless of our anticipations, its irruptive actuality will always by necessity undo and outdo our prognoses and intentions. If the virtue of exposure calls for a preparatory stance, it must also at the same time acknowledge that the forbearance of what is to come will be unforeseeable and unimaginable. Hence the readiness it calls for cannot but be in the mode of a psychosomatic *welcome* to the unknown to take us where it will. Its attitude can only consist of a resolve to let a foreign future break us out of ourselves. Exposure, in this sense, is a *blind yes* – to the arrival of the unpredictable and exceptional. On no account must we consider this ineffective. Without the affirmation endorsed by exposure, it is probable that in most cases our ethical interaction with situations that our conscience enjoins us to respond toward might be deterred or impoverished as a result of our compulsive self-serving mindframe. By force of habit and for reasons of self-protection, we often tend to look but not see.

If the virtue of exposure invites us to suffer, it is not for suffering's own sake. Suffering is in itself the necessary preliminary for our aspiration toward the good life of which all existence is to partake. The infinite negativity of experience is essential to suspend our own worldview in order to be free to inhabit others. The disorientation affected is but a step toward a reorientation toward unforeseeable modes of perception. For this reason, the welcome of exposure is never aimed toward our own personal representation of the good life but rather at the structurally indeterminate definition that grounds it: 'the good life with and for others in just institutions'. Otherwise, any knowledge eventually gained would simply mirror our preconceptions.

To welcome experience for the sake of a better future as an open-ended schema is to acknowledge that experience can also teach us how such a future can come to be. The world around us must be heard if our goals are to be sufficiently informed, inclusive, and realistic. Our ideas must be premised on the outside present conditions in order to work for a time to come that would pragmatically and effectively resolve our predicament.

The dialogue of exposure with the other virtues

In its dialogic relationship with the other virtues, exposure has a crucial role to play. It is exposure that *stimulates* especially the practice of the two virtues that are more specifically concerned with the hermeneutics of experience: imagination and practical wisdom. In submitting us to what is foreign to us, exposure incites us to comprehend it. In revealing the outside as *conflicting* with our worldview, it *drives* us to seek some form of reconciliation through the imaginative and rational plane of practical wisdom. Because our hermeneutics are derived from this conflict, they address the outside as authentically as they can. By braving experience on its own foreign terms, we attempt as much as possible and often at our expense to capture it *as it is* in our comprehension. We are enjoined to drastically reconfigure our horizon of understanding in order to incorporate it into our vision of existence and its ideal of the good life. What often results from our efforts is an expansion of our worldview.[42]

At the same time, however, exposure sustains the virtues with a reminder that their work is inevitably *cognitive* – while the experience as irreducibly other to us happened *empirically*. A focus is thus placed on the disjunction that lies at the heart of our hermeneutics, which reveals our knowledge to be always already an imperfect translation of what factually happened. The clarity and depth of our knowledge cannot but be an approximate representation of what really took place. Experience will always *exceed* our attempts at assimilating it with our horizon of understanding. It will always undermine and demand more of our efforts.

Consequently, an implacable discrepancy is to inevitably remain between what we suffered and how we resolved it mentally. This is captured in the conjunction 'and yet' in the statement designating the refiguring decision: 'I expose myself to the foreign in experience, *and yet* I imaginatively reconcile myself with it as well as discover through practical wisdom what moral projects need to be done at its behest . . . ' *Despite* the fact that we cannot ever really reconcile ourselves with what happens to us in the outside world, we *still* attempt to. A contradiction is inherent to all endeavours at interpretation.

Through the influence of exposure, outside events are thus not allowed to lose their *sufferance* effect upon us. Exposure ensures, even postfactum, that we are not to forget their ineradicably self-disruptive nature. The dismissal of memory can incline us toward the temptation to believe that our subsequent interpretations *are* equivalent to what actually took place, that the signifier *is* the signified. The inability to affectively and cognitively maintain an irredeemable distance between the two poles can easily cause a disregard of all alternative views on the source in the unquestioning conviction that our view is definitive and that no more reflection on the matter is required. Forgetfulness might not take us too far from arrogance and complacency.

In spite of a necessary confidence in our hermeneutical achievements, a consciousness of exposure thus ascertains at the same time an underlying attitude of scepticism toward them, in regarding them as inevitably incomplete, even unwittingly defective in some manner. We are therefore encouraged to constantly reassess them and find alternative ways for their further development. We are urged to understand our horizon of understanding as an unending work-in-progress.

▼

From Consumer Creativity to Imagination

Creativity as the site of authenticity

In the consumer culture, we are meant to realize our authenticity predominantly through the value of creativity. The expression of our individuality – our ideas, personality, feelings – entails an originality, which, we are told, will provide us with the acquisition of self-knowledge. To invent ourselves according to our worldview or personality is to find out who we really are. Our inventiveness ideally requires a complete alteration of anything involving us and our quotidian life, including no less our appearance, behaviour, profession, leisure activities, relationships, and product choices. In order to capture our inimitability, our whole way of life needs to change. We have inherited an ideology, Charles Taylor writes, where 'We discover what we have it in us to be by becoming that mode of life, by giving expression in our speech and action to what is original in us'.[1]

The idea that self-revelation is the product of creative utterance captures a popular *expressivist* definition of the contemporary self-realized individual. In *The Ethics of Authenticity* (1991), Taylor derives this belief from a genealogy of reverence granted to artists and their imagination. Since around 1800, artists have been perceived as paradigm cases of persons who have managed to find their authenticity through their expression. In defining themselves through the production of unprecedented and experimental works of arts, they have come to experience their truest sense of self. 'I forge a new artistic language', Taylor writes, '– new way of painting, new metre or form of poetry, new way of writing a novel – and through this and this alone I become what I have it in me to be. Self-discovery requires poi sis, making'.[2]

The artistic act and the life of the artist have since become a general model for the way of life we are to follow. They have come to metaphorically embody the mode of conduct to be aspired for. In order to find ourselves, like the greats, we are encouraged to create an original 'work' out of the different aspects of ourselves and our deeds.[3]

Consumer creativity is the combinatorial game of products

Of all the lifestyles advertised by today's public media, it is in the characterization of the entrepreneur that creativity seems to take the most central role. In *Business Cycles* (1939), Joseph Schumpeter indeed hinges the entrepreneur's success on innovation when he attests that it is the only process that is fundamental in history.[4] For Schumpeter, innovation is the impetus for the development of the economy in reforming or revolutionizing the current pattern of production. It ruptures the economy out of its consistency, its static mode, or 'circular flow', and sets it on a progressive path that is discontinuous in proceeding at irregular intervals. Innovation for Schumpeter can flow through five channels: the introduction of a new product, the introduction of a new method of production, the opening up of a new market, the conquest of a new source of supply of raw materials or semimanufactured goods, and the new organization of an industry.[5] The great entrepreneur transforms the state of the economy 'by exploiting an invention or, more generally, an untried technological possibility for producing a new commodity or producing an old one in a new way, by opening up a new source of supply of materials or a new outlet for products, by reorganizing an industry and so on'.[6] The motive behind the entrepreneur's innovations, Schumpeter points out, is not limited to the pecuniary profit. There is also involved the joy of creation, of having brought something into the world, the related joy of achievement, and finally, a joy in the sheer exercise of energy and ingenuity.[7]

In the consumer society, as Jean Baudrillard illustrates so well, the most promoted mode of creativity involves our *combinatory choices* between commodities on offer. We are enjoined to define our authenticity by experimenting with different assimilations of the shopping options that are displayed for us. We involve ourselves in a game of trying-this-or-that-together to finally come up with what we believe captures best our special individuality. Integral to what Baudrillard terms 'personalization' in the consumer world are the singular bricolages each and every one of us is expected to construct.[8] In his essay, 'Style' (1961), Meyer Schapiro points out that there is today a lack of interest in the creation of our own coherent, unique style that would enable us to express our inner self. What seems to be more popular is playing with a range of familiar styles and expanding on them.[9] Contemporary mainstream creativity tends to be interpreted through a *ludic* dimension.

For Baudrillard, the differences in consumer options to combine for self-personalization are not in actual opposition or contradiction to one another. They belong rather to a system of abstract differences designed by the industry and expressed through signs exhibited on the commodities. To read a commodity sign is to read its value *in relation to other commodities*. Products in the market signify only by reciprocal allusion. Their differential significance can change from one day to the next depending on the underlying dictates of their manufacturing companies, which are communicated to us as what is *au courant*. The exchange-value is contingent on the fashion codes of the moment.[10]

Despite all appearances to the contrary, therefore, for Baudrillard, the combinatorial game of creativity we indulge in as consumers is highly manipulated by *preset models* that determine the worth of what we are to select and combine. Though we experience our conscious behaviour 'as freedom, as aspiration, as choice',[11] we are often in truth unconsciously perpetuating the commodity code system of the moment. Which is to say that what we consider to be achievements in self-expression through the right shopping decisions are often precisely experienced as achievements insofar as they unwittingly follow the prestige hierarchies that the market has already established for us. In the consumer culture, our ascension in authenticity, which also means an ascension in status, *is* an ascension paradoxically to the extent that it reinforces the fashion code system. 'Each individual', Baudrillard claims, 'experiences his differential social gains as absolute gains; he does not experience the structural constraint which means that positions change, but the order of differences remains'. 'In the very act of scoring his points in the order of differences, each individual maintains that order, and therefore condemns himself only ever to occupy a relative position within it.'[12]

The cult of personalization that issues out of the consumer culture is therefore indifferent to our singular specificity as individuals and its creative manifestations. It substitutes for our differences its own manufactured, prearranged differences that only apply or signify within the ideology of commodities. In taking over the role of expressing and realizing our individualities, these differences end up homogenizing us.[13]

The combinatorial game of consumer creativity is also strongly recommended by the industry as *the* method that should organize our pursuit of the lifestyles it advertises. Essential to the way we are to conduct a lifestyle is a creativity informed by a mix-and-match from an assemblage of services and goods, with choices determined by whatever fits our personal aesthetic and stimulates our interest and curiosity. We are encouraged to construct our individuality above all through our *whims* and *tastes* of what is on offer at the moment. Our creative expression, which is supposed to deliver us to our true self, would be the resulting bricolage. And this, in most cases, ends up reproducing one or more combinations that happen to be in vogue.

The world of specialized fashion, for instance, is today premised on the idea of conjugating certain clothes items and beauty products with one another in order to bring about a customized look. The same items can then be discarded or reconjugated with others in order to conform to newer fashion standards. In the same vein, as fitness-seekers we are free to take any ideas and regimes that suit our preferences in order to form our own personalized path toward the high-status body, wherein we are to discover ourselves.

As self-spiritualists, we are also charged with liberally adopting and appropriating different systems of thought and practices to syncretize our preferences in our own 'unique' belief system and program. The 'unique' meta-theories of the gurus themselves are a bricolage of elements from Eastern and Western traditional religions, theories and practices from psychology and psychotherapy, as well as Western and Eastern scientific theories.[14] Andrew Dawson in 'New Spirituality as "Mystified Consumption"' (2011) thus reveals that new spirituality gives 'an *individualistic* emphasis upon the self as the ultimate arbiter of religious authority and the primary agent of spiritual transformation; an *instrumentalized* religiosity driven by the goal of absolute self-realization [...]'.[15] It categorically instructs us to pursue its posited goal through any means at our disposal and at any available opportunity. We are to pick, amalgamate, and use whatever works for us as long as it will help us reach our destination point.

It is also agreed among many scholars in tourist studies that a change has taken place in tourism since its Fordist years, when it was centred on readymade itineraries and targeted toward the mass consumption of standardized products, activities, and sites, such as holiday camps and cheaper packaged holidays. Many post-Fordist tourists now design their holidays by choosing from the array of services made available by the industry in order to plot their own version of the ideal itinerary.[16] In *Tourism, Technology, and Competitive Strategies* (1993), Auliana Poon highlights the conversion of the travelling lifestyle into a segmented, flexible, and customizable experience. We are now expected to assemble a program for a journey that is explicitly intended to express our unique self.[17] As Scott Lash and John Urry argue in *Economies of Signs and Space* (1994), flexibility in the industry is now a prerogative. An ever increasing diversification of holiday-types, visitor attractions, and activities are consequently required to satisfy the ever-changing plurality of tourist preferences. For instance, the growth of alternative, real, ecological, and responsible tourism and nonmass forms of refreshment and accommodations such as country house hotels are clearly indicative of services tailormade for a peculiar consumer scene that is not interested in what is considered to be the popular variety of vacation.[18]

Consumerist lifestyle discourses also frequently index each other by endorsing many of each other's ideas and techniques. They tend to urge us to make time to pick-and-mix elements from other lifestyles in order to enhance the desired results. As Mike Featherstone stresses in *Consumer Culture and Postmodernism* (2007), consumer culture intermediaries 'do not seek to promote a single lifestyle, but rather to cater for and expand the range of styles and lifestyles available to audiences and consumers […]'.[19]

Heidi Hanna's article, for instance, 'How to Use Physical Exercise as a Spiritual Practice' demonstrates several ways how we can cross-train our body, mind, and soul. When exercising especially in nature, she recommends practicing mindfulness toward our surroundings as well as to how our body feels while moving. During our workouts, we are also to reflect on anything we feel grateful for, including people we know, so we can imagine sending them positive energy and prayers. Meditating on our breathing patterns or on a personal mantra is also recommended.[20] In *Meditative Fitness* (2015), Clark Hamilton Depue, a CrossFit athlete and coach, proceeds to prove that our fitness plan can itself be validated as a spiritual practice in that many of its activities and their effects are not so different from any kind of meditation. Depue in fact calls 'fitness' 'an active physical meditation' that can lead to mental or emotional breakthroughs. To execute our workout, we focus on the task at hand and learn to control our breathing. This quietens the mind and we are fully present in the moment, wherein we discover a greater self within us. Through fitness, Depue confirms, our karma changes and our mental and physical thresholds expand. Our will is also continuously tested.[21]

By a similar logic, as Andrew Dawson makes clear in 'New Spirituality as "Mystified Consumption"', self-spirituality regards the body and its material environment as essentially 'principal loci of spiritual fulfilment'.[22] It is through them that the spiritual realm can manifest itself to itself. To take good care of our physical well-being, to include fitness regimens in our lifestyle, is therefore highly advised as a way of improving on our spiritual life and get more in touch with our transcendental self.[23]

Self-spirituality has also been incorporated into financial and corporate circles. Its influence, David Graeber reveals in *The Utopia of Rules* (2016), extends to the peculiar idiom they use that is 'full of bright, empty words like vision, quality, stakeholder, leadership, excellence, innovation, strategic goals or best practices',[24] that can be traced back to the discourse of self-spiritual movements such as Lifespring, Mind Dynamics, and EST. Their popularity in corporate boardrooms in the seventies left a legacy in the business-world vocabulary. Nowadays, many entrepreneurs also integrate spiritual exercises in the daily running of their firms, including various forms of meditation, mantras, positive affirmations, future visioning, the consultation of tarot or angel cards, breathing techniques, journaling, and visualization, and so on. The promotion of wellbeing and fitness in the company culture is also implemented by installing a private gym or setting up a corporate membership at a discount with a local gym. Some entrepreneurs also plan team workouts and race activities for the staff and stock healthy food at the workplace.[25] Being spiritual and fit in the business is believed to reduce our stress levels, cut healthcare costs, increase brain power and motivation, foster better relationships, increase tolerance, and reduce negative conflict as well as absenteeism, among innumerable other benefits.[26]

Along with entrepreneurship, the world of travel now also tends to incorporate fitness and self-spiritual elements in its activities and events. We witness this overlap, Mauro Dujmović and Aljoša Vitasović explain, in the rise of so-called 'themed vacations' or 'hobby vacations', that are expressly intended for the pursuit of 'personal intensive and permanent interests'[27] while on holiday, with the most popular being sports (tennis, skiing, horseriding, golf, diving, etcetera) and the acquisition of new knowledge and skills (language proficiency, painting, dancing, etcetera).[28]

Showcasing our look in fashion is also often indissociable from showcasing a fit body. If fashion is nowadays aimed to evoke ideals related to youth and sensuality, then, a high-status body with its own youthful and sensual connotations can only enhance the effect of our choice of wear and beauty products.

Lifestyle crossreferencing can only take place due to the goals that every lifestyle shares with the other. Like any other product in the market, they are all geared toward status achievement and physical stimulation. To synthesize components of the philosophies and practices of other lifestyles with the one/s we primarily uphold is believed to amplify, speed up even, the two goals we are chasing.

The consumer culture homogenizes commodities and objectives

If enjoyable feelings are the effect intended by all lifestyle goods and services, the differences they exhibit through their sign-value are only differences in view of the *quantification* of these feelings. Every article comes to allude to a certain level of status and arousal and therefore it comes to constitute a code referencing a place in an abstract hierarchy based on the degree of feelgood to be experienced upon consumption. As a result, what distinguishes each and every article in meaning becomes *minimal*. An item's particular significance becomes a simple question of extentness.

The same system that differentiates according to feelgood also paradoxically dedifferentiates in the appearance and content especially of those products that pertain to the same lifestyle.

The market's continual multiplication of product types tends to their overall standardization while only producing distinctions in marginal details. A plausible reason for this is that in a consumer culture there is no longer the need for a differentiation that is radical, based on opposition or contradiction. If what matters is the degree of feelgood, then a particular detail signalling this result is sufficient.

Another factor that contributes to lifestyle standardization is the way the particular conditions surrounding their feelgood goals are usually simplified and generalized in description. There can be several short-term and long-term states of being aspired for in a lifestyle that are inherently different from one another and which are yet not accurately explained and distinguished but often assimilated under a single category or name. If empirically the circumstances of the goals pursued have diverse affective-cognitive impressions, their discourses yet often treat them as identical.

Lifestyle experts and followers tend to express goals by generic labels that are used interchangeably. The varying attributes of the destinations we are exhorted to chase are therefore befuddled, deterring any attempt to circumscribe them with any precision. A plausible reason for this tendency would be indifference on everyone's part. If what matters is that ultimately our purchases and activities would reward us with more arousal and status, then by implication the particular character of the new territory we would be entering ceases to matter as much.

Another reason for the discursive homogenization of goals lies in the fact that each goal entails, as Zygmunt Bauman states in connection to fitness, a *'subjective experience* (in the sense of "lived" experience, "felt" experience – not a state or an event that may be observed from outside, verbalized and communicated)'.[29] Self-spirituality, fitness, fashion, and travel all aspire to various personal states of being which we can only properly comprehend by going through them ourselves. They are consequently not easy to articulate and distinguish with universal criteria. What lifestyle discourses resort to instead are vague definitions that are often more akin to extended advertising slogans targeted to produce a sensational effect.

As a result of the vagueness that inheres in our lifestyle goals, our only point of reference in our pursuit is often ultimately no one and nothing else but ourselves, how we are feeling. This makes our progress notoriously ambivalent to measure as we are never really certain how far we still have to go to reach the designated goal or whether we have already reached it. In the lifestyles' culture, as Bauman indicates again in connection to fitness, you can never really know 'whether your sensations are as deep and exciting, or indeed "pleasurable", as those of the next person'.[30] Our successes or what we are told are successes thereby often feel incomplete. Lingering doubts remain concerning the inadequacy of our accomplishments: doubts as to whether we have done enough and that perhaps more, always more, needs to be done.

Self-spiritualist systems of thought and self-help books, for instance, dilute all experiences of the transcendental self to a handful of typical phrases and terms such as 'peak experiences', 'enlightenment', or 'ultimate consciousness' that are often evoked through various testimonials. Contrary to classic religions, spiritual gurus emphasize that there is no need to believe any doctrine or narrative in order to access these states of being. What is important is the need to experience. Dominica Motak in 'Postmodern Spirituality and the Culture of Individualism' (2009) confirms that the intimate singularity of these episodes, however, makes them tough to describe. They 'can only take the form of generalized statements on a broadly understood *sacrum*'.[31] Furthermore, as Jennifer Rindfleish shows in 'New Spirituality as "Social Product"' (2005), the ideas and techniques proposed are extracted from large and complex traditional belief systems, scientific, and/or psychological theories. Isolated from their cohesive bodies of knowledge, the insight they provide is impoverished and in many cases deteriorates to overgeneralization and abstraction. Rindfleish confirms that decontextualization factors as well behind the 'oversimplification, homogenisation, and a reduction in the meaning of the knowledge [spiritual gurus] use to develop their meta-theories'.[32]

In spite of standardizing its set goals, the same self-spiritualist market is yet perpetually releasing new meta-theories that express them with new techniques for their realization. The differences in content between the philosophy-technique packages released, however, are minor in significance. As Rindfleish discloses, they all comprise of a slightly altered perspective and focus on the same theme of 'the promise of transformation from one state to another via a teleological process'.[33] Their narrative typically commences by discrediting current explanations of our lived reality as flawed to suggest instead their own superlative vision of what is real. They bemoan our entrapment in an inferior or illusive reality that is complicit with our ego to emphasize on the importance of sacrificing this lesser self through practices that require the continual examination of our thoughts in order to exercise a modification, contemplation, and obedience to their patterns. In doing so, we will gain access to unitive experiences through some version of our 'truer' or transcendental self that is always evoked as unknown and yet infinitely desirable.[34]

The practices prescribed for our 'enlightenment' are likewise often close to identical despite being termed differently and altered in some minor respects. By and large, their methodology and their described effects remain unchanged in being regurgitated variations of Oriental practices, namely of a Buddhist and Hindu orientation, such as meditation, yoga, mantras, energetic body focus, nature-immersion, visualization, breathing exercises, and so forth.

The fitness market follows the same commercializing procedure in generating a multiplicity of regimens in the pursuit of various objectives that are all supposed to lead us toward the one vague ideal of the high-status body. The regimens rehash the rigorous mindset and activities necessary for progression but the very construal of progression is often hard to ascertain in that the goals we set ourselves and the high-status body desired so much capture for the most part personal experiences that cannot be satisfactorily pinned down through an intersubjective vocabulary. Any successes gained on the way toward the ideal can only be measured and demonstrated, albeit crudely, in their effects on our physique, beyond which they can be confusing to gauge as clear stages in our journey, let alone formulate. There are very limited resources through which we can objectively calculate as well as articulate our coordinates in the fitness hierarchy. In an effort to showcase what we believe is our advancements, and having hardly any other reassuring evidence, we resort to images and videos on social media that capture our exercises and our flexing, posturing bodies. Other typical photos that are supposed to mark our success include changes in our calorie count and weightloss over a certain period of time, before-and-after parts of our body – namely, the arms, belly, and backside, along with our dietary intake. Social media in this respect serves to reinforce our conviction that we *are* factually progressing. If talk on our fitness 'evolution' can ever take place at all, it would have no choice but to focus obsessively on numbers that abstractly signal our position in the race toward final happiness.[35]

The ambiguity inherent to lifestyle goals is a much capitalized on resource. The uncertainty and insecurity it breeds legitimates the industry to issue ever newer commodities that are advertised as delivering more effective and efficient results. It is part of what makes the commodities' perpetual reinterpretations and reinvented techniques convincing as better substitutes for 'older' variants. Objective ambiguity *creates demand*.

Contrasting the refiguring imagination from consumer creativity

The mode of creativity the consumerist lifestyles endorse is not as original as they portray it to be in that its method of freely combining readymade options is heavily limited by what is available at that moment as well as the trending models the industry wily directs us to follow. If by 'creativity', we are meant to understand a self-expression that illuminates our interiority, then the creativity at work in the consumer culture falls woefully short of this ideal. Even if we were to put all our efforts at resisting fashion codes in our purchasing decisions, there remains the issue of the quasi-uniformity of many options in appearance, thought, strategy, and practice. There is also the likelihood that what we choose will reflect more on our current personal tastes than on any proper introspection.

This is not to say that we cannot actually be creative with consumer lifestyles. Our assemblage of purchases, say, a vacation in rural Japan followed by a Jaffna cruise topped with a mushroom trip in Amsterdam or a complete Kardashian-inspired makeover coupled with an Atkins Diet and a new brand's seasonal wear, can in theory supply us with previously undisclosed knowledge about ourselves and the world, perhaps directing us toward new perspectives on our life. The problem as I see it is that the perspectives disclosed are for the most part quite superficial. They are not and will never be *radical enough*. Not radical enough to inaugurate ways of seeing, involving all or most aspects of existence, that are distinctively *other* to our own. They do not constitute alternative *worldviews* – and they are therefore incapable of illuminating ways of how we can understand ourselves and the life we are to live in a singularly different mode. Behind the lifestyles' incapacity for the possibility of authentic self-insight and transformation lies the essential character of any commodity. Commodities are specifically designed to be enjoyed. Constructed on a secure and reassuring expectation, they will always be familiar to us even if we have not purchased or tasted them yet. Their nature also makes them easy to conjoin with one another. Several of them, as already indicated, presuppose and reference others in connection to their hedonistic purposes. Because of their overarching common aim, many commodities are manufactured to be combined, which makes most of our creative ploys paradoxically hardly creative and incapable of any breakthrough in perceptivity. Any experimental combination of them is therefore likely to be already not original enough.

The refiguring identity's equivalent to consumer creativity is the virtue of the imagination. Like creativity, the type of imagination implemented in our identity model is tasked with combining different components with one another in order to reveal a new self-understanding. Whereas the task of creativity is the reconciliation of products, however, the task of imagination is the reconciliation of *realities*, which comprise of our reality and the reality evoked by what is foreign in experience. Whereas the products creativity reconciles are therefore preknown, the reality imagination has to reconcile with ourselves is *unknown*. Products carry a predisposition to be reconciled while the realities imagination has to work with are averse to reconciliation: repulsion governs their difference from us. If creativity works with existent materials, imagination works with the very *problem of existence* or the problematically existent in having to comprehend an actuality that contradicts and undermines *our* actuality. It is precisely this aporia that provokes its intervention.

The imaginative image (Ricoeur)

The imaginative process takes place as a dialectic that is analogous to the dialectical functioning of the metaphor as explored by hermeneutical thinkers like Paul Ricoeur, I.A. Richards, Max Black, Colin M. Turbayne, Monroe Beardsley, and Douglas Berggren.[36] Through the practice of exposure, our horizon of understanding with its own representation of the good life finds itself in irresolvable conflict with experience. *Despite* this discordance, however, *and yet because* of it, a concordance of the two poles takes place. Their opposition galvanizes the imagination to unify them. The first and second clauses of the refiguring decision statement allude to this: 'I expose myself to the foreign in experience *and yet I imaginatively reconcile* myself with it …'

The reconciliation conjured by the imagination finds its determination from the fundamental enjoinment to live the good life. In its efforts it thus aspires for an ideal time-to-come that is only schematic in form. The radical open-endedness of its futural ideal ensures a freedom and flexibility in its creations that it would otherwise not possess had it directed itself toward an idea of the future that was more strictly defined. To focus the imaginative process on a clearly stipulated telos is to stifle its originality in forcing it to produce ideas that tend to reflect our prejudgements.

What the imagination evokes is a potential way of seeing ourselves and the world around us that had formerly been inconceivable. An alternate vision or visions of existence is suggested that would not have been possible were it not for our disarming exposure to a particular event. What constitutes the unprecedented nature of the imaginative vision is its integration of *what contradicts* and therefore undermines our customary worldview. It therefore pertains neither to our worldview nor the event in question, but instead converges upon an unforeseen way of understanding the good life. In its assimilation, its perspective is autonomous of both, and cannot be reduced to either.

Ricoeur describes the imaginative possible vision as a cognitive image.[37] In works like 'Pastoral Praxeology, Hermeneutics, and Identity' (1995), 'Metaphor and the Main Problem of Hermeneutics' (1991), and 'Poetry and Possibility' (1991), he explores its character by drawing attention to the distinction between two types of referentiality. The descriptive type of referentiality is what preordains ordinary spoken discourse as well as any discourse that pertains to the theoretical-conceptual like the scientific. Underlying all these discourses is the dependence of signification on a world external to us, with attributes that are understood to be universal for everybody. Relevance is here predicated on ratifying what one says with facts. Between two or more interlocutors or the text and its reader is the presupposition of a shared reality against which we verify or falsify all our claims. Descriptive referential communications are therefore established on empirical description. Their form of referentiality assumes an uncritical ramification of a certain idea of truth that is objective and as a result can be measured. Truth is here informed by the separation of subject from a reality populated by distinct objects that can be gazed upon to analyze and dissect.[38]

Poetry, metaphor, and any fiction or nonfiction narrative in film, novel, or drama that is innovative in style and content are structured on an altogether different type of referentiality that Ricoeur calls 'nondescriptive'. The nondescriptive, Ricoeur argues, signals toward 'modalities of our relation to the world that are not exhausted in the description of objects'.[39] The convergence of the work's succession of events and their totality with its form and style evokes a particular *state of being* through which our world is perceived from a different angle. A unique mindset is narrated into possibility that articulates a way of belonging and behaving in the world around us, *a way to be*. Nondescriptive referentiality unfolds a peculiar, ontological mood that therefore takes place prior to the 'normative' attitude of things understood as 'objects' that confront us as 'subjects'. For nondescriptive referentiality, the descriptive is just one more perspective among others, special only in being generally considered as the standard way of interacting with the world.[40]

In its nascence, the worldview inhering in an original poem, metaphor, or narrative is revealed as a mental image that conveys a certain emotional personality. It impresses upon our cognition *what it feels like* to see things in a certain manner and as such it has a sensorial and emotional coherence. Despite the attitude it expresses, it is irreducible to words and concepts in the same way as music.

In its basic state, the imaginative image is *suggestive* of a type of worldview we can dwell in. It can thus be described as a schema or a sign that invites us to formulate it in detail. It offers the sensorial and emotional rudiments of a potential vision that awaits our reflective actualization. In unfolding the immediate beginnings of a potential mindset, we are called upon to elicit its concrete significance with its themes and values as well as find ways how we can adopt it in our practical life. The preconceptual nature of the image allows itself to be recognized by a variety of interpretations each of which can do it justice. Its importance overall is that it enables us to understand ourselves further, to think and act through perceptual horizons that are not our own. Our motivations are reoriented in accordance to another possible world. It is in this sense that Ricoeur compares the nondescriptive reference to when 'we speak of the Greek world, [or when] we speak of the Roman world, that is to say, a horizon of possibilities which constitute an environment for people . . . where we could dwell'.[41]

The imaginative image as defined by the refiguring identity differs from the Ricoeurian imagination in inferring an original way of living the good life. The possible world it alludes to is indicative of an ideal future that we had not anticipated. Its ethical hermeneutics thus characterize it as more focused type of imagination than the regular idea of the imagination we usually presuppose. In making possible innovative ways how we can lead a better life, its visions perhaps carry a certain import and depth that are normally absent in accounts exploring an everyday imagination that synthesizes sense perceptions as well as one that produces new ideas in the realm of art. In suggesting a path toward an unprecedented representation of a better future, the refiguring imagination reassesses our own idea of a future, laying it open to possible improvements or change.

Discovering the imaginative image in two literary samples

To elucidate further on the Ricoeurian imaginative image and its mode of function, I will analyze two literary texts that invoke it with a particular emphasis, briefly exploring how they disclose its possible world and what it entails. The challenge at hand would be the paradoxical attempt to trace a literary effect that does not easily lend itself to verbal description. Perhaps it would be more accurate to designate my study of the two possible worlds as intimation rather than proper description. Intimated are two particular sensorial atmospheres that express a way of life.

The first text to be considered is 'To Autumn' (1820)[42] by the Romantic poet, John Keats. The poem alludes to the early augurs of autumn in summer captured through thickly sensuous imagery. A diminuendo, a gradual fading, pervades the configured scenery through lines that in the words of Thomas McFarland are 'so tactile, so heavy, so luxurious in their summoning of swelling and plumping and ripeness [...]'.[43] A shift in mood eventually takes place from a sense of stasis steeped in a sheer joy in the now to a sense of the impending that gradually leads to an expectancy of the inevitable – the looming winter. The images of waiting presented for us, however, capture an immeasurable patience, serenity, even reverence, for what the near future is going to bring.

All the components of the poem, from its diction to its stylistics, conspire to create feelings that converge on a particular state of mind that alludes to a passion for life that is founded on the bittersweet awareness that everything will soon pass. 'To Autumn's' imaginative image seems to refigure all possible contradictions of the permanent and the ephemeral into a sensorial aura that expresses a poignant beauty that coexists intimately with a tragic acceptance of transience.[44]

On a more modern note is Cormac McCarthy's bildungsroman, *All the Pretty Horses* (1992),[45] which tells the story of John Grady Cole, a sixteen-year old who in 1949 flees home in San Angelo with his best friend to cross the Mexican border in search of the ideal cowboy life. He believes that unlike the United States, Mexico is still an untouched, primitive land, ripe for his recreation of the frontier myth. What he finds instead is a vast geography that alternates between the beauty of rich nature and the desolation of wastelands and which grows wilder and more barren the further on he travels. The traces of ancient hunters and warriors found across the land along with the behaviour and vernacular of the locals that is alive with poetic expressions, references to the Bible, and legends and myths, suggests a present that has an intimate connection with a living past and its stories.

Heralded by the constant cries of wild, strange animals in the backgrounds, a harsh and mindlessly vicious natural world is eventually unfolded, with a scale and origins that are beyond fathoming for the two wanderers. The rugged and cruelly civilized settlements encountered also call for a dangerous living accorded by the laws of nature. The wanderers' days are spent trying to tame and control this world through sheer physical strength and cowboy skills. As synecdoches of these efforts are a number of young male 'fetishes', which do not only include a variety of weapons but all sorts of farm tools, ropes, boots, hats, saddles, bridles, and trucks. Fighting for survival, the protagonist and his friend yet find themselves progressively plunging into a primal state of being that is constantly captured through images of a living fire. Heart fires, gun fires, cosmic fires, and campfires abound throughout the journey.

The relentless struggle to stay alive is mercifully punctuated now and then with moments of reprieve that often take place when the duo is camping. Drinking coffee around the fire and sleeping under the stars brings peace of mind and renewal. Grady's relationship to horses likewise seems to transcend the everyday toil and violence by giving him a sense of fulfilment and unity with nature and existence.

In the same fashion the Keats poem is experienced, the diverse elements capturing the Mexican world of *All the Pretty Horses* converge into a sensorial mood that seems to refer us to a mindset. Like the tragic vision of 'To Autumn', this mindset has the potential to be ontologically comprehensive in significance and as such can constitute a worldview. At its heart there seems to be the fundamental necessity of our conflict with a natural world that remains cruel and ruthless despite our attempts at civilizing it. It also perhaps entails the search for the beliefs we cling to when life deprives us of all comforts and attachments that are henceforth understood as illusory and deceptive. Grady's silent and practical character epitomizes this stoical embrace and fight against the very real hardships life throws at us. The harsh acceptance and confrontation that emerge out of the gritty landscapes of the novel can be variously interpreted in more particular ways through close attention to the places and events that mark the narrative.

Both Keats's 'To Autumn' and McCarthy's *All the Pretty Horses* invite us to see and inhabit a world that is other to what we are accustomed to. Attuning ourselves, at least for the time of reading, to their perspectives, can augment our self-understanding and help us reconcile ourselves with factual issues that we had previously denied or found difficult to comprehend.

VI

From Instrumental Reason to Practical Wisdom

Entrepreneurial and fitness rationality

To interpret experience, consumer culture life-strategies and the refiguring identity model both endorse a form of rationality that is oriented toward a certain *conduct*. A cognitive knowledge is devised that focuses on a certain mode of practice rather than a theoretical and conceptual knowledge. What this reflection aims to accomplish is a set of concrete behavioural directives that cohere around a particular mindset.

The behavioural mindset that is exhorted by the consumerist lifestyles is often known by philosophers and sociologists as 'instrumental reason'. The reason at issue engages our environment by way of finding the *most efficient procedure* through which it can yield us the most profit. It perceives any situation in an *exploitative* manner in conceiving how best it can maximize our self-gain. What is sought for in any object is its potential optimal instrumentalization for our profit. Means are prioritized over ends, whose consequences are dismissed. To regard the world through instrumental reason, Charles Taylor explains, is to 'calculate the most economical application of a means to a given end. Maximum efficiency, the best cost-output ratio, is its measure of success'.[1]

Instrumental reason for entrepreneurs is targeted singularly on the interests of their firm. In his works, Hugh Willmott exposes the tendency in today's business organizations to promote the employees' autonomy but *as reframed* through core corporate values. Programs of corporate culturism, human resource management, and total quality management inculcate the idea that it is highly significant for the employees to be self-determined at work as long as this is committed toward a love of the company's product and its financial profits.[2] All choices and actions, as James H.

85

Michelman points out, must at all times be guided by the dictates of the one single rule: 'Let the maxim of your action be that which advances the profitability of your firm'.[3] Entrepreneurs are taught that success in life, and therefore self-esteem and purpose, is contingent on the standards set up by this principle. Their wants are redefined according to its pregiven system of values. Subjective independence is appropriated into an economic resource with its deliberations and creativity firmly delimited to furthering the firm's ends, through, for instance, product design, marketing, industry organization, or investment strategies. No leeway is given for any other principles and courses of action.[4]

What the corporate ethos aims at ultimately is a restructuring of the entrepreneurs' very identities. All independent reason is to be deployed to fulfil the internalized company values in the quickest and least costly manner. Rational performance in a typical company is in fact premised on the most efficient use of the means of production, including other employees, as well as a focus on the production and exploitation of those products for sale that optimize revenue. It also means the purchase of resources – which again, includes other people – at the cheapest possible. It is the entrepreneurs' 'morality' to see and use their coworkers, vendors, customers, and other firms as instruments to their firm's advantage (which is to maximize its income and amass ever more capital).[5]

In 'Business Ethics and Bauman Ethics' (1997), René ten Bos adds that if the corporate ethos emphasizes the importance of teamwork and team development among its promoted values, it is done to hammer home the idea that all outsiders, especially the competitors, are to be treated as potential threats to the company's wellbeing, which by implication means a threat to the staff's wellbeing since their identities have been reconstituted around that company. A team morality is thus upheld in order to foster the 'us against them' mentality. The defeat of anyone deemed to be an opponent becomes a value and objective in its own right. In assuming the status of just another obstacle to be outmanoeuvred, ideally with minimal effort and expense, opponents lose their humanity; they become faceless.[6] As ten Bos remarks, 'The moral capacity of competitors, customers, and other stakeholders who do not belong to the team is mangled in the wringing-machine of efficiency and speed'.[7]

Michelman argues that in the unremitting competition of

business, it virtually does not matter whether opponents are bested in what appear to be relatively inconsequential matters, such as one month's increase of sales for a product, or in matters serious enough to bankrupt them. The harm caused in either case is often extensive. That moral fact, however, is usually overlooked by both winners and losers in that they regard it as a necessary part of the game of business, and as long as the game lasts, what is usually considered as moral behaviour is suspended.[8] Gary Hamel and Coimbatore K. Prahalad in *Competing for the Future* (1994) confirm that 'Feelings of beneficence, even of compassion, are effectually blocked; they have no place in this world'.[9]

The value of teamwork only stands insofar as the firm is pitched against external opposition. When internal affairs are concerned, the value is just as easily dismissed as soon as it gets in the way of the firm's interests. Any repercussions involved in an action designed to promote the firm are ideally disregarded or at best side-lined in priority. The potential exploitability of anything for the sake of the firm as prime objective means that any corollary damaged incurred must always be judged as secondary in importance if at all. Justifying this objective is the firm's survival. If return on invested capital is not maximized, it would in all likelihood lose out to its competitors and become insolvent.[10]

Business instrumental reason is also analyzed by Peter Vardy and Paul Grosch in *The Puzzle of Ethics* (1994) in connection to Alasdair MacIntyre's capitalistic archetypal character of the 'bureaucratic manager' that is also integral to the entrepreneur identity-type defined in this work. 'Manipulating others and manip-ulated by the system he has created', Vardy and Grosch maintain, 'the manager examines economic resources and has no qualms about shutting down factories wholesale in order to achieve the best return for his shareholders. His area of expertise is efficient management which, for him, has no moral dimension'.[11]

Norbert Elias, in works such as *The Court Society* (1983), *The Society of Individuals* (1991), and *The Civilizing Process* (2000), explores the brand of instrumental reason that is practiced in the fitness industry. Rationality in fitness is exercised by weighing what-ever we do with how closer it would position us relative to the high-status body. It operates by calculating whether any decision we make, trivial or significant, conforms to the standards that the objective has set for us. A continuous self-monitoring is consequently required. The extent of our rationality depends on how driven and capable we are at separating ourselves from demoralizing feelings such as sadness, apathy, physical discomfort, fatigue, pain, and stress for conduct that is believed to produce the more lasting states of confidence, self-esteem, satisfaction, pleasure, success in the future. Immediate moods and emotions are thus to be sacrificed for diet and exercise regimes. Strict consistency and order must prevail at all times.[12]

Both Louise Mansfield in *Gender, Power and Identities in the Fitness Gym* (2005) and Chris Shilling in *The Body and the Social Theory* (1993) disclose that self-surveillance in fitness also extends to an envious and obsessive observation of those others who have attained (or are close to attaining) the high-status body in our eyes. These individuals – from the models and actors in the media to people we meet at the gym and at work – tend to serve as markers for our own achievement. Our constant measurement with whom we regard as representatives of the upper echelons of fitness compels us to keep refashioning our looks. Our critical consciousness is further reinforced by the sight of our reflections in the mirrored walls of the gym and dance studio as we practice and workout.[13]

'You must have fun (or else you are to blame)'

Rationality in the consumer culture and its popular life-strategies is generally geared toward the realization of enjoyment and success. For our behaviour to be 'rational' – which is also considered to be a descriptor for 'normal' or 'sane' – we are to evaluate anything we think or do in terms of a variant of these two objectives as articulated in the particular lifestyle we are following. Our perception of the outside world is thereby reduced to the purposes of the stipulated happiness we are to constantly acquire. Our proper sensitivity to the singularity of places, people, and events is suppressed in an appropriation to how much satisfaction they can provide for us. Existence is consequently disenchanted of its otherness or transcendence. It is hermeneutically flattened to one exploitative dimension.

For Jean Baudrillard, the principle and finality of consumer culture does not pertain to fun but the *imperative* to have fun. Fun, he announces, 'is now something which is forced upon us, some-thing institutionalized, not as a right or a pleasure, but as the *duty of the citizen*'.[14] Just as it is now our 'duty to be happy' so it is also our duty to be 'loving, adulating/adulated, charming/charmed, participative, euphoric and dynamic'.[15] Consumerist life-strategies educate us into what Baudrillard calls a *'fun morality'*,[16] a guide toward living that is seriously committed toward the increasing of pleasure. They instruct us on how we are to see ourselves as a busi-ness with a profit currency of enjoyment. They also expect us not just to act for the absolute maximization of our pleasure and well-being but to find new sources that can enhance their realization. We are now duty-bound to seek innovative routes that can augment our arousals. Every person, Baudrillard points out, 'must constantly see to it that all his potentialities, all his consumer capacities are mobilized. If he forgets to do so, he will be gently and insistently reminded that he has no right not to be happy'.[17]

To be professional consumers and lifestyle professionals we must therefore always be active. At all times, we are to invest ourselves in untried products and activities to procure a different and/or better arousal, to procure more status. We are required to capitalize full-time on any opportunity that promises more feelgood results. To motivate us in this accumulative race, consumer culture drills into us the importance of being 'open-minded', 'daring', and 'risk-taking'.[18] Baudrillard sums up these qualities in the mainstream promotion of a *universal curiosity*, which is revived 'in respect of cookery, culture, science, religion, sexuality, etc. "Try Jesus!" runs an American slogan. You have to try *everything*, for consumerist man is haunted by the fear of "missing" something, some form of enjoyment or other. You never know whether a particular encounter, a particular experience (Christmas in the Canaries, eel in whisky, the Prado, LSD, Japanese-style love-making) will not elicit some "sensation"'.[19]

Our quest for the 'always more' means that there is no natural end to the pursuit of lifestyle objectives. No definite benchmark is ever agreed upon. Instead, norms are established *in order to* be surpassed once reached. To this effect, a narrative is propagated on the urgency to always break our limits, to leave already achieved standards behind, to do better, to be better. 'Targets may be set only for the current stage of the never-ending effort', Zygmunt Bauman writes in relation to fitness, 'and the satisfaction brought by hitting a set target is but momentary'. '[T]here is no time to rest, and all celebration of the success-thus-far is but a short break before another round of hard work'.[20] One thing that we as travellers, fashionistas, self-spiritualists, entrepreneurs, and fitness-seekers know for sure is that we are not well-travelled, fashionable, spiritual, entrepreneurial, and fit enough, yet, and that we must keep on improving. The road toward greatness, we are told, depends on how much we are 'on top of our game'. A status is conferred on the endeavour to always overcome ourselves, which pressures us in turn to spend ever more time, energy, and money on our quest to feel great about ourselves. It has become prestigious to always be 'on the go' – always intent on meeting intenser and harder challenges, always raising the bar.

The consumer morality of happiness insists that we are capable of accomplishment *no matter what* the obstacle. Through the sheer force of our will, we can realize any dream we put before ourselves. The 'can' in this narrative is elevated to a potential omnipotence while the 'cannot' is prohibited and stigmatized. It is in the fitness discourse that the prominent role assigned to our determination is the most emphasized. Fitness is centred by way of our body with *me*, and what my self can accomplish with that body. It extols a firm belief in my self as the final author of my body and, by extension, my life. What matters in any situation is the capacity to turn it into a conduit for my physical improvement.

In 'Paradoxes of the Flesh' (2014), Margaret Carlisle Duncan and Lori A. Klos demonstrate how health and fitness magazines tend to portray dieting as a matter of taking initiative over our body. The magazines reiterate that we are completely responsible for whatever physical changes we would like to see in ourselves. They seem to insist that if the models they are showing us have made it, so should we. What they therefore implicitly suggest is that if we have not changed our body, if we still do not look like the models they display, we only have ourselves to blame.[21]

An indirect accusation therefore often hangs upon fitness discourses should we fail to comply with the standards they preach. What this tends to lead to is an exacerbation of our disillusionment and guilt when we take a wrong step or fail to attain a targeted stage in our progress. We are consequently pressured to be harder on ourselves, subjecting ourselves to harsher criticism for any difficulties faced along the way rather than considering, for instance, the unrealistic rigour, discipline, inefficiency, and/or ineffectuality of the regimen recommended along with the exorbitant demands of the goals proposed.

The time of instrumental reason is now

Instrumental reason is relentlessly focused on the next thing to work for, the next best thing to enjoy, which inclines it to be dismissive of the past and its attendant knowledge. Its single-minded pursuit of new and 'improved' experiences labels those that are no longer as outdated and useless. Any sense of a future beyond the upcoming enjoyment is often equally dismissed despite the tendency to adopt a consumerist lifestyle primarily for its far-reaching goals. If our initial focus is on the long-term, it is eventually replaced in prominence by a recurrent focus on our immediate plans for that same lifestyle: our concerns on whether the plans we have just made to feel good are the *right* plans to feel good. Our preoccupations come to dwell on whether our next pursuit will secure the happiness and success it promises – or if there are other affordable opportunities out there that can deliver better results that we are missing out on. Our deliberations are often incited by an urgency caused by the consumer culture's insistence that *now* rather than later is the time to make the most out of our life.

Despite the long journeys necessary for the realization of their high ideals, lifestyle narratives paradoxically seem to imply that the same journeys can be taken by simply staking everything on the present moment. They enjoin us to seek and satisfy as many opportunities as we are capable of seizing in the shortest time possible. We are compelled to deploy an ongoing strategy to acquire everything we want (or that we are supposed to want) as soon as we can. Not a moment is to be missed for every moment comes equipped with its own new chances. The rewards we anticipate must therefore arrive almost instantaneously. Aspirations must be gratified quickly, ideally in the very moment they are conceived. In contemporary life-strategies, Bauman points out, a desperate impulse is evident for desire to be satisfied by 'immediate, "on-the-spot fulfilment" […]'.[22]

Instrumental reason is driven by consumer culture to do and feel as fast and as much as it can. It encourages us to absorb ourselves by the sensations of our currently chosen experience to leave it shortly for the next one, provoking as a result an alternative sense of time. A peculiar mode of 'temporality' is conceived that is severed from any recollection or prospection in immersing itself totally from one present moment to the following moment. Frederic Jameson in 'The Cultural Logic of Late Capitalism' (1991) refers to schizophrenia as a paradigm for this archetypal postmodern state of being. The schizophrenic mind brings about a breakdown of all connections between signifiers whereby the moment is dissolved of its intimate relationship with memory, history, and anticipation. The condition, he explains, induces isolated, discontinuous, unrelated material signifiers which are incapable of synthesizing into a coherent sequence. Deprived of a before and after and consequently deprived of a personal identity, the schizophrenic perpetually inhabits a present that is immediate and undifferentiated.[23] Saturating this instantaneity is an emotional intensity, 'a mysterious and oppressive charge of affect'.[24]

Bauman explores the expert consumer's episodic temporality or '"nowist time"'[25] in such works as *Liquid Modern Challenges to Education* (2011), 'A Short History of Identity' (1996), *Liquid Love* (2003), and *Liquid Modernity* (1999). In our society, he argues, we are encouraged to live the present *unconditionally as* the enjoyment of the experience we have purchased. The present comes to amount only to the capaciousness of the experience's enjoyment. Nothing is to restrict, bind, or direct the present elsewhere. No memories, projects, and responsibilities are to refer it outside of the immediacy of its commodified arousal. In its freedom to enjoy itself without the least constraint attached to the past and future is an experience of *infinity*. A boundless indulgence of its sensorial instantaneity is licensed by a devaluation of the no longer and the yet to come.[26]

Between the immediacy of one experience and another occurs a liminal state where nothing much happens save for the unease incited by uneventfulness. To have unoccupied time, *to have time* is to squander yet more chances to be ahead in the race for happiness. We must therefore be hard at work at having no time left at our disposal. The intervals between our experiences need to be shortened as much as possible by always already ensuring that we have the next plan in mind.[27]

An awareness of passing time also inevitably intrudes in the nowist life when the effects of our experience start to diminish. We must therefore be quick enough to recognize the first signs of affective decline in order to leave that experience for another, which we would then treat in the same manner. To be able to preempt the beginnings of obsolescence is necessary if we are to avoid disappointment. Bent as it is on erasing time, the nowist life is a '"hurried" life'.[28] If its instantaneous excitement is to be sustained indefinitely, and ideally escalated, it must discard early to swiftly try the next new over and over again. 'The hurry', Bauman stresses, 'ought to be at its most intense when one is running from one point (failed, failing, or about to start failing) to another (yet untried)'.[29]

The joint fear that our experiences will let us down and the demand to always improve on them leads us eventually to a life predicated on a series of new starts that are barely allowed to develop as, Bauman remarks, 'the finish would have come right after the start, with pretty little happening in between'.[30] Our phobia of endings accelerates our life further by compelling us to taste our choices in their very early stages to be dumped as soon as we believe that they are about to grow familiar. In the chance event that they might fail us at any point soon, we enjoy them insofar as they still retain their novelty.[31]

Practical wisdom as critical solicitude (Ricoeur)

The refiguring identity's fuller counterpart to instrumental reason is the virtue of practical wisdom. If the virtue of imagination invokes the aesthetic of a possible worldview capable of integrating the exceptionality of an experience, practical wisdom is knowledge geared toward coherent directives on *how* to act ethically in view of that exceptional experience. In recognition of a circumstance's singularity, it formulates a praxis directed toward the good life. While imagination is preconceptual and cognitively sensorial in its visionary hermeneutics, the hermeneutics of practical wisdom is above all *rational* and *verbal* in its reflections. Its role can be summed up in the fourth clause of the statement that captures the refiguring decision:

Because I hope for a better life, I expose myself to the foreign in experience, and yet I imaginatively reconcile myself with it *as well as discover through practical wisdom what moral projects need to be done at its behest*, while all along accepting it as always foreign to me.

Practical wisdom, or its ancient Greek term, 'phronesis', has a long history in philosophy. Finding its origins in Aristotle's Book VI of *Nicomachean Ethics* (340 BCE), it has since been explored, revised, and developed extensively by a number of thinkers, including no less some of the hermeneutic-phenomenological thinkers that form the backbone of this work, namely, Hans-Georg Gadamer, Paul Ricoeur, and Richard Kearney.

Ricoeur associates practical wisdom with my solicitude toward the you of the vulnerable stranger.[32] To identify with your suffering is to identify with the unspoken enjoinment to take care of you without conditions. Your singularity as a person asks this of me. Your summons, however, is too exorbitant to reconcile with my life plans and the moral system I already inhabit. It refuses to be incorporated in my worldview with its duties on behalf of other people who might also be in need, including especially those with whom I already share a relationship. You are the exception. To help you, I am to set everything else aside and devote myself completely and utterly to you. You awaken me to the *inadequacy* of those customs of behaviour by which I have been taught to understand you and everyone else. Your presence, John Wall explains in 'Phronesis, Poetics, and Moral Creativity' (2003), 'consists [...] in the recognition of others as ultimately irreducible to one's own understanding or interpretation of them'.[33]

What practical wisdom attempts to achieve for Ricoeur is a way of reconciling my principles with your needs *despite* their anomaly. It seeks to figure out to what extent I am to forego and revise my rules of conduct for you. If I surrender or alter too much of my norms, I might end up neglecting other vulnerable people, who are also a you, as well as other significant projects in my life, like my career and social engagements. If I stand too much by my norms, I might misconstrue your needs and impose on you my own prejudices. A practical trade-off must therefore take place. In my moral arbitration between me and you, I am to aim at accommodating you as much as is possible but within sensible boundaries. Practical wisdom, Ricoeur argues, must ensure that my kindness toward you is effectively integrated in 'global projects, including, for example, professional life, family life, leisure time, and community and political life'.[34] The evaluative deliberation that is required to balance your needs with my goals is why Ricoeur calls the procedure, '*critical* solicitude'.[35]

The dialectic of practical wisdom in the refiguring identity model (and its other functions)

Practical wisdom, as Ricoeur illustrates it, is thereby a form of reasoning that aims to make a 'judgement in situation'[36] or 'on the spot' moral guidelines that are drafted specifically for a very specific circumstance. In seeking a golden mean between my principles and your needs, it is necessary that the interpretation I formulate is prudent, fair, balanced. Since it is aimed at moral action, it is also required to be pragmatic and realistic in what it can achieve.

The practice of phronesis in the refiguring identity model is not limited to people in need. It can include any other situation insofar as it provokes a reassessment in different degrees of our preconceived ideas of the good life and its attendant conduct. Mundane or exceptional, any situation that conflicts in some way with our personal vision of how to live well calls upon practical wisdom for resolution.

In the refiguring identity model, the virtue has other related roles. It figures as a judge to whether a situation merits an ethical response, and hence whether we should engage it with the refiguring decision. Not all instances require us to interpret them according to our ethical knowledge. It is patently also important for our wellbeing that we act for our own personal enjoyment or the satisfaction of material needs. Practical wisdom, here often exercised on a preconscious level, helps us distinguish the times when we can employ self-regarding decisions and those that call on us to employ the five virtues as aimed toward the good life.

It goes to show that if the virtue of exposure motivates the practice of practical wisdom, practical wisdom is *at the same time* as well a key motivator for the practice of exposure to experience. In such role, it performs a cautionary function mostly toward certain people, activities, and places whose unfamiliarity to us is too extreme. It is counterintuitive to unquestioningly give ourselves to *any* otherness that we cross paths with: a certain level of vigilance is crucial to ascertain whether our decision is as far as we can tell a sensible one. A baseline rudimentary understanding of what we might be going to expose ourselves to is worked out in order to determine whether it is prudent enough to trust the situation or leave it alone. Without some element of trust, minimal and vague as it might be, allowing the experience to affect our life can be self-destructive.

In its dialectical logic, the actual procedure of phronesis in the refiguring identity model is analogous to the imaginative procedure. One side of the dialectic references our life projects and the background of moral beliefs acquired through education, culture, experience, and the counsel of others that compose our own idea of what it means to live well. Insofar as we attach ourselves to this knowledge, our reflections would be to a large extent deontological by nature in conforming to preset life rules and duties that we would have developed from our past. To base our sense of worth on obedience to preestablished norms is to have what Ricoeur calls, *'self-respect'*. Self-respect derives its validation from the moral law, which is a reified expression of the call to live the good life. To have self-respect therefore is to act as agents of the moral law.[37] On the other side of the phronesis dialectic is the unprecedented context that contradicts this law and any law. What it asks of us is an unreserved ethical care that sabotages the rules we stand for. A level-headed interaction between our morality and the context's demands is required that is predicated on compromise and consensus.

Quite unlike instrumental reason with its ambitions to subdue the effects of the past and future, practical wisdom operates fully on the time factor. It enacts a reciprocal dialogue aimed at a calibration between our moral past and the anomalous present in order to construe a moral knowledge that can pave the way for a praxis to come that is more suitable for that present.

A close affiliation can be traced between the phronesis dialectic and the active methodology known in philosophy as 'reflective equilibrium'. The reflective equilibrium procedure assumed prominence in ethics after John Rawls in *A Theory of Justice* (1871) explained its integral function in his development of moral and political theory. Stelios Virvidakis defines it as 'a state of coherence of our thoughts about one or more issues, resulting from a deliberative process of mutual adjustment of beliefs, principles, theories, and arguments'.[38] Its starting point entails a consideration of our initial beliefs, judgements, or intuitions about particular and sometimes general features of a relevant domain of philosophical inquiry. Followed would be the drafting of an initial set of theoretical principles that can consistently account for the preliminary beliefs. At the final stage, any possible conflict between the beliefs and the principles laid out, along with any other conflict between the members themselves of either party, is brought to relief and resolved.[39]

The phronesis dialectic likewise resolves the discordance between our rules and the situational demands through a diplomatic process of a back-and-forth movement. In the interests of reconciliation, it is compelled to eliminate from, add to, balance, and alter our rules in view of the present's exceptional requirements.

Practical wisdom's recourse and origination in self-esteem

To settle the dialectical dispute of phronesis can yet be difficult to achieve in most cases. The context's exceptionality can prevent us from finding some form of agreement. The procedure of practical wisdom, as Ricoeur infers in *Oneself as Another* (1992), therefore has to fall back on our susceptibility to the underlying call of conscience to live the good life. We are to repeal all our injunctions on how to live well to renew our faith in living well *without* injunctions – *prior to* them. What is revitalized is the wish to aspire for the good life as absent of any determinations. In dispensing with its attachment to rules, our self-respect is returned to its originary drive, our self-esteem, whence all its moral knowledge is derived. Our hope is that our redirectedness toward the call would revive the attitude required to conceive the possibility of an interpretation that can reconcile us with the current predicament. Our reorientation can renew the faith, humility, and conviction needed to construe an ethical resolution that we had previously not foreseen.[40]

To have recourse to the mainspring of practical wisdom, the call, is to confirm above all the identity of our self-respect as a mode of expression of our self-esteem.[41] It discloses its fixed, rule-governed behavioural strategy as a concrete manifestation of our desire for the good life. As Ricoeur elucidates, self-respect deals with the moral, that is, the injunctions drawn up to live the good life. Self-esteem deals with the ethical, or the originary instinct to live that life anterior to any of its representations. Both 'refer to the intuitive idea of *mores*, with the twofold connotation of that which *is considered to be good* and of that which *imposes itself as obligatory*'.[42] 'Ethics', he writes, is 'the *aim* of an accomplished life and the term "morality" for the articulation of this aim in *norms* characterized at once by the claim to universality and by an effect of constraint [...]'.[43]

Ethics is premised on 'I wish' while morality is premised on 'I must'. The first is an implacable impulse or hankering and the other is the rationality of this impulse through procedures that ask for our obedience. Both, however, originate from and are directed toward the same destination. Morality is a necessary stage of ethics. 'It is held to constitute only a limited, although legitimate and even indispensable, actualization of the ethical aim, and ethics in this sense would then encompass morality'.[44]

The type of knowledge that practical wisdom devises (Ricoeur)

Phronesis is not interested in appropriating its object into a definitive and comprehensive system of knowledge. It refrains from categorizing or theorizing it in any manner. In its role as a hermeneutics of experience, it seeks to elicit an authentic interpretation by allowing the virtue of exposure to reveal the singularity of experience as much as possible without the imposition of any cognitive judgements. In doing so, it addresses experience precisely as a *response to its 'revelation'*. Before all else, its hermeneutics is thus an *answer* with intentions that are modest at best in that they seek a commonsensical interpretation that is targeted *solely* toward what needs to be morally done. In its very manner of understanding the circumstances as authentically as possible is an acknowledgement that the circumstances are irreducible and that other, more ambitious efforts at comprehension – and even its own to an extent – are bound to fail. Its ad hoc efforts therefore will still only ever be a rough and incomplete guide on what needs to be done. The unpretentious mode of its knowledge testifies to its humility.

Ricoeur acutely calls phronetic knowledge, 'universals in context' or 'potential or inchoate universals'. In its devoted focus on the peculiar situation, its construals are almost always incomplete and decentred. They have not as yet gained the status of universal rules; nor might they ever in being possibly irrelevant to other scenarios. In intending on being nothing other than a estimation of how the moment at hand can be viewed on a morally practical level, they might not be able to stand the test of time.[45]

There is often an inevitable high degree of inaccuracy or distortion endemic to phronetic interpretations in that they can never fully accommodate the excess of the experience's demands. No matter our endeavours to cohere its demands with our norms, more modifications are always in order. In the universals in context configured, an *inbuilt* inadequacy will always remain that is based on this implacable lack. As such, the universals must be constantly subjected to review with the aim of further developing on our moral understanding of the experience addressed as well as others. An intrinsic part of the process of practical wisdom is precisely the exigency to endlessly reappraise its universals in context in an attempt to ever improve on its reconciliations of the general with the singular. In his reference to Ricoeur's 'critical solicitude', Wall writes that 'practical wisdom is charged, for Ricoeur, with an essentially *dialectical* task, in the sense […] of an imperfect mediation of others' "proposals of meaning that are at first foreign" in the direction of an endless "path of eventual consensus". The end or goal of critical phronesis, never completed but always to be pursued, is an ever greater "mutual recognition" of self and other […].'[46] It thus functions in the direction 'of moral practices in common that are ever more genuinely and hyperbolically inclusive […].'[47]

Universals in context are yet in most cases the result of the virtue's direct recourse to the call of conscience. In expressing our faith in the call, they are full of what Ricoeur would call '*conviction*'. They carry an authority that is derived from the way they successfully *conjoin* in some measure not just our morality and the exceptional present's demands – but the call of conscience no less. They constitute above all a resolution between our moral duties or self-respect, the experience at hand, and our originary longing for the good life or self-esteem. What they attest to thereby is the *integrity* of our ethical sense. To act upon the 'potential universals' is to act out of our holistic ethical being where ethical desire and moral duty are brought to a general synchrony through the intervention of the foreign event. In my performance, the 'I must' here returns to recalibrate and develop itself from the 'I wish', delivering me to the 'I am'. The conviction of my actions emerges from this innate process, through which I can finally claim, 'Here I stand. This is all that I am. This is the all that I can be.'[48]

In evolving out of our ethical integrity, it is possible that the universals in context can in some cases become universals *for all contexts* or what we would call 'norms'. Some can disclose a potential relevance to other situations that are typical and/or that we consider as exceptional. In other words, they can assume the status of standards that can guide us to resolve future situations that we would have otherwise found irresolvable through our former standards as well as addressing other 'mundane' situations in a more insightful and integral manner. This would require the universals in context to develop further through a reflective equilibrium with our moral system, where both are revised and modified for an effective assimilation to ensue. By the same token, our personal vision of the good life can likewise go through a reinterpretation. It is therefore not unlikely that phronesis can eventually affect an alteration in how we conceive a better future along with the kind of actions it encourages. At the same time, the universals we have incorporated in our moral knowledge and conduct are to remain open to future renegotiation given their inevitable inherent incapacity to ever fully satisfy the requirements they were created for.[49]

Consumerist lifestyle rules versus the 'moral impulse' (Bauman)

Another crucial difference is evident between those rules derived from practical wisdom and those derived from instrumental reason. Whereas phronetic rules are perpetually reevaluated, readjusted, and even reinvented in their endeavour to be more just toward experience, the rules deployed by instrumental reason arrive as *prepackaged*. They are prepared for us wholesale by self-professed experts and dilettantes of the five commercial life-strategies

Consumerist lifestyle conduct in fact tends to unquestioningly follow the guidelines stipulated by influencers, wellness gurus, travelling agencies and guides, media celebrities, and fitness trainers among others. This intense reliance on what is offered us comes with its own selection of options with our decisions to drop some rules and take up others justified exclusively by the promise of quicker, easier, and better results. If the market celebrates our autonomy of choice, the version of autonomy it celebrates is limited to the lifeguide offers that it sets for us *itself*. Our freedom is thereby always already exploitable by what it deems we should adopt. Free will is in reality the compulsion to select from among the selections already exhibited for us. Generic consumers, Bauman remarks in 'The Self in a Consumer Society' (1999), 'are the judges, the critics, and the choosers. They can, after all, refuse their allegiance to any one of the infinite choices on display – except the choice of choosing among them'.[50]

It is in the world of business that the pursuit of readymade instructions is often taken to a blind extreme. As Bauman in *Modernity and the Holocaust* (1989) and ten Bos in 'Business Ethics and Bauman Ethics' (1997) both illustrate, the *morality* of a deed in bureaucratic organizations depends at all times on the extent of its compliance with rules 'from on high', whose sole intention as always entails the interests of the company. For any choice to be moral, it must conform to the regulations already laid down by managerial ideology along with contractual obligations. Morality therefore, ten Bos explains, 'no longer has to do with self-respect, integrity, empathy, autonomy, conscience, or individual responsibility, but, instead, self-sacrifice, obedience, docility, duty, and discipline'.[51] It is no longer the quality or virtue of the act that is esteemed anymore but its technology or how well it serves to fulfil certain commands. What results is an *instrumental morality*, where the idea of good or bad is in direct proportion to how effective are the means rather than the ends of an action.[52]

Companies, for Bauman, affect a neutralization of what he calls the 'moral impulse', which can be interpreted as his own version of practical wisdom. The moral impulse is provoked by the vulnerability of the other, which calls upon me for succour. In its ineffable intensity, this prelogical cry asks of me to do everything I can for it and more, what is possible and beyond. Akin to practical wisdom, the moral impulse thus charges me with the urgent yet impossible task of formulating a reconciliation of its exorbitant demands with my preset morality. It is therefore neither 'the knowledge of what is to be done' nor 'the duty correctly performed' but 'the urge to do', the instinct to act for a defenceless plea.[53]

By virtue of the exceptional character of the plea, I have no preplanned knowledge that can enlighten me on how I am to behave toward it. I am left alone to my own devices, thrown into a *complete accountability* for my deeds. Placed upon me is the unique role of being unconditionally responsible for what is going to happen to the vulnerable one. I find myself, Bauman claims, as 'different from all others, the irreplaceable I, not a specimen of a category [...]'.[54]

Because of the other's infinite need, however, I am always already put in a position of *doubt* as to whether I have given them enough justice. The conduct that ensues from practical wisdom or the moral impulse is always fraught with the possibility that I could have done more, that I could have done things differently. 'This uncertainty with no exit', Bauman explains, 'is the foundation of morality. One recognizes morality by its gnawing sense of unfulfilledness, by its endemic dissatisfaction with itself. *The moral self is a self always haunted by the suspicion that it is not moral enough*'.[55] It is the anguish of its deficiency that motivates the moral impulse or practical wisdom to continuously evolve its moral vision with its norms. This virtue, like exposure, imagination, acceptance, and hope, is chronically premised on ambivalence.

As Bauman and ten Bos show, business executives regard the choices made by the moral impulse as too disruptive and deregulative for the smooth running of their organization. The impulse's unpredictable and nonpecuniary intentions are a direct confrontation to the profit-maximizing norms of the business culture. Various strategies are therefore designed to relegate the impulse to the margins, if not to abolish it completely. These procedures are gradually ingrained into the instrumental moral mindset that sets the standards for workplace conduct.

In *Postmodern Ethics* (1993), Bauman draws attention to a popular strategy that encourages the employees' moral exculpation from the grave consequences of some of their actions. Their blamelessness is justified by explicit reference to the complications of the situation at hand as well as the involvement of a large number of intermediary people that have brought the action into effect. What is thereby achieved is a distraction by directing attention on the overwhelming complexity of the scenario and diminishing responsibility by spreading it out among a lot of people. As a result it becomes conveniently difficult to trace clearly the harm that has been caused by the employees.[56]

Another popular strategy that has already been briefly referenced is the insistent claim that anyone outside of the company's team – competitors, customers, and stakeholders – is to be strictly regarded as an object that can either facilitate or obstruct the interests of the company. 'Being in business', ten Bos remarks, 'is being merciless with respect to the competitor and there is no place for moral concern here: the competitor is faceless'.[57] The customers are likewise turned faceless in their perceptual reduction to an opportunity for the firm. Writers on business management like Gary Hamel, Coimbatore K. Prahalad, and Tom Peters in fact disregard the customers' holistic being in their studies, treating them instead as a bundle of needs and demands. Customers are worthy of investigation only insofar as their desires can be analyzed for exploitation.[58]

Instrumental morality *relieves* company employees from the agony of having to make moral choices. Having the rules prepared for them excuses them from the very real struggle of having to decide what to do in situations where the moral choice is not so clear-cut. In his article, Ten Bos alludes to the common instance of a consultant whose ideas on, say customer-friendliness, are unquestioningly taken up by the managers, who overlook the simple fact that their company decisions will henceforth be based on someone else's idea of the customer rather than their own. Sanctioning all the rules handed down from an external authority in a business is often justified by the conviction that we are no qualified specialists in the field treated by those rules and that thereby we should grant full authority to those who claim so. Placing all responsibility for a line of action on others' shoulders on account of our confidence in their superior competence absolves us, or so we believe, of our moral responsibility.[59]

The other four life-strategies of fashion, fitness, self-spirituality, and travel likewise dismiss moral issues from their discourses, which constitutes perhaps one of their major selling-points. It explains above all the appeal of turning them into *identity-types*. Elevating them to the status of biographical narrative schemes legitimates their amoral instructions to dictate our life, which can grant us reassurance and security. Peace of mind is here tantamount to the absence of practical wisdom and its hardships from the life map they chart for us. Substituting the anguished moral choice, the lifestyle discourses give us the consumer choice instead. This is perhaps their 'true' cure: to decide on *any matter as a consumer*, that is, according to simple, straightforward, and manageable goals. At all times, our decisions are to be based on what makes us feel good about ourselves, what brings us prestige: the same decisions which are usually safely directed by the models and codes of fashion.

An important influence on our eagerness to interpret consumerist lifestyles as identity-types is the way their instructions are presented. Travel, self-spiritual, entrepreneurial, fashion, and fitness gurus tend to display the rules we are to abide by not only as guides on how to perform certain activities meant to improve our life – but rather as guides *to life*. They counsel us to follow them not to enhance our wellbeing but to find *salvation*. In our journey toward this end, they profess to know *what* difficulties in life we are to confront and how to overcome them. By formulating for us what is supposed to constitute a problem, they emphasize some aspects of life that are only defined *as problems* insofar as the goals they stipulate are being chased. Otherwise the prominence of these instances or their very definition as obstacles would not have factored in our day-to-day life. Among the typical scenarios we are asked to treat as highly undesirable are a lack of motivation or energy, not having enough time, finding no support in friends, the expenses of the lifestyle commodities we are supposed to buy, a lack of self-worth, doubt, idleness, moodiness, setting standards that are too high, trying to be someone we are not, and having too many family caregiving obligations.

Lifestyle discourses tend to subtly *substitute in significance* the difficulties they mark for us for the usually far more complex and turbulent difficulties of our actual life. Hardly ever addressed are the very real potential problems associated with relationships, career, love, illness, death, etcetera. What seems to be implied rather is that it is *their* difficulties we should be worrying about in interfering with the achievement of their objectives, which means an interference with our true happiness.

The difficulties we are told to commit to are in fact elevated to a heroic scale. They are themselves made appealing to fight against by being broken down into a succession of smaller difficulties to concentrate on sequentially along with day-to-day minitasks targeted toward digestible goals. The carefully dissected challenges are clear in explanation as well as manageable through easy-to-follow methods. It is one of the crucial tasks of lifestyle experts to explain what needs to be overcome in an accessible and simplified manner.

The projects illustrated by the lifestyles therefore *act as* comprehensive visions of life with their own exhaustive compendiums of difficulties and solutions (to be taken in small steps that, however, accrue in time). Everything is clarified and predictable in the life simulacrum they design; every action and event marking a stage on a measuring tape that extends toward our final happiness. At every point in the journey we are encouraged to feel that this happiness is within sight. It is no wonder that we are more than willing to replace the challenges that feature in this simulacrum of life with the infinitely messier, more painful and disorienting challenges that beset us in the world outside.

VII

From Surrender to Acceptance

Therapeutic surrender in self-spirituality and travel

A lot of literature on self-spirituality explores and prescribes a mindset that often goes by the term, 'surrender'. Derived from the precepts of Hinduism, Buddhism, as well as in part from the Ancient Greek philosophy of Epicureanism, it is an outlook that is predicated on a relinquishment of what is usually a difficult situation to a benevolent higher power in which we place our unconditional trust. It involves the admission that the situation is beyond our control and that it is inevitable that we give up all possessive attempts at directing it. In recognizing that we are helpless to affect a change in our circumstances, we unburden ourselves by giving them up to the forces of the cosmos, through whose mysterious wisdom all will be resolved.

What, for instance, Patanjali in *Yoga Sutra* (500 BCE–400 CE) calls 'Ishvara pranidhana', translated as 'surrender to the Lord',[1] or wellness gurus such as Marianne Williamson in *A Return to Love* (1996) or Kathy Cordova in *Let Go: Let Miracles Happen* (2003) call 'spiritual surrender', converge upon the same practice of offering an experience, or even offering *all* experience, to a beyond that will take care of us.[2] The beyond reality can be represented as our deeper intuition, the Cosmic Energy, Spirit, God, the Universe, and the Life Force, among other appellations. The skill of surrender, writes Sally Kempton in her online yoga journal, 'involves an attunement to the energetic movement that is sometimes called universal or divine will, the Tao, flow, or, in Sanskrit, *shakti*. Shakti is the subtle force – we could also call it the cosmic intention – behind the natural world in all of its manifestations'.[3] To give in to this force, we are told, is to transform ourselves from self-centred to selfless beings, opened to and reflecting the will of the cosmos. Kempton points out that one of her spiritual mentors, Gurumayi Chidvilasananda, 'once said that to surrender is to become aware

106

of God's energy *within oneself*, to recognize the energy, and to accept it. It's an *egoless* recognition – that is, it involves a shift in your sense of what "I" is'.[4] To 'let go', to 'surrender a problem', to 'go with the flow', to 'give in to love' . . . all seem to articulate a shift to a methodology and a point of view that is at the heart of self-spirituality.

The contemporary literature on travelling also tends to emphasize a way of being that is akin to surrender but expressed in a secular vocabulary. Often we are enjoined by social media, TV programs, magazines, adverts, and tourist agencies not to regard our trip as a *plan* with an itinerary on what to do every day. Rather, we are to relinquish our control of the trip along with any attached anticipations to let it take us wherever it will. We are advised to be carpe diem, to trust contingency, to seize the opportunities thrown in our way in the belief that life has its own unforeseeable but benevolent designs for us. The idea of 'spontaneous travelling' in the discourse captures this increasingly popular attitude.

To travel spontaneously is to pick destinations we would not usually consider on a whim. We are encouraged to keep an open mind to random events and have faith in their serendipity. A typical article that argues for this travel philosophy, for instance, 'The Art of Not Planning' (2008) from *The Guardian*, presents a number of extracts from books by traveller writers that share their own advice and insight on the intuitive form of holidaymaking. Owen Sheers invites us to let the foreign city itself be our guide, and he gives as an example the city of Manhattan, where we can decide our route according to the never-ending pattern of stop and go lights. Annie Hawes, moreover, advises us to put our faith in the locals' hospitality for the next steps of our journey; Jason Webster counsels against booking for our trips; while Geert Mak tells us to slow down and spend some time in one place in a location without venturing too far so we can become more intimately acquainted with it.[5]

In a similar vein, Rick Steves in 'The Beauty of Spontaneous Travel' stresses on 'the value of tossing the schedule once in a while and living in the moment': 'free to go where the spirit moves you'. 'With no agenda', he claims, 'you can blow like the wind freely through Europe'. 'Make an art of taking the unexpected in stride, and turn mishaps into adventures'.[6] Meanwhile, Dean Seguin in 'The Key to Happiness?' (2019) confirms that new research by Travelzoo reveals that Canadians who travel spontaneously tend to lead a happier life. Some of the tips provided on how to be this kind of tourist include getting deliberately lost and 'being fine' when things go wrong, knowing that you can turn the unexpected odds to your advantage.[7]

Experienced travellers assure us that various rewards await those who take trips by following their instinct. We can discover what is new and surprising in the familiar. We can discover new places we would have never dreamed of visiting as well as local traditions and ways of life we might have ignored if we were abiding by a schedule.[8] We are told that if we let go of the need to take charge and let events unfold on their own, our experience of the foreign country will be that much more authentic and fulfilling. It is for the sake of a higher personal satisfaction that spontaneous travel is so celebrated in consumer culture. If travel gurus exhort us to pay closer attention to our surroundings and let the moment determine our thought and action, it is because they believe that this will grant us so much more happiness than a strict adherence to a planned route.

In self-spiritualist discourse, the exercise of surrender is likewise often tied to the guarantee that it will make us feel better about ourselves. Whether it is described as the ideal process for finding solutions to problems we cannot seem to resolve on our own, releasing ourselves of negative feelings or energy toward a partic-ular event, reaching an inner state of peace and intuition, or living a healthier, stress-free life, the final objective is always without exception our personal happiness. Notably absent in fact is the practice of surrender as a stimulus for solicitude toward others and societal institutions. No goal that is inclusive of our concern for what is outside of us is usually referenced. Akin to all other activ-ities encouraged by the consumerist lifestyles, the activity of surrender is for the most part encouraged for our psychological, emotional, and physical wellbeing. In excluding its potential to help us care more for our surroundings, it is here turned into a self-regarding act.

There is an irony in the self-spiritualist portrayals of surrender in that they depict it as bringing us close to a transcendent reality that is yet interpreted as just another means for our satisfaction. The spiritual realm comes to be defined as a function for how it can change me and only me for the better. What transcends us is here devoured as well by instrumental reason to be exploited for our individualist gain. It is utilized as *therapy*, which is in most cases the prime motivation why self-spiritual systems are adopted in the first place as well as their overall purpose. Christopher Lasch in *The Culture of Narcissism* (1979) argues to this effect when he states that 'People today hunger not for personal salvation [...] but for the feeling, the momentary illusion, of personal well-being, health, and psychic security'. They seek 'neither individual self-aggrandize-ment nor spiritual transcendence but peace of mind [...]'.[9] 'The world view emerging among us', Peter Marin states in *The New Narcissism* (1975), 'centers solely on the self' and 'has individual survival as its sole good'.[10]

The philosophy of surrender in spontaneous travelling and self-spirituality thus turns out to be yet another self-gratifying lifestyle theme in reflecting an overwhelming preoccupation with the internal reality of the self at the expense of an awareness of the external reality of our bonds with individuals and institutions. We can infer that the success of its practice *depends* for the most part on the pretence that our place in history and our present environ-ment is irrelevant, or at best, of little importance to our salvation. The world around us is marginalized in that we are told that it is through our interior world alone that sure enlightenment can be reached. In the grandiose vision of self-spirituality, it is the feelgood consumed from its therapeutic, higher power that is presented as superlative in reality and value to anything else. Along with travel and the rest of the lifestyles, it drastically diminishes the crucial role of our responsibilities to the other-than-self in an exchange for the solipsistic responsibilities it prescribes. All lifestyles assure us above all that we owe it to ourselves to be happy. And everything will be fine if *I* am fine. Adopting any of the lifestyles as an identity-type is thus tantamount to castrating ourselves from the intersubjective field of which we are necessarily a constituent.

To accept is to accept facticity

'Surrender' bears a strong resemblance to that virtue the refiguring identity calls 'acceptance'. 'Acceptance' is here given a specific characterization that we will henceforth for the purposes of clarifi-cation differentiate from the concept of surrender *as characterized* by the self-spirituality and travel lifestyles. Like surrender, acceptance refrains from manipulating circumstances to force out a predetermined outcome. It, too, derives its practice from the understanding that all control is at the end of the day futile, in that life has a way of taking its own unforeseeable path in spite of all our intentions and calculations. The awareness that characterizes acceptance regards any interpretation of experience as perforce illusory in that it cannot ever capture the *actuality* of the foreign in experience itself. The experiencing of what is other to us in the outside world cannot but be irreducible to any mode of comprehension. With surrender, acceptance thus lets experience run its course without interference. It allows it to take place without any cognitive and affective investments.

Along with the virtue of exposure, acceptance can also be seen to dwell in the psychology of what Hans-Georg Gadamer in *Truth and Method* (1960) calls 'experienced persons'.[11] Experience has taught such individuals to expose themselves to what is other in all experience to come. In their willingness to submit is an attestation to their 'insight into the limitations of humanity', that they are 'master neither of time nor the future', 'that all foresight is limited and all plans uncertain'. They are defined by the knowledge that anything that happens or will happen will always exceed and in many ways undo their attempts at controlling it according to their desires. In this lies the 'truth value of experience' or the *facticity* of existence, whose ineradicable immediacy is obstinately *external* to our subjective reality. All experience in some measure attests to this impersonal outside force that is blindly indifferent to our endeavours. It is, says Hans-Georg Gadamer quoting Leopold von Ranke, the unknown '"what is," here, [which] is not this or that thing, but "what cannot be destroyed"'.[12]

To accept the facticity of all we go through is to accept our finiteness. It is, by Gadamer's account of the experienced person, the acknowledgement of 'the limits of the power and the self-knowledge of his planning reason'.[13] Acceptance's affirmation of experience as foreign allows experience to return *to itself*, to its fundamental autonomy. Along with surrender, it urges a renunciation of the possessive and autonomous self by regarding it as a perpetual offering to the unknown principle in everything that is outside us. No longer seen as a 'for-itself', the self becomes a 'for-otherness'. It discovers itself as a submission to the unforeseeable processes of life to take it where they will. In many ways, our inveterate drive to control, however, deters us time and again from fully achieving this psychosomatic abandon.

The future for which we accept

If both the concepts of surrender and acceptance are premised on a self-givenness to a higher reality, they differ predominantly in the *reason* why this givenness is pursued in the first place. In contrast to the therapeutic future that surrender aspires for, the future acceptance aspires for is above all *ethical* in its focus on the good life. Its primary incentive is to help realize a reality to come that involves not just me but everyone and everything else as well.

The *manner* acceptance pursues the future is not *active*. In order to progress toward its destination, it does not engage with experience through a positive intention, that is, an intention with any distinguishing features. In fact we can say that it does not 'engage' at all: its intention is *negative* in having no aims and expectations of any sort. This makes it unique from all five virtues for even the virtue of exposure is exercised through an intention that constitutes a certain character in its readiness to suffer the difference of experience from ourselves. The resolve of acceptance toward experience, however, is as it were, to be without resolve. In this is revealed a humility that understands that all our efforts are insignificant in the great scheme of things, that history ultimately develops by its own driving force. If a better future is to arrive, it will do so with or without our consent, beyond our plans. We can never comprehend how it will come to pass, how it will even be an improvement to the present. Like the rest of the virtues, though for reasons that issue from a different perspective, its vision of what is not yet thus always remains *indeterminate* in character.

Acceptance surrenders to the process of experience by virtue of its *faith* in the call of conscience. It sees in the call a higher intention that enjoins existence toward a certain inevitable future where everything will finally be reconciled. Its will to have no will expresses an unconditional trust in a transcendental will that directs us all toward certain unfathomable routes with time. To accept is thereby to believe in an inconceivable fatedness. We let life take lead because we believe that it is steered by the call.

The final state of catharsis and ataraxia

The acceptance mindset is not so far off from the state of being that defines the final stages of catharsis. 'Catharsis', derived from the Greek 'katharsis', literally signifies 'purification' or 'cleansing'. Aristotle in Poetics (330 BCE) was the first to affiliate the concept to the dramatic genre of tragedy, and it has since also been associated with literary narratives. Catharsis tends to allude both to a particular experiential process of a character in the narrative and the potential reaction of the audience to such a process. All narratives evoking catharsis seem to be centred in different measures on episodes of loss and suffering that are visited usually upon the protagonists, compelling us as audience to identify. Our care for the protagonists, Richard Kearney explains in On Stories (2002), makes us feel pity and fear for them as well as awe at the horrifying misfortunes they endure.[14]

The tragic circumstances of the characters eventually reach a certain pitch that is irrevocable. Their loss arrives at an irreversible limit where all concern for surviving and overcoming is recognized to be futile and absurd. In the extremity of their predicament, their self-protective instincts are revealed to be a deceptive illusion. All sense of care, along with ours for them, is thereby given up. Their self-attachments are surrendered in the accession that there is nothing that can be done. In letting go of all attempts at controlling their fate, they cave in to its implacable facticity.

In its reconciliation with the loss of our powers, catharsis over-laps with the virtue of acceptance. At this point, the all-consuming fixation with loss is lost, its affective purchase lost. What results from our severance from all concern with ego is an experience of liberation. We are delivered to a state of ineffable calm that reveals a detached and therefore much more lucid perception on our life. Released from our myopic self-interested perspective, we acquire a vision whose distinterestedness provides us with existential clarity.

The type of serenity that catharsis and acceptance inspire also entails the goal of Epicureanism, an ancient school of philosophy founded in Athens that taught emancipation from physical and mental pain. Through its concept of the tetrapharmakos, Epicureanism sought to liberate its followers from all psychic disturbance that was usually caused by the belief that the gods will judge us for our deeds, the inevitability of death leading to the possibility of postmortem punishment, the worries accompanying unfulfilled desires, and the concern with the impure intent of our actions. The removal of all worry led to what the Roman politician and general, Torquatos, calls 'the greatest pleasure'[15] or 'ataraxia' by the Epicureans. To dwell in ataraxia is to enjoy *the absence* of all self-preoccupation. Ataraxia, as Peter Preuss explains in *Epicurean Ethics* (1994), is a katastematic pleasure in that it is not experienced as a feeling or sensation but rather as a conscious state of imperturbable being.[16] Premised on the strict lack of desire, it opens us to a deep equanimity. Highly influenced by this philosophy is the self-spiritual life-strategy itself.

Catharsis in three literary instances

Three instances of catharsis will be briefly explored from literature for further elucidation. The extracts are from John Synge's tragedy, *Riders to the Sea* (1904), Maurice Blanchot's reçit, *The Instant of My Death* (1994/1998), and William Shakespeare's *King Lear* (1606).[17]

Synge's play, *Riders to the Sea*, ends with the protagonist, Maurya, coming to the realization that she has lost the last of her sons to the sea. As the corpse of Bartley, her last son, is carried into the house, she is led to remember the tragic deaths of all her previous sons, testifying to a whole lifetime spent in misery. Maurya's soliloquy and actions here articulate a climax of loss that has exhausted all capacity for suffering. In particular, her gesture of placing an empty cup downward on the table while laying her hands together on Bartley's corpse symbolically expresses life's pain having been drained to the lees. What follows is a diminuendo of acquiescence where her release from all worldly claims takes her to what T. S. Eliot in *Four Quartets* (1941) calls 'A condition of complete simplicity (Costing not less than everything)' (4.V). There is an intense pathos in this final resolution by virtue of the fact that Maurya only manages to find consolation through the deaths of those she loves. Only in the awareness that there is nothing more to lose does she finally accept loss: 'They're all gone now, and there isn't anything more the sea can do to me . . .' Comfort only comes for her in total defeat. 'It isn't that I haven't prayed for you, Bartley, to the Almighty God', she says. 'It isn't that I haven't said prayers in the dark night till you wouldn't know what I'd be saying; but it's a great rest I'll have now, and it's time surely. It's a great rest I'll have now, and great sleeping in the long nights after Samhain [...]'.[18]

In transcending suffering through its acceptance, Maurya gains insight into suffering as *the* fundamental human condition, death as sovereign. She accordingly discovers compassion toward the plight of everyone else. '[M]ay [the Lord] have mercy on my soul, Nora', she tells her younger daughter, 'and on the soul of every one is left living in the world'.[19] In *Tragic Pleasures* (2014), Elizabeth S. Belfiore draws attention to the contemplation evoked by catharsis through the vivid realization that our lot is also everyone else's. The finitude of all living beings or the facticity at the heart of existence is brought home to us, awakening a universal empathy.[20]

The sense of freedom found by catharsis and acceptance is also indicated in the ending to Blanchot's *récit, The Instant of My Death*, where the protagonist narrates his alarmingly close encounter with death before a Nazi firing squad. Lined up to be shot, just about to be executed, he embraces his own imminent demise, and with this comes 'a feeling of extraordinary lightness, a sort of beatitude (nothing happy, however) – sovereign elation? The encounter of death with death [...]? I will not try to analyse. He was perhaps suddenly invincible'.[21] Later on he writes:

> There remained, however, at the moment when the shooting was no longer but to come, the feeling of lightness that I would not know how to translate: freed from life? the infinite opening up? Neither happiness, nor unhappiness. Nor the absence of fear and perhaps already the step beyond. I know, I imagine that this unanalysable feeling changed what there remained for him of existence. As if the death outside of him could only henceforth collide with the death in him. 'I am alive. No, you are dead'.[22]

As the author discloses, what is accessed through release from care is, again, a state of being that seems to be transcendent and in some indescribably significant way enlightened. Above all, it is captured through a form of expression that is common to apophatic theology where an ineffable divine reality is expressively approached by negation: a sublime source evoked by language that progresses in terms of what may not be said about it. In the passage, the repetitive use of paradox in particular serves such a purpose.

The final state of catharsis is further explored in the first scene of Act V of *King Lear*, where the former king, now stripped of all authority and facing possible death, tries to comfort Cordelia, the only daughter who has not betrayed him:

> Come, let's away to prison.
> We two along will sing like birds I' the' cage.
> When thou dost ask me blessing, I'll kneel down
> And ask of thee forgiveness. So we'll live,
> And pray, and sing, and tell old tales, and laugh
> At gilded butterflies, and hear poor rogues
> Talk of court news, and we'll talk with them too –
> Who loses and who wins, who's in, who's out –
> And take upon 's the mystery of things
> As if we were God's spies. And we'll wear out
> In a walled prison packs and sects of great ones
> That ebb and flow by th' moon. (V.18–19)

Lear seems to be telling his daughter to surrender to the inevitable, their impoverishment of fortune, as a precondition to their freedom. An acceptance of their fate, he seems to claim, will renew their vision of the present moment. It will let experiences 'ebb and flow' on their own. It will free 'things' to shine forth in all their 'mystery', uncontaminated by judgements and ambitions. To be 'God's spies' is to see the 'gilded butterflies', the 'poor rogues', the wins and losses of people at court without our controlling desires and thereby in all their dissociative original wonder. To let go of our possessive hold on life is to bear witness to its free singularity in even its simplest and most ordinary events, to find beauty therein and rejoice in it. True happiness seems to be derived from this selfless recognition.

To dwell fully in the present is to find happiness (Epicureanism)

With an acceptance of our finitude comes a vivid concentration on the present. Severing all possessive attachments with the world and acknowledging wholeheartedly our lot opens us to a susceptibility of the world around us right now as not 'for us' but 'for itself'. The moment is given back to its own proceedings – and in its otherness we recognize an infinite value for which we find we are illimitably grateful. The Epicureans similarly taught that by meditating on our death and the death of everything else, a deep appreciation and enjoyment of the present *as it is,* is acquired. Training ourselves to be ready for death paradoxically intensifies the processes of life happening now and a beauty is revealed therein that is precious because fragile.[23] As Pierre Hadot claims in *Philosophy as a Way of Life* (1995), 'Each of life's moments surges forth laden with incommensurable value'. '[I]t allows us to accede to cosmic consciousness by making us attentive to the infinite value of each instant, and causing us to accept each moment of existence from the viewpoint of the universal law of the *cosmos*'.[24] We have reached the condition of ataraxia.

For the Epicureans, our acceptance of mortality immerses us fully in the present because life is always lived fully there rather than in the past and future, which are always independent of us and ever beyond our intentions. The present is all we can really know. It is the only actuality we can ever be certain of when we ponder on the certainty of death's nothingness. Pondering on what has gone and what is to come will only provoke passions that will alienate us from ourselves. The encroachment of nothingness, however, stimulates focus on where our life always dwells. Horace's famous carpe diem thesis in his *Odes* (23 BCE) attests to this now-consciousness that can open a path to a way of life: 'Life ebbs as I speak: so seize each day, and grant the next no credit' (1.11.17).

Ataraxic happiness is consequently indifferent to the influence of time. In its intense awareness of the here and now, its fulfilment is undisturbed by recollection and prospection. It no longer either desires or dreads a past or future: it does not need them. Its quiet abides in an 'eternal present'. For this reason, the Epicureans associated ataraxia with the immortality of the gods. On their account, it is a perfect happiness of the present that makes the gods immortal rather than a happiness that comes from being immortal. Adelmo Barigazzi remarks that 'Immortality and blessedness constitute the fundamental attributes of the gods. Their primary advantage with respect to the human is neutralized by virtue of the fact that happiness does not know time, because it is already fulfilled in the moment and as a result it becomes senseless to desire infinity'.[25]

The dialogue of acceptance with the other virtues

As the practice of the Epicurean 'ataraxia' proves so well, the mindset of acceptance need not evolve from any tragedy, even though this cause tends to be prominent in the case of catharsis in literary narratives. Like the other virtues of the refiguring identity model, acceptance is treated as an innate disposition that we ratify and that requires experience and deliberation to develop. We are not to ever assume that its practice has been perfected inasmuch as its relationship with some past episode can always be partial or disingenuous while new episodes can bring unprecedented challenges toward its attempts at self-renunciation. It must therefore be constantly reviewed and renewed in light of changing circumstances. To this end, the unified and individual impression of the other virtues along with the narrative's overarching focus on the good life telos can help steer it toward the right directions. Without these guiding influences, its activity would come close in nature to the narcissistic surrender of self-spiritual discourses.

The dispassionate and lucid attitude that acceptance leads to reciprocally also acts as an affective premise for the other virtues' performance. It encourages their distantiation from the bounds of our acquisitive self to derive their practice more authentically from the call to live well. Its mood helps loosen them from our egotistic fixations so they can deepen their susceptibility to the call of conscience.

At the same time, acceptance also *discourages* the virtues, imagination and practical wisdom in particular, from furnishing experience with *any* interpretation. In its awareness that all our attempts at understanding life are intrinsically fallible, it helps maintain an endemic distrust in all hermeneutics despite its necessity for moral praxis. In all such endeavours to understand, no matter how receptive, it instigates a quotient of disengagement or noncommitment. The underlying scepticism helps ascertain a nonreliance on our horizon of understanding as well as any nascent understanding that imagination and/or practical wisdom work out. In our confrontation with the outside world, acceptance not only demotivates us to lose our judgements and biases as much as possible but also demotivates a reification of our interpretative outcomes, which helps in turn to avoid the chance of their eventual fetishization. It thereby helps ensure that the disruptive foreign of the outside retains its affective authority upon us regardless of any form of incentive at determining it and its necessity. The role of acceptance as outlined in the refiguring decision statement testifies to this countermovement character:

> Because I hope for a better life, I expose myself to the foreign in experience, and yet I imaginatively reconcile myself with it as well as discover through practical wisdom what moral projects need to be done at its behest, *while all along accepting it* as always foreign to me.

Acceptance's inherent faithlessness in our hermeneutics is shared by the virtue of exposure. Both mindsets are built on the conviction that the only way we can really 'know' experience is to discard all evaluative criteria to give ourselves uncompromisingly to its process, wherever that might direct us. In this regard, both have a similar effect upon the rest of the virtues. There is, however, a significant contrast between them that requires emphasis. Their mode of affirming experience is different – on account of their distinctive stances on the self. In exposure, the affirmation is in the manner of a *suffering*, while in acceptance, it is in the manner of an *abandon*.

On the one hand, exposure proceeds from the premise of an appropriating subjectivity that faces an experience that is *in conflict* with it. In this mindset, a discordance between our self-reality and the reality of the outside world is made prominent – so that our openness to that outside must by necessity take place as an *endurance*. On the other hand, acceptance proceeds from the premise of a renunciation of this self and its concomitant attachments. There is in this mindset *already* no appropriating subjectivity to engage the outside. As a result, the outside is not approached through conflict but through an egoless receptivity. Whatever happens to us we let it take over with a flexibility that attests to the loss of our judgemental self. Like a liquid taking the shape of any vessel it is poured into, we indiscriminately 'become' any event that arrives in that moment. We become a variant of what John Keats famously called 'the chameleon poet'. Acceptance, therefore, does not affirm discordance but concordance. It conveys an abandon to whatever takes place around us.

The difference between exposure and acceptance becomes clearer when we consider the *reasons* why these two virtues practice affirmation. On the one hand, exposure affirms an experience because it has faith that its singularity might develop our worldview and choices tending toward a closer realization of the good life. Assent is therefore given to the experience *in itself* and not any other. On the other hand, acceptance affirms an experience because there is no controlling self to hold on to, because nothing else is really 'real'. By acceptance, we affirm because to do otherwise would be illusory and disingenuous. For this mindset, an experience, any experience discloses what is inexorable, the facticity of life, to which we give all our esteemed attention. Our assent is therefore not tied to the particularity of an experience but the necessary nature that it shares with all the others. We welcome it insofar as it is inevitably foreign as the rest. For acceptance, it is precisely this universal truth – the only one we can know – that opens each and every experience to its inherent truth. From our surrender to the principle of alterity in life, we then surrender to the individual (and different) alterity of each and every moment.

There is perhaps a partial continuity between exposure and acceptance insofar as exposure entails the extrication of our ego from our relations with the outside world. If the suffering of exposure leads to a dispossession of our hermeneutical powers, then, it might have a preparatory role for the practice of acceptance, where the presence of an empowered self has already been removed from the picture. It is therefore plausible that for acceptance to be considered, exposure must first be learned.

VIII

From Consumer Desire to Hope

Consumer desire and its utopian fantasies

Goods and services offered by the mainstream lifestyles of today are intended to stimulate a desire that is consumerist by nature. Russell W. Belk, Guliz Ger, and Søren Askegaard in 'The Fire of Desire: A Multisited Inquiry into Consumer Passion' (2003) explain that commodity desire originates from our fantasies of a better life for ourselves. We aspire toward a utopian future that is to a large extent shaped by our social and historical circumstances. The objects we would like to possess are believed to be conduits for this future. If we are drawn toward this car, shirt, phone, or wellness seminar it is because we are convinced that it will help us realize in some way an ideal self that is to come. In our mind, commodities become instrumental in the road toward our perfect happiness.[1]

Consumer desire, writes Julien Freund in 'Théorie du besoin' (1971), is in fact very different from what we call 'needs'. Needs are concerned with physiological requirements, linking objects to definite functions. To perceive an object through need is to affix it with a rational finality. Despite our occasional awareness that needs are heavily influenced by our social institutions, we still tend to interpret that influence as ultimately biological. If needs refer us to clearly circumscribed ends, then, only some goods and standards are required to satisfy them. Beyond a certain limit, there would be no use for more of the same goods or any other good.[2]

If desire is the product of our imagination, however, there is virtually no limit to the things we can desire. Our imagination is free to attach itself to anything that is possible and it is therefore one of the primary roles of the market to manipulate it toward what it is offering. As Belk et al. point out in 'Metaphors of Consumed Desire' and 'Consumer Desire in Three Cultures' (1996), the strategies of advertisers, retailers, peddlers, and other marketing agents, as well as the consumption behaviour of real or imaginary others, ensure that commodities that are as yet unpossessed can enthral and appear to provide magical results in life.[3] Their mode of presentation can evoke fanciful ideas of the bliss to be experienced upon consumption. 'Because desire has to do with fantasies', Belk et al. explain, 'it takes on a mystical, childlike, or enrapturing quality that is felt to be antithetical to reasoned calculation'.[4] In the intense anticipation that it is capable of inciting, desire is in fact more akin to an intoxication that excites our imagination and emotions. Aroused, both feeling and thought reciprocally fuel one another in an escalating process that only climaxes once satisfaction is reached.[5]

As much as we are seduced to buy and consume, we also often *want* to be seduced: we enjoy it. We play an active and not insignificant role in the evocation and cultivation of images of desire affixed to an object. The hold that desire has on us is a product of drives that arise from both the market and ourselves. As Belk et al. point out, 'We find that the person who feels strong desire has almost always actively stimulated this desire by attending, seeking out, entertaining, and embellishing such images. The desires that occupy us are vivid and riveting fantasies that we participate in nurturing, growing, and pursuing, through self-seduction'.[6]

Dwelling on what we have not experienced yet and idealizing it constitutes its own form of arousal. Jean Baudrillard illustrates this psychology in connection to the character of the seducer. In *Seduction* (1979), he claims: 'Doesn't the seducer end up losing himself in his strategy; as in an emotional labyrinth? Doesn't he invent that strategy in order to lose himself in it? And he who believes himself the game's master, isn't he the first victim of strategy's tragic myth?'[7] Abandoning ourselves to the emotions and fantasies of what is as yet unpossessed is just as much a reason for desiring it as the idea of its possession. Nevertheless, we usually refrain from acknowledging our part in this seduction and instead blame everything on the object and its stylistic representations. Rather than owning up to our complicity in a product's attractiveness, we employ what Pasi Falk in *The Consuming Body* (1994) describes as a plot that justifies our desire exclusively on the basis of the object's intrinsic, irresistible attraction.[8]

As a phenomenon, desire is always affixed to something *specific*. As Gabriel Marcel makes clear in works such as *Being and Having* (1949), *Faith & Reality* (1951), 'Desire and Hope' (1967), and

Presence and Immortality (1967), desire is defined by its sharp focus. It is always a particular commodity that is wanted rather than any other. The undeviating definiteness of desire's goal attests to its obsessive and overpowering character. For Marcel, this goal has to do with *having* rather than *being*. The mode of realization that we orient ourselves toward is the acquisition of something rather than the prospect of being anything.[9] In my view, however, we need to take this logic further back to trace the roots of our desire to own an object as the belief that it will transform us, that it is the key to some version of perpetual happiness. We fantasize at a particular time and place that this or that object will be the means to our sublimation. We endow it with the potential to work a miracle. To finally own it is therefore tantamount in our thoughts to a certain mode of being. The radical change we believe it will affect is always strictly concerned with us alone. In our desperate longing to be transformed, the pleasure taken from anticipating ownership of the object is never enough. We also *do* want to have it as soon as possible. Desire is inherently impatient. '[I]t brooks no delay', Marcel writes in 'Desire and Hope', 'for this defers satisfaction; it hears no objection, for objection means delay. Hence desire as such has a relation of time that involves rejection of time: there is "no question of waiting"'.[10]

Consumer desire is the desire of the new

If desire is known to be volatile and capricious, it is primarily because it finds novelty irresistible.[11] Consumer culture tends to elevate the status of new products and models not just on account of claims that they perform better than their predecessors. A more significant subtext in their promotion is the idea that we have *not tried them yet*. How they will improve our life and what they will improve are less mandatory than the opportunity to (always) try something different. Use-value is once more superseded by the thrills of unfamiliarity. As Zygmunt Bauman in *Liquid Modernity* (1999) states:

> Even if any of [the new goods] proved to be working in just the way which was expected, the satisfaction would not last long, since in the world of the consumers possibilities are infinite, and the volume

of seductive goals on offer can never be exhausted. The recipes for the good life and the gadgets that serve them carry a 'use by' date, dwarfed, devalued and stripped of their allurements by the competition of 'new and improved' offers.[12]

In many cases, new products in the market are considered to be prestigious by virtue of their novelty. What is recent is instantly regarded as desirable because owning it will show that we are 'in the know', that we are updated. If recent models are fashionable because they are recent, then the older ones are as a result quickly degraded into obsolescence, no matter how satisfactory their performance. If the ownership value of any commodity is compulsively short-term, the market has to cultivate a mindset that is contingent on enjoying them insofar as we never attach ourselves to them so that we can remain ever open to the desire for the next newer commodities, updates, and models that would supersede them in value. At all times, Bauman claims, we are to 'keep the options open'[13] or enjoy them 'until further notice'.[14] Loyalty and commitment are to be denigrated in preventing us from desiring the novelties to come.

The free-floating personality that is encouraged in the consumer culture can also contribute to insecurity over *what* we should desire *as we are desiring*. Not only must we be on a constant lookout to desire the fashion of the season but our decisive pursuit of what is fashionable is always going to be at the expense of other, perhaps more fashionable and/or prestigious commodities that we ought to be pursuing instead. Given the virtually limitless and ever-renewing options at our disposal, our choices always face the unwitting danger of being relatively inferior in status and arousal to others. By this reasoning, our vigilance must also ensure that the pleasure we derive from our purchases does not take too long. Otherwise we could be missing out on 'better' offers in stock. Our desire and its consummation are as a result sometimes experienced as inadequate or as not intense enough in our worries that there can be other possibilities out there that we could be relishing at this very moment. The FOMO phenomenon or the fear of regret that there are better opportunities out there while we are not present insistently prevents us from the full enjoyment of our purchases. Our frenzied pursuits toward owning and consuming can be laced with an anxiety and an anticipatory disappointment.[15]

Consumer desire dreams of an everlasting happiness

Intrinsic to consumer desire is the dream of a future that is meant to convey some form of hedonistic enjoyment that will last indefinitely. In Bauman's words, it is bent on securing 'happiness into a permanent and safe condition [...]'.[16] The mode of time it aspires toward is an eternal present of euphoria. Since product effects are incapable of lasting, however, it settles for a *succession* of such presents by endlessly and swiftly chasing one product after another. The 'second-best' mode of time it has to opt for therefore is a series of brief euphoric presents. Each one of the instants pursued is discontinuous from the rest on account of its complete devotion to the pleasures afforded by a product. In its abandoned absorption in the sensations unlocked on purchase, it is indifferent to what came before and what will come after. Once the effects start to diminish, the experience is instantly aborted for the next chase.[17]

Desire's endeavours to prolong enjoyment are also often threatened by the fact that the product effect *itself* never delivers on its promise. Neither does its pleasure affect a deep-set transformation, nor does it last long. Disappointment is exacerbated by the fact that the product's actual effect can never match the expectations set for it. Its consumption never proves to be as arousing as the fantasies conjured while it was still being desired. Cultural thinkers like Georg Simmel, Colin Campbell, and Dean MacCannell all refer to desire's constancy of disillusionment in such works as *The Philosophy of Money* (1900), 'Sex Sells' (1987), and *The Romantic Ethic and the Spirit of Consumerism* (1987).[18] Because desire ascribes to its object what Simmel calls 'a peculiar ideal dignity',[19] it underwhelms the empirical experience it extracts from it.[20] Satisfaction 'breaks the spell' of desire, whose 'rude awakening' is worsened further by the deterioration of the product effect as well as its swift replacement in value by more fashionable products. As a result, we are pressured to move on to 'greener pastures' in order to feel good again as quickly and as long as possible.

Desire is thus propelled by its attempts to escape the imprint of time on products, their disaffection and expiration. This provokes it to always desire elsewhere, to always desire more. Inherent to its trajectory is its endless extension into the future in the insatiable race toward yet another object. In its elusiveness, the utopia it is always striving for is perpetuated as a repeated postponement.

To desire is always to desire more but if the 'more' turns out to be consistently disappointing, then perhaps there is in addition another source to account for its inexhaustible stimulation. To be frustrated time and again by the objects we idolize is likely to result in exhaustion and subsequent apathy. It is then perhaps more plausible to regard desire's *own* emotion and wild imagination as its primary incitement. If it is to sustain its motivation, it needs to derive it from its own momentum, while the objects targeted would to a large extent act only as pretexts. No object turns on desire more than itself for nothing else seems to compare to its self-inflicted intensity. What desire really desires is *its own desiring*. It has to be by necessity its own object of obsession for the instant it is satisfied by anything is the instant it is let down. It is only in its own unconditional indulgence that it seems to come closest to its dream of an enduring and unspoilt state of happiness. Nothing else seems to compare. Therefore, as Belk et al. claim, it follows that 'If we harbor a desire for desire, it might seem that indefinite postponement of desire fulfilment could allow us to remain in this pleasurable condition'.[21]

The self-fixation of desire itself further explains why it inherently has no boundaries and no reason to ever cease or slow down. If its mission is indefinite self-intoxication, it is intentionally or unintentionally dismissive of anything that goes on in the world 'out there'. It puts reality and its unresolved issues 'on hold' for its escalating drive to carry on uninterrupted and undiminished. Bauman draws attention to its masturbatory nature in *Liquid Modernity* when he claims that 'Desire becomes its own purpose and the sole uncontested and unquestionable purpose. The role of all other purposes, followed up only to be abandoned at the next round and forgotten the round after, is to keep the runner running [...]'. 'It is the running itself which is exhilarating and, however tiring it may be, the track is a more enjoyable place than the finishing line. It is to this situation that the old proverb "It is better to travel hopefully than to arrive" applies. The arrival, the definite end to all choice, seems much more dull and considerably more frightening than the prospect of tomorrow's choices cancelling the choices of today [...]'.[22]

The dialectic of hope

The counterpart to consumer desire in the refiguring identity is the virtue of hope. Like consumer desire, hope is indissociably associated with an unsatisfactory present from which it anticipates deliverance. For Joseph J. Godfrey in *A Philosophy of Human Hope* (1987), the future it looks forward to is *restorative*. It will redress or renew our current predicament. It can be 'so much more' than we can ever conceive. What is to come might be an unforeseeable *advent*, the inauguration of a new reality of superabundance.[23] Contrary to consumer desire, hope bypasses the necessity to possess objects for its future to be realized. If desire believes and depends on ownership to be happy, hope simply has faith that I *will* be happy. Desire aims *to have* in order to be while hope only aims *to be*.

The determination and magnitude of hope are often proportionate to the level of constraint endured in the present. The more constraining the present, the stronger is the hope that emerges. Our circumstances deprive us in some way of our freedom, of our powers to think and act as individuals in society. Situations such as imprisonment, exile, entrapment, sickness, death, and so forth prevent us in variant ways from being fully ourselves. Dispossessed of our capacities in some measure, we are no longer able to take charge of our life. Consequently, we suffer alienation from ourselves and the world around us. It is precisely due to our severe limitations that the very idea of a future attributed to reversal and transcendence is evoked. As Godfrey rightly remarks, '[S]aying that hoping means holding or declaring or finding the future open makes sense only if it is frequently held or declared or found to be closed'.[24]

To suffer the present and its concomitant future as absent of possibility is never so far away from despair. It is, however, that same proximity of despair that can awaken hope. As the philosopher of hope, Gabriel Marcel, reminds us in *Homo Viator* (1945), 'The truth is that there can strictly speaking be no hope except where the temptation to despair exists. Hope is the act by which this temptation is actively or victoriously overcome'.[25] A paradoxical phenomenon is here in effect whereby the absence of deprivation instigates a fullness of presence. Hope, as Paul Ricoeur illustrates in his essay, 'Hope and the Structure of Philosophical Systems' (1995), is an 'excess of sense over non-sense', 'the "superabundance" of meaning" as opposed to the abundance of sense-lessness, of failure, and of destruction'.[26] *Because* there is nothing to hope for, we hope. *In spite of* hopeless prospects, we hope. Invoked is a virtue that derives its lucidity, resolve, and seri-ousness precisely from its current scarcity. It is a virtue that only performs as a *resistance* to its extreme opposite.

At the root of the phenomenon of hope is the inexplicability of its causation. No law of necessity, no plausible explanation can be given as to why one state of being can motivate its contradiction. This leads Paul Ricoeur to call 'hope' 'irrational', placing it as an instance of what Søren Kierkegaard would call an 'absurd logic'. He then wonders if another form of rationality, equally truthful in its own way, is developed within the bounds of this faculty. 'Only a logic of identity and equivalence – the equivalence between sin and death, crime and punishment – is overcome', he claims. 'Is there not another logic – which we may already call a dialectical logic?'[27] The form of rationality disclosed in hope is dialectical in nature.

Hope as exercised in the refiguring identity concerns itself with our affirmation of the foreign in experience. Insofar as we *suffer* experience, that is, insofar as it disempowers our horizon of under-standing, we find our freedom to be and act seized from us. Our susceptibility to the outside necessarily deprives us for a certain time from the ability to take control of what is happening to us. Despite its temporariness, we endure our subjection as *irremedi-able* and consequently as hopeless. It is through the anguish that emerges from this sense of finality that hope is seen to take place. In impossibility, it chooses to see signs of possibilities to come. William Desmond's declaration about hope in *Beyond Hegel and Dialectic* (1992) again illustrates its transformative capability: 'The sense of the irreversible, the Never, is transfigured through hope to the "marvel of a once again"'.[28]

The orientation of hope toward our current distress is fundamen-tally different from that belonging to consumer desire. Whereas desire seeks to escape from distress – to postpone, forget, suppress, distract itself from it – predominantly by its self-absorption, hope *acknowledges* distress but refuses to give in to it. Hope, Godfrey reminds us, entails 'non-capitulation in face of even the inevitable, yet it is compatible with recognizing the inevitable as precisely just that'.[29] As Marcel declares, we are first to accept 'the trial as an integral part of the self, but while so doing [we consider] it as destined to be absorbed and transmuted by the inner workings of a certain creative process'.[30]

The futures of desire and hope

If desire is motivated by a denial of our shortcomings, the future it envisions is meant to be sharply *discontinuous* in nature from our present. The self-transformation it anticipates is meant to be altogether different from the actuality being lived. An infinite gap is conceived between the now and what is yet to come. This is why the future intrinsic to desire is a fantasy. For the informants on whom Belk et al. conducted their research as reported in their paper, 'The Fire of Desire':

> a fundamental appeal of desires lies in the promise of escape or alterity. Themes of magic and mystery are replete in the projective results, pointing to the transformative power of desire and the desired object [...]. The anticipated transformation can be to the past, the future, or another place, all of which offer escape from present conditions [...]. In each case the desire is to escape to something far better, to a life diametrically opposed to the one currently being lived, to a condition of sacredness that transcends the profane present.[31]

Conversely, the future of hope resides in a mysterious *continuity* of the present. It is conceived as intimately yet unforeseeably affiliated with the now. This is seen in the *manner* the present is believed to be eventually transformed as restoration, a renewal, or a transcendence. What is to come is seen to inaugurate a superlative time, perhaps even a climactic endpoint *relative to* the condition we are in. It is seen to be the manifestation of the now *as* fulfilled. The now is consequently regarded as somehow yet intrinsically relevant to what will arrive: a duration that *needs* to be endured for everything to get better. The affirmation of suffering as a finality is sublimated into a suffering as a *way-toward,* a necessary *stage* in a development. It is turned, as it were, into 'the darkest hour just before the dawn'. What had previously been senseless is thus given an ineffable purpose or direction.

On the one hand, hope grants its future its remoteness and is willing to wait it out for as long as is required. On the other hand, desire is impatient on account of the manner it believes that future will be realized. Its stubborn fixation on acquisition as the *only way* it can find transcendence accounts for a restless race against time to purchase as soon as possible whatever it deems will transform it. There is no time to waste, no reason to wait if the 'cure' is already on offer, often regardless of whether it is affordable or not.

Provoking desire's impatience are the displays of the commodities themselves that constantly pose as guarantees of our emancipation. They hinge on the extravagant promise of a complete and utter transformation upon consumption, thus bringing the not-yet desire dreams of teasingly close to the now. The future, as often proclaimed by consumerist lifestyle adverts, is *already here* in the tangible present. The utopia of consumers, Bauman claims in connection to fashion, 'brings forth a land of solutions and cures from the "there and then" of the distant future to the "here and now" of the present moment. Instead of a life towards utopia, [consumer] hunters are offered a life in utopia'.[32]

Hope harbours no fixation on the how and the when. It neither imposes any criteria on the way its future will be realized, nor does it pretend to define what kind of future will take place. From its refusal to have any expectations comes its infinite patience. Hope, Godfrey claims in allusion to Marcel, is not 'psychic stiffening, a rigid clinging to one's own self, ideas, or projects. It involves relaxation'.[33] Rather than dictating its terms of salvation, it entrusts inscrutable forces to take us there, and is therefore at peace with the understanding that all will somehow turn out well in the end. It is a matter of no significance if our impoverished condition appears terminal. Our liberating confidence operates on a different phenomenological plane than the empirical plane. It exists on the plane of faith, whose dialectical process entails a *determination in spite of* all evidence to the contrary. Faith proceeds by exceeding the closures of factual and scientific knowledge.

'I hope for us'

The structure of hope in the refiguring identity inherits Marcel's structure of full hope, formulated as: 'I hope in thee for us'. For

Marcel, the future we wait for is an 'us', where 'us' refers to possible realizations of a 'shared life'. What we anticipate is a communal life that inaugurates a resolution to our predicament. If the resolution is an 'us' and not just me, then the predicament it is a development of involves others as well. As a group, a society, a nation, humankind, life, we all partake of a common suffering that will be cured in the time to come. We do not know what *type* of shared life is yet to save us. From where we stand, the 'us' is indefinite and pluriform. If its content is unclear, its function of emancipating us is nonetheless clear. The way out is glimpsed but not grasped.[34]

In expressing a bond of sorrow, full hope, for Marcel, gains its strength by being shared with others. Its conviction and reality are established in part from its consensual premise. Marcel maintains that 'it is precisely only in the light of intersubjectivity that one can speak of salvation'.[35] Exploring his concept of 'full hope', Godfrey writes:

> Hope at its best is not hope for me. It is hope for us. Indeed, hope at its best holds both myself and you as equiponderant, not for separate outcomes, but for an outcome – not thoroughly known – which joins us together. Such joining is not to be understood in terms of competition or of purely functional interplay [...]. The forms of 'us' may be manifold. But hope for salvation, from whatever captivity, is hope essentially for us.[36]

The highest form of hope that Marcel conceives can thus take place between an invalid and a close friend, a group of activists fighting a corrupt government, prisoners of war, a trade union protesting against unfair conditions at work, a family that cannot make ends meet, and so forth insofar as there are two or more parties oppressed by the same sufferance. Constrictions that are common to two or more people can inaugurate a common faith in their eventual overcoming.

Conversely, the hope enjoined by the refiguring identity need not be shared. No one else needs to be aware of it or have any hope at all for that matter, for its resolve and clarity to be upheld. If anything, it is likelier to be exercised in solitude insofar as it is incentivized by my personal exposure to episodes that can also often happen to me alone. Nonetheless, what this hope anticipates is by no means solipsistic. The suffering endured by the foreign in experience is not the only obstacle it believes it will overcome and transcend. If it is an experience's particular suffering that first sets my hope in motion, it also subsequently integrates in its motivation all the sufferings of my society, and by extension, all other societies. My finitude is expanded to the idea of the general finitude of all humankind so that from the hope to reconcile myself with a singular event grows the hope that everyone alive and yet to be will reconcile themselves with one another and the world around them. The assimilation of the consciousness of my fallibilities with a universal consciousness of humankind's fallibilities transforms my situational hope to a hope for the world to heal and evolve. Regardless of what others may or may not hope for, I hope for such an ideal reality. This is how hope in the refiguring narrative conceives the prospect of 'us'.

Like the other four virtues, the 'us' that drives hope entails 'the good life with and for others in just institutions'. Intrinsic to its 'us' is thereby not just the fulfilment of our personal life plans but also the twin objectives of solicitude in relationships between people and a social administration built on institutions that ensure equality and justice among the citizenry. I act in view of a hope for this transformative communal future despite what others desire and act for. Beyond its tripartite schema, the 'us' has to be as indefinite as the 'us' that orients Marcel's 'full hope'. Marcel warns that to dictate conditions and fixed representations on the manner my hope is to be realized is to set myself up for disillusionment, even despair, when these criteria fail to be met. The more my hope slides toward specific forms of liberation, the more 'I myself put up limits to the process by which I could triumph over all successive disappointments […]. Indeed, I own implicitly that if my expectations are not fulfilled in some particular point, I shall have no possibility of escaping from the despair into which I must inevitably sink'.[37]

Our hope must surpass any reified meanings imposed on it. It must always be *exceeding itself* in any of its possible interpretations. As Marcel claims, 'The more hope tends to reduce itself to a matter of dwelling on, or of becoming hypnotised over, something one has represented to oneself, the more [illusory it will be]. On the contrary, the more hope transcends imagination, so that I do not allow myself to imagine what I hope for, the more this objection seems to disappear'.[38] While the utopia of desire is always about to arrive, it is always already uncertain when and how hope's future will arrive. Always it is to be seen as a nebulous endpoint, immeasurably distant in time from the here and now. Unlike desire's destination, it is never in postponement because it precisely *should not* arrive anytime soon.

If the future hoped for in the refiguring identity is the good life, its indeterminacy is crucial because of its schematic inclusion of an external environment that must be allowed to *hermeneutically participate* in its vision. To lay out the terms for the good life by myself is to disregard the role played by that outside in the development of its meaning: a role which is often vague and unpredictable. Tying ourselves to a fixed picture of how the world will transform for everyone is to deny the necessary involvement of elements that are beyond our control, such as the lives and life plans of other individuals, the projects of societal, national, and international organizations, and the effects of unprecedented, contingent, and even mundane events. We would be closing ourselves off from the input of that actuality that is itself integral to the constitution of the good life – other people and their institutions.

Fixating definite objectives, methods, and standards to what we hope for would therefore be in direct contradiction to the good life ideal that hope should be oriented toward. In this regard, the other four virtues might help steer hope back to its original indefinite concentration. In affirming what is other to our worldview in their variant ways, exposure and acceptance especially can influence the restoration of hope to its authentic attitude. The more extensive and uncompromising their susceptibility, the more persuasive their impression is likely to be.

In its focus on the refiguring identity's telos, hope in turn can act as an affective and cognitive reminder of the why of our decisions. It can recall us to the purpose we exercise exposure, imagination, practical wisdom, and acceptance for in the first place. In the abstract ideal it points us toward, it ensures that we regard the present as unfailingly *imperfect,* thereby motivating us to always improve on ourselves and the world around us.

'I hope in thee'

For Marcel, the blind faith of full hope finds its foundation and constancy before all else in the 'thee' to which it addresses itself and from which it acquires its constant solace and conviction. The 'thee' stands for a benevolent force that predicates existence and guides it toward its best intentions. Its motivations, Marcel claims, are always in alignment with ours. Believing in 'thee' means 'asserting that there is at the heart of being, beyond all data, beyond all inventories and calculations, a mysterious principle which is in connivance with me, which cannot but will what I will, if what I will deserves to be willed and is, in fact, willed by the whole of my being'.[39] To hope is to believe in a providential power that is capable of making possible the impossible. We cannot deign to understand its designs but we are to put our unconditional trust in it.

For the hope of the refiguring identity, Marcel's 'thee' is the call of conscience. The call invites hope to have faith that the refiguring decision it asks of us, with the ethical hermeneutics and praxis it engenders, will bring the good life always closer to reality. We are to dedicate ourselves to the selfless activity of the virtues because we are willing to believe that they are its gifts needed to deliver us to emancipation. To hope is to trust in the call's enjoinment to be virtuous for its kingdom on earth to be realized. It means loyalty to the way of life the call asks us to follow in the 'irrational' knowledge that all will be well eventually if we do so. Insofar as our hope comes from our belief that it is being guided by conscience, it is anything but a passive expectancy. It urges rather *our* collaboration to change the world for the better. It is because we hope for a trans-formed future that we undertake a work of ethical interpretation and action toward certain experiences.

IX

The Case of Limit-Experiences
Refiguring Identity at the Limits

Limit-experiences in philosophy and critical and cultural theory

An issue that has not been addressed so far is whether there exists any type of situations that are perhaps too foreign for the virtues of the refiguring identity model to work with. Can we conceive of episodes that inversely undermine the practice of the virtues and their underlying narrative despite their intrinsic valuation of the foreign outside? Facing up to this scenario is important in order to assess the refiguring self-narrative's efficacy under extremely adverse conditions, and thereby consider the measure of its relevance for all manner of situations.[1]

The prime example of the kind of challenging episodes that concern us here are those related to what are famously called 'limit-experiences'. These have been a prevalent theme in critical and cultural theory as well as various branches of philosophy such as poststructuralism and deconstruction, along with the broad discipline of existential phenomenology. Their characteristic role in our thought experiment comes from the way they are insistently invoked as a breakdown of all conditions of knowledge, the undermining of all our sense-making faculties. As such, they are suffered as an incessant inability to take control of ourselves, to be ourselves. What Georges Bataille, for instance, calls 'inner experience' and 'sovereignty', Maurice Blanchot calls 'neuter' or 'outside', Jacques Lacan calls 'the Real' and 'Other', Jacques Derrida and John D. Caputo call 'khora', and Mark C. Taylor calls 'altarity', all refer to a subjugation by an otherness that is so other that it radically deprives us of the capacity to reconcile ourselves with it while under exposure. We are here at what Michel Foucault would call 'the point of life which lies as close as possible to the impossibility of living, which lies at the limit or the extreme'.[2] Charles Taylor in *A Secular Age* (2007) presents a similar category of event that 'unsettles and breaks through our ordinary sense of being in the world, with its familiar objects, activities and points of references [...]', 'when "ordinary reality" is 'abolished' and something terrifyingly other shines through"'.[3]

Limit-experiences are not limited to loss and pain but can also involve episodes of intense joy such as the birth of our child, a spiritual revelation, or certain moments in an intimate relationship. Here, we are likewise laid bare to what irreversibly exceeds and undercuts the categories of our perceptual awareness, delivering us to an unfathomable beyond. Limit-experiences come in many forms, ranging from abandonment and fascination to madness and even poetry. For Lacan, they include 'Desire, boredom, confinement, revolt, prayer, sleeplessness [...] and panic'.[4] For the purposes of this chapter, however, the term will be limited to those experiences that are predominantly suffered *as loss and distress* in that they are the ones that are much more likely to threaten and dissolve the foundations of our faith in the refiguring narrative model not only while we endure them but also possibly afterward in the traumatic effects they might leave behind.

Can we practice exposure and acceptance in suffering without aiming for the good life?

It is plausible to consider the possibility that episodes of extreme loss and suffering, in their affective violence, can drastically undermine the refiguring identity. A large extent of the identity's success indeed finally stands or falls on whether it can be sustained during such events. If it is not capable of *guiding* us, psychologically, emotionally, and ethically in trying times, then, a fundamental part of its purpose has been lost. The strength of any self-identity is especially tested in its capacity to signify in moments where all signification seems to have collapsed.

In what follows, I will demonstrate, however, how the refiguring identity *is* capable of integrating limit-experiences in its narrative. Our hardest tribulations *can* find a place in the framework of its plot on conscience and the virtues. In not relying on any predetermined body of knowledge, the basic schema of its narrative of the call with its good life telos is aimed precisely to be flexible, absorptive, and adjustable to whatever befalls us in the outside world. Given the limit-experience's extreme alterity to our subjectivity, however, this same narrative, minimal and indeterminate as it might be, could still be considered as a condition of knowledge. It is still after all a *basis* or a *means* through which we are to comprehend experience. In its absolute foreignness, the limit-experience would still be seen as disempowering us of this mindframe. The affective immediacy of its suffering would break open the temporal continuum of our sense of a past as heading toward a future guided by the good life formula, subjecting it to a devastating futility in making sense of anything that is happening to us. The constancy of our self-understanding with its virtues and life purposes is ruptured by a harrowing process that seems to have no end.

If we are deprived of any objective in extreme distress, it still might not mean that we would lose all motive for the practice of some of the virtues. As hermeneutical practices, imagination and practical wisdom would in all probability prove to be inoperable in such circumstances. It is plausible, however, to see the virtues of exposure and acceptance as still capable of performing in that they are both in principle forms of unrestrained submission to alterity, no matter how drastic in nature. Without the good life they customarily base their decisions on, their accession can still be justified on account of their uncompromising faith that alterity would somehow improve our life and/or lead us to a better place or reality. They can still derive their motivation from the belief that our submission to alterity with its unforeseeable course and outcomes holds an inconceivable value. We can hang on to them, that is, insofar as they testify to a trust that is predicated *strictly* on the unknown of any experience in the unknown ways it would transform us. Their attachment to the good life can thus be removed perhaps without much ruinous effect on our esteem in the mindsets they characterize.

Severing exposure and acceptance from their original destination, however, opens up new problems. The overarching purpose of the refiguring narrative model would have gone, and with this, the ethical nature of their resolve. Furthermore, in placing all stakes on alterity, the mindset prescribed by the two virtues can easily deteriorate into resignation, despair, or depression. Without a final 'meaningful' purpose, indeterminate as it might be, the simple belief that our suffering holds some form of *necessity* is a fragile belief. It can easily be lost should that suffering exacerbate and/or lead to unanticipated consequences. The resolve to see alterity as incalculably significant is much too obscure and conjectural to sustain. It is perhaps also prone to masochism or a self-destructive enjoyment in our disempowerment for its own sake, instead of seeing the process as justified in being an essential stage toward our futural development in some radically unimaginable way.[5]

Having faith in the caller of our conscience as we suffer

What is required is a realignment of exposure and acceptance toward a life-affirming or ethical aim that does not impose any inter-pretative conditions on experience, whether they are schematic or more particular in their criteria. The refiguring identity model provides a way how we can meet this requirement through the way it understands conscience. Conscience, as conceived *on a funda-mental level*, can characterize the virtues of exposure and acceptance as unaffixed to any form of knowledge. Doing so can enable them to be practiced in situations where all modes of knowledge are being incessantly disrupted.

How does the refiguring self-narrative view 'conscience', then, in such a way that the two virtues are stripped of all defining objec-tives? Prior to its call to live the good life is the call *itself*. The call to live well presupposes the more rudimentary call by the who or what of the caller. Before we are called to be or do anything, we are already *as called*. To hear the enjoinment of how to be, we would have always already heard the enjoiner enjoining us. Our yes to a better time to come is always already derived and built on a more primal yes to the one who wishes it so.

Our commitment to the good life therefore depends on a predating commitment to the source that asks us to commit to that life. We are called *to it* before we are called to any thought and action. We are invited to be *for it* prior to our invitation to be for anything that we can cognitively understand. Our attachment to an invoked cause is pre-established on an agreement to have faith in the invoker, a willingness to open up to it unconditionally. The character of self-esteem as explored by the refiguring identity can indeed be viewed according to this preliminary affirmation. If our sense of self-value is contingent on our receptivity to the wish to lead a better life, it also means that it is contingent, before all else, on our receptivity to what wishes us to do so. Authenticity here begins with the decision to welcome the bond we share with the voice of our conscience.

In calling us before and beyond any schemes of interpretation, our faith and love in the voice of conscience can be thereby retrieved during (and after) our subjection to limit-experiences. Its authoritativeness, which comes from its paradoxical transcendence and intimacy, can survive the limit-experience precisely because it too comes from the *unknown*. Much like the nature of the suffering we are going through, it too belongs to an extreme otherness. It can therefore potentially rival it in its singularly affective intensity. Both phenomena can equally exert upon us the irreducible claims of their distinct sovereignty. The subjugation exacted by the limit-experience can be as compelling as a 'truth' to our faith and love for the call of conscience. For its sake, we are consequently capable of exercising the virtues of exposure and acceptance despite our 'dark night of the soul'. Our exposure and acceptance of pain can be sustained if we see such decisions as stemming from the originary decision to welcome conscience.

There are, nonetheless, crucial differences to highlight between our faith in the call and the ordeal of the limit-experience. Whereas the limit-experience entails an otherness that is an inhuman, blind force, the call's otherness constitutes an *intent* that has a *humane* dimension. One follows a determined though indeterminate course while the other, though likewise indeterminate, is believed to *determine* its course. The limit-experience has no who; it does not care. But the call cares for us; it comes to us as a benevolent appeal. It is an inner yet foreign presence whose inarticulate invitation is a sign of its immeasurable compassion toward our predicament. By virtue of the fact that it calls *us*, it entails a communication, or perhaps the beginning of one, even though it is irreducible to any message and language.

We can understand the way we experience the call more closely if we compare it to what Emmanuel Levinas in *Totality and Infinity* (1961) describes as 'signifyingness' in the context of our ethical susceptibility to the vulnerable other. The other, Levinas tells us, does not only express perspectives that are outside our own. They do not only communicate to us by revealing significations that are unprecedented to our horizon of signification. They also above all communicate themselves as the very *signifying* of these innovative significations and any other signification. What they express to us precedes the intelligibility and actualization of meanings in constituting the *possibilizing* of expression itself, the intentional process of giving meaning, the visceral act of signifying or signifyingness. In the ethical scene, we are opened to a foreign intelligence that is fecund with nascent meaning.[6]

By the same token, the refiguring narrative's call of conscience cannot be fixed to any signification. It predates signification because it is an *intention* that conceives signification. It signifies, perhaps, *the* willingness to signify that makes possible signification. While the limit-experience proceeds as a withdrawing of all communication, the call proceeds *as* communication, or more accurately, as a *giving* of all possible communication. Through it, we *can* have meaning/s, we mean. We are anything, we are, because of the call. It calls us to ourselves – and we are ourselves as for it.

Our hope in the call as we suffer

The call calls us to be for it *in order to* be a part of it. It invites us *to it*. Its invitation is an anticipation of our communion with it. Our yes is a yes to an eventual union. To have faith in the call is to have faith that we will be as one. Intrinsic to the call and our response is thereby a *hope*. Hope is this prospect of a better time to come. If hope derives its resolve and lucidity from its antithesis – an oppressive situation – then, limit-experiences offer paradoxically the ideal grounds for its motivation. By virtue of their radical self-deprivation, the 'darkest nights of our soul' can constitute the perfect opportunities for the stimulation of the most resolved hope. Hope thrives especially when there is the least cause to hope for anything.

Even in exceptional distress, hope still retains Gabriel Marcel's structure of hope as 'I hope in thee for us', where 'thee' stands for the caller that calls us toward communion. The efficacy of hope is here premised on its character as a hope *in* rather than a hope *that* something will take place. As Marcel remarks in *Homo Viator* (1945), hope-that refers us toward a precise objective, a reliance on a particular vision of the future, which therefore assumes certain criteria that we are to depend on for its realization. It is a hope that attaches itself to particularities, without which it will easily plunge into disappointment.[7] Given that limit-experiences abound in relentless suffering and loss, this form of hope cannot survive them.

Hope-in, however, *can* assimilate them in its workings. It can gather its determination from their 'negativity'. Hope-in, or what Marcel calls 'full hope', does not hold on to a circumscribed meaning of the future. It does not demonstrate any fixation on a defining and definite ideal What it longs for is to be with someone, the 'thee' or 'you' of its schema, but how this will come about and what it will involve, it does not pretend to know. Instead of focusing on an object, it has the character of an objectless disposition, a *readiness* or *willingness* – for an unspecified time to come. In its uncompromising love, it entrusts the 'you' with its hope. It has faith that the 'you' will bring 'us' together, that it will make this unified reality come to be. As such, the 'you', as Marcel states, is 'in some way the guarantee of the union which holds us together [...]'.[8] In its surrender to the 'you', hope-in demonstrates its nonpossessiveness, wherein lies its steadfastness. It is, as Joseph J. Godfrey explains in *A Philosophy of Human Hope* (1987), 'conceivable without specific demands, the disappointment of which will not vitiate the bond that links I and you together'.[9]

Hope, as practiced by the refiguring identity when faced by the limit-experience, amounts to a hope in you, the infinitely unknown caller that calls me. I hope in you, the unknown, that you will deliver me at some point, equally unknown, from this suffering. I hope in you that we will be together in a future whose reality is also unknown. The vitality of this hope, especially in connection to limit-experiences, relies completely on its *inconceivable* element. Not knowing or pretending to understand its giver and destination enables its suitability and effectiveness in such times, when all our attempts at understanding anything are removed from our scope. The more limit-experiences deprive us of control in fact, the more they empower this hope.

In his explanation of Marcel's writings on 'full hope', Godfrey, offers some more specific indications on how this virtue can be exercised in limit-experiences. '[R]ather than being determined by evidence', he claims, '[hope-in] shapes the evidence; it brings it about that certain aspects of a situation shall count as evidence

[…]. [It] can shape what is possible rather than be held within possibility's boundaries'.[10] By this logic, hope chooses to see in the limit-experience's incomprehensible suffering *itself* evidence of the salvation that is to come. It *possibilizes* what seems impossible in reading it as a *sign* of a futural communion. Our faith in the call can refigure pain from a dead end to a necessary conduit toward freedom. Suffering *for nothing* is here reframed as a suffering *for the caller that calls* in the belief that suffering will lead us to it. Our adverse circumstances are seen as a crucial transition toward another state of being. What seems irreversible is *redeemed* as a component of a larger emancipatory vision. A future is opened up where before there was none.

It is perhaps through hope that the virtues of exposure and acceptance acquire their efficacy in the limit-experience. Hope's faith in a 'you' that promises me an 'us' sustains them. I expose myself to and accept the pain because I choose to see in its absence of any future, the plenitude of a new future; in its never, an unprecedented maybe. In this way, the refiguring narrative remains a significant source of counsel and purpose in desperate times.

Innate to our suffering is always a perceptual decision

To have the faith that is particular to hope, a *hermeneutical decision* is to be made through which we interpret our predicament on a rudimentary level. How we perceive our pain is a *way of understanding it*, minimal as this understanding might be. For many thinkers of limit-experiences, however, the very existence of such a decision *as* we suffer is categorically impossible. Again, they insist on the active subversion of all our capacity for understanding. We are subjected to an interminable process of dispossession. We endure not as ourselves but as a perpetual powerlessness to be ourselves.[11]

It is implausible, however, to think of extreme otherness as *exclusively* undergone through the disempowerment of our faculties. This, I wager, is only *an aspect* of the experience. A quotient of standard awareness must always inevitably remain struggling during the episode. Otherwise it is highly probable that it would virtually never or hardly have existed for us at all, especially since it would be difficult to remember, if not impossible. Rather than an 'experience' or an 'event', it would be more synonymous with a blackout or at best a barely discernible memory. If we are to speculate on limit-experiences it is because on some level we are *aware*, and therefore on some level, disconnected from, their affective intensity and its postfactum psychological and emotional effects. In some irreducible and rudimentary way, we *know* that they are happening or that they happened and that are happening *to us*. If they are unbearable, if they divest us of our control, it is because we are aware of what they are doing or what they did to us. A constancy of consciousness, diminished as it might be, must persist in order to register our subjugation. And consequently, this registering presupposes a certain detachment from our subjugation. It is such a self that the various thinkers of limit-experiences often fail or even refuse to address in their phenomenological (or quasi-phenomenological) descriptions of the subject.

With our distantiating consciousness comes a degree of *cognitive empowerment*. Awareness inherently provides the potential for interpretative choices to be made, no matter how powerless our condition. If we agree that some degree of standard consciousness persists in limit-experiences, then we can factor the capacity to make perceptual decisions as we are suffering them. Even if our cognitive and/or physical powers are drastically impaired, it is not impossible to sustain sufficient awareness to gain a perspective on our situation. We can decide to exert our belief while subjected to the most severe of tribulations.

Configuring the peculiar relationship between the refiguring call and the limit-experience

Reconciling the limit-experience with our faith in the call is often not an easy feat. If in the limit-experience, the good life ideal loses its certitude on account of its (schematic) representability, our faith in the call can paradoxically lose its own certitude on account of its *nonrepresentability*. The call has no foundation in knowledge and we have therefore no assurance if its summons is to be trusted or that it even exists as its own reality. If its invitation cannot be articulated in words, we can never be sure of what it is asking us to think and do. We may even come to believe that it would lead us down delusional paths that would only aggravate our situation.

If the site of the call cannot be comprehended by our reflective efforts, then it can in principle be anything, if it is anything at all. It can be a lie, or worse, the interiorization of societal norms acquired out of habit.

It is common for our doubts to surface when our distress takes a certain toll. At wit's end, our faith can degenerate into suspicion, disappointment, even faithlessness. What can result is a perceptual shift toward the call that reinterprets it as traitorous, as abandoning us to our fate. Our suffering is in turn worsened as any sign of reprieve or resolution further withdraws from our horizon.

If limit-experiences can unwittingly empower our faith in the call, they can therefore also lead to its disempowerment. What is indicative in their paradoxical influences is a peculiar relationship that is often found to occur between any faith in a higher reality and deep suffering. We can elucidate further by drawing a parallel with the relationship between two other experiential polarities that are analogous in several respects – the God of theology and khora. Richard Kearney in *Strangers, Gods and Monsters* (2003) explores their dynamic in ways that can prove insightful to the subject at issue.

Addressing Derrida's and Caputo's seminal notion of khora in Plato's writings, Kearney refers to this limit-experience as 'a void of empty space'.[12] Khora takes place as a somewhere that is nothing or less than nothing in that it turns to nothing anything that passes through it. Ideas, hopes, beliefs, and so forth are invalidated by its 'experience'. Khora is outside or without being. It is neither an entity nor an object but an anonymous no-place that remains deserted: 'a night without end'; '[j]ust ashes and ashes, without ascensions into heaven'.[13] We approach this liminal site in our descent into despair and other forms of severe anguish. Its abyssal nature thereby stands in stark opposition to the transcendent heights of faith. God or the call as an experiential object of faith can be considered as equivalent insofar as they both signal toward a foreign reality beyond being that is personified by a benevolent disposition toward us.

At first, Kearney draws attention to the radical *divergence* between faith and khora. Khora dwells in the desertification of meaning and all possibility below being. Faith aims for a compassionate will above being that gives meaning and possibility.[14] This distinction reveals, in my view, an active estrangement between them. By virtue of the extent of their opposing nature, experiencing one will intrinsically distantiate us from the other. Hence to suffer khora is to suffer a loss of faith and to have faith is to be indifferent to such suffering. The 'reality' one discloses devalues and alienates the 'reality' of the other. Precisely because of their reciprocal repulsion, it is often difficult to transition between them. If the transition is to take place from khora to faith it would call no less for a Kierkegaardian 'leap of faith' or 'qualitative leap'. Or conversely, the conviction and constancy of faith can keep us out of khora despite its proximity in adverse situations.

Yet, as Kearney makes clear, faith can on occasion capitulate to khora just as khora can stimulate a renewal of faith. 'My faith comes forth from the crucible of doubt',[15] Fyodor Dostoevsky confessed, where the crucible can represent any limit-experience that involves loss and pain. It is my wager that this reciprocal traversal happens to the extent that the polarities are *also similar* in nature. Whether transcendent or abyssal, they both essentially signal toward a reality outside being at the limits of all representation and thought. They are events of what is impossible to our cognitively conditioned reality: the approach of the wholly other. Because they share this fundamental character, faith and khora can sometimes lead to each other.

Phenomenologically, the two polarities overlap in the mode of a reciprocal *predisposition*. Faith can find itself being attracted toward khora and khora toward faith. A plausible reason for the mutual inclination is the equal or stronger force of authority and conviction each can exert upon the other at any point in time. By itself, however, the attraction would not suffice for the 'leap' between the two to be realized. An autonomous resolve to resist the experience we are going through to be for the other must prevail.

In belonging to a phenomenological field that is outside reason, the sharp differentiation between faith and khora, and correlatively, the refiguring call and the limit-experience, does not follow a straightforward either/or law. Just because we dwell in one does not mean we will not end up dwelling in the other. Neither does their relationship follow the strict law of causality. It is never a simple matter of faith necessarily leading to suffering or the inverse. '[I]f the theist does choose God', Kearney reflects, 'it is always in fear and trembling and can never be more than a hair's breadth from the underlying, undecidable abyss of *khora* – a common pre-original void from which faith issues and from which it is never definitively removed, to its dying day. Indeed, were it so definitively removed it would no longer be faith'. Despite their antagonistic natures, on some occasions, very little seems to separate faith and khora. Though 'they beat with different hearts', though 'they think different thoughts and signal different options', '[t]he two are inextricably linked as Siamese twins [...]'. They could be in fact, as Kearney reveals, 'two sides of the same coin. And maybe in a strange way [...] they need each other'.[16]

Constructing a Dialogue between the Consumerist Lifestyle and the Refiguring Identity Model

The comparative study of the consumerist life-strategies and the refiguring identity model has confirmed among other things that the former are above all ethically problematic if adopted as identity-types. As a result of their hedonistic focus, to define ourselves in accordance to their narratives is bound to narrow our scope of significance in our life. Retaining them precisely *as lifestyles*, as routinized activities performed to an extent because they *express* our self-identity rather than *construct* it, can steer clear of their egotistic dispositions. Insofar as they are not given the role of composing our self-biography but are practiced as its supplements, their benefits to our wellbeing can indeed be considerable. We could enjoy a healthier life, a more attractive appearance, a calmer attitude, financial gains, a diversity of foreign cultures, and so on without allowing these results to dictate our primary life plans.

Perhaps, however, the proper lifestyle treatment of fashion, fitness, self-spirituality, entrepreneurship, and travel can still induce a certain toxic effect. The self-indulgent values they endorse can still influence the relationships and decisions we take outside of their jurisdiction. The case of entrepreneurship is perhaps stronger in its effect than the others. It has also been demonstrated how all five life-strategies are precisely designed to be *addictive*. In pivoting their theory and practice on consumer desire, they are meant to consume us by the never-ending mission for arousal and status. This, as we have seen, is the unavoidable outcome of the pervasive consumer culture they inhabit along with their appropriation by market forces and their logic.

Nonetheless, to outrightly condemn and give up on the five lifestyles is inadvisable and ultimately unrealistic.

The overwhelming presence of their culture in today's world cannot be simply ignored. They are here to stay, at least for a long time to come. Moreover, self-oriented as they might be, their values and narratives are still commendable if followed with a certain measure of caution. Perhaps we can find a way of practicing them without falling into the trap of embracing them as philosophies for our life. Perhaps they can be adopted in conjunction with a self-created ethical identity, such as one that is premised on the schema of the refiguring narrative. It can therefore be compelling to chart the rudiments of a possible relationship between the two. The attempt could also settle a yet unexplored potential limitation of the narrative: if the refiguring identity's structure is ethical, how does it justify actions taken solely for purposes of the individual's gratification, which are, as we know, *also* needed for a balanced and fulfilling life? How can it affirm and uphold strictly self-benefiting activities pursued only for the sake of material gain, relaxation, and/or simple fun? It would appear that the ethical seriousness of its narrative would outrightly devalue this category of actions.

I suggest that the refiguring narrative can justify self-pleasure in its scope of motives via the first dimension of its objective's definition, 'the good life', *to the extent that this is regarded as separate* from the other two dimensions of solicitude and just institutions. As explained in Chapter 2: 'The three constituents of the good life schem', the first component of the good life focuses on the life plans that give us purpose irrespective of whether or not they summon any responsibilities undertaken on behalf of the other and/or any social institution. It can therefore include goals strictly pertaining to our personal gain, which can encourage certain leisure interests and entertainment projects pursued only for our satisfaction.

The virtue of practical wisdom can here provide the function of distinguishing which occasions are to be dedicated independently to the first dimension of the good life and which ones are to also involve the other two. This task of course is not practiced exclusively by the refiguring identity model. It is a discernment that we exercise in our everyday life regardless of whether our identity coincides in some degree with the refiguring narrative. We are often required to choose and recognize which decisions are to involve our own private needs and which ones are to be ethical almost intuitively, without much self-deliberation. There is a difference when the refiguring identity model is concerned in that it puts an added emphasis on which ethical dimension practical wisdom is to address. We are enjoined to consider whether our choices will aim toward our care for the other, our care for social institutions, or a convergence of both.

If the first dimension of the good life objective allows for self-centred activities and projects, then a way how to reconcile the consumerist life-strategies with the identity model can be articulated. A main reason for this is the role of the virtues that motivate our actions within this dimension. Absent of any goals related to other people and social institutions, they no longer in fact hold the role of virtues but become closer in character to the life-strategy values themselves. Exposure, imagination, practical wisdom, acceptance, and hope as geared toward subjectivist enjoyment bear a broad resemblance to open-mindedness, creativity, instrumental reason, surrender, and desire. A general reconciliation between the two can be acknowledged. The refiguring identity model can thereby accept the mainstream lifestyle practices as consistent with its story without having to alter them in any manner.

Not only can the lifestyles have a relevant role in the identity model but they can also motivate their virtue counterparts themselves. In other words, the lifestyle values can *dispose* us to or *improve* the exercise of the virtues in our endeavours to care for others and our social institutions. This influence is due to their simulational affiliation with the virtues. A certain degree of intrinsic similarity is shared between the two sets of qualities despite their embeddedness in different frameworks: a capitalist-consumerist framework on the one hand and an ethical-hermeneutical phenomenological context on the other.

It is not implausible therefore to conceive the open-mindedness or courage and will promoted in fitness regimens to exceed our endurance and strength, to try healthier diets, or adventurous sports, or in travelling, to visit places and participate in traditions that are different from our culture (despite the predominantly aesthetic purpose of these actions), as incentivizing us in *other* unrelated scenarios to suspend our entrenched worldview in our willingness to expose ourselves to experiences that are not familiar to us at all so we can learn other possible ways of understanding ourselves and the world. Perhaps the resolve to try new things, to challenge ourselves to be different as practiced in the lifestyles can even incline us to be more sensitive to what is foreign to us in any experience we come across. Or perhaps as entrepreneurs, the creativity and instrumental reason needed to implement innovative strategies to sell a product in the market can unwittingly assist our ethical imagination and assist, even inspire our practical wisdom to devise its situational rules as well as encouraging us to realize their projects in actuality. Being creative in what we wear and how we look can also perhaps stimulate and/or enhance the imagination required to assimilate experiences with our worldview, while the desire to discover our 'cosmic self' through the pursuit of diverse workshops, therapies, practices, and products, can inspire or provoke our hope for a future of universal reconciliation. Surrendering our problems to the 'life-force' or undertaking spontaneous travelling might also deepen our acceptance of life as a journey that should be allowed to take its own course without any intervention of our controlling intents.

It is of course often far from certain if the mainstream lifestyles are in actual fact helping our ethical endeavours. Unless we are vigilant, they might instead end up blurring the boundaries between occasions deserving their values and those deserving the virtues' expertise. They can easily abet our confusion, forgetfulness, or indifference to the crucial demarcation between the self-centred and ethical fields of thought and action – and again, practical wisdom would here prove invaluable in assessing which type of mindsets would be ideal for the situation at hand.

The mainstream lifestyles and the refiguring identity model can also overlap in an inverse direction. We can intend the virtues to *redirect* the lifestyle goals in order to involve all three dimensions of the good life instead of just the first. The virtues would be allowed to *guide* the lifestyle values to a behaviour that is also solicitous toward society. The practices that define the lifestyle would be maintained but as reoriented toward the good life ideal. There are numerous methods how we can achieve this directed integration and it is up to us to draw out the particulars for the project depending on the lifestyle/s we would like to focus on and the resources at our disposal.

There are already plenty of evident instances in our time where lifestyle activities are assembled for a cause that reflects the general ethical goals of the good life. We see this taking place by way of nonprofit organizations that prepare fundraising marathons and other fitness-related games for charity, or fashion designers and influencers who appropriate their wear to make a political or environmentalist statement. Business and financial companies also tend to commit themselves to ethical projects like donating a generous percentage of their profit to humanitarian groups and developing countries, sponsoring voluntary services, or addressing a social or political issue through their advertisements and products.[1] There has been moreover a surge in the popularity of travel philanthropy, where the ideal of travel to developing countries is no longer limited to entertainment but also incorporates different ways of helping the locals, from the education of the youth to medical assistance provided in conditions of poor health. Other more daily examples can involve business decisions that are premised on respect for the employee's and employer's integrity more than on financial profit; the repurposing of feelgood results in, say, fitness and self-spirituality, as sources of stimulation to develop projects to help marginal and minority groups or to improve some aspect of a social institution; a focus on compassion in the self-spiritualist philosophies we follow and their discourses on meditative exercises, and so on and so forth. There is virtually no limit to the ideas we can come up with.

By realigning the mainstream lifestyles' ends to the good life, we extricate them, in different degrees, from their absolute conformation to the hyperindividualist and hedonistic logic of the market. In this way, we choose in various manners and respects, to free ourselves from the pervasive idolatry of the screened image held as standard for the means of our arousal and search for status. Whether the integration of lifestyles with ethical horizons is happening often enough in our life and the lives of others is an issue we need to constantly reassess and aspire toward improving and expanding as the consumer and corporate culture fostered by many multinational businesses grows ever more dominant by the day.

Notes

INTRODUCTION: The Age of Identity

1   'Grand narrative' or 'master narrative' is a term introduced by Jean-François Lyotard in *The Postmodern Condition: A Report on Knowledge*, trans. Geoff Bennington, Brian Massumi (Manchester: Manchester University, 1984).

2   Gilles Lipovetsky, *Hypermodern Times*, trans. Andrew Brown (Cambridge: Polity, 2005), p. 64.

3   Philip A. Mellor, Chris Shilling, 'Modernity, Identity and the Sequestration of Death', in *Sociology*, 27:3 (1993), pp. 411–14, 427.

4   Charles Taylor, *The Ethics of Authenticity* (London: Harvard University, 1991), p. 26.

5   Erich Fromm, *The Fear of Freedom* (Oxon: Routledge, 1942), pp. 1–32, 117–77.

6   Fromm, *Freedom*, p. 218.

7   Fromm, *Freedom*, p. 218.

8   See Jean-Paul Sartre, *Existentialism and Humanism*, trans. Philip Mairet (London: Methuen, 1948).

9   See Fromm, *Freedom*, pp. 117–177.

10 Zygmunt Bauman, *Postmodern Ethics*, (Oxford: Blackwell, 1993), p. 20.

11 Bauman, *Ethics*, p. 20.

12 Bauman, *Ethics*, p. 21.

13 Zygmunt Bauman, *The Art of Life* (Cambridge: Polity, 2008), p. 88.

14 Bregham Dalgliesh, 'Zygmunt Bauman and the Consumption of Ethics by the Ethics of Consumerism', in *Theory, Culture & Society*, 31:4, p. 102.

15 Taylor, *Authenticity*, p. 35.

16 Anthony Giddens, *Modernity and Self-Identity: Self and Society in the Late Modern Age* (Cambridge: Polity, 1991), p. 52.

17 Giddens, *Self-Identity*, p. 54.

18 Giddens, *Self-Identity*, pp. 54–5.

19 Giddens, *Self-Identity*, pp. 54–5.

20 Giddens, *Self-Identity*, pp. 54–5.

21 Zygmunt Bauman, 'From Pilgrim to Tourist – or a Short History of

Identity', in *Questions of Cultural Identity*, ed. Stuart Hall, Paul du Gay (London: Sage, 1996), p. 19.
22 Lipovetsky, *Hypermodernism Times,* pp. 64–6. Much like consumerist identities, the adoption of a cultural identity can be dangerous if we unquestioningly affirm all its beliefs and rules, applying them to *any* situation regardless of its possible exceptionality. The absence of any critical stance toward our cultural identity can also lead to intolerance and dismissal of outsiders and their perspectives.

I
Turning Lifestyles into Identities
1 Erich Fromm, *The Fear of Freedom* (Oxon: Routledge, 1942), pp. 221–37.
2 In *The Consumer Society: Myths and Structures* (1998), Jean Baudrillard claims that late modern culture is precisely based upon the ingrained belief that our wants or needs lead us toward objects capable of satisfying them. Since we are nonetheless never satisfied – and we are indeed criticized for this – this same pursuit begins over and over again ((London: Sage), pp. 69–70).
3 Zygmunt Bauman, 'From Pilgrim to Tourist – or a Short History of Identity', in *Questions of Cultural Identity*, ed. Stuart Hall, Paul du Gay (London: Sage, 1996), pp. 25–6.
4 Gilles Lipovetsky, *The Empire of Fashion: Dressing Modern Democracy*, trans. Catherine Porter (Oxford: Princeton University, 1994), p. 155.
5 Lipovetsky, *Fashion*, pp. 125–26.
6 Cited in Zygmunt Bauman, *Culture in a Liquid Modern World*, trans. Lydia Bauman (Cambridge: Polity, 2011), p. 18.
7 Bauman, *Culture*, pp. 19–20.
8 Lipovetsky, *Fashion*, p. 29.
9 Lipovetsky, *Fashion*, pp. 106–7.
10 Cited and translated by Joseph Donohue, 'Salome and the Art of Wildean Theatre', in *Modern Drama*, 37:1, 1994, pp. 88–9, from Charles Baudelaire, *Oeuvres complètes* (Paris: Gallimard, 1980), p. 807.
11 Note that 'marginal differentiation' as explored here in the sphere of fashion is different in interpretation from Lipovetsky's use of the term, which has to do with the diversity of products available for the consumer, where small differences between products are multiplied in excess (see Lipovetsky, *Fashion*, pp. 131–32).
12 Lipovetsky, *Fashion,* pp. 98–102.
13 Bauman, *Culture,* p. 20.

14 Cited and translated by Bauman, *Culture*, p. 21, from Georg Simmel, *Zur Psychologie der Mode; Soziologische Studie,* in *Gesamtausgabe,* vol. 5 (Berlin: Suhrkamp, 1992).

15 Bauman, *Culture*, p. 22.

16 Lipovetsky sees the three main characteristics of consummate fashion as belonging to 'ephemerality', 'seduction', and 'marginal differentiation' (see Lipovetsky, *Fashion*, pp. 134–241).

17 Cited by Vance Packard, *The Waste Makers* (New York: David McKay, 1960), p. 71.

18 The influence pertains mainly to the mindset known as 'instrumental rationality', which will be illustrated in detail in Chapter 6.

19 David Graeber, *The Utopia of Rules: On Technology, Stupidity, and the Secret Joys of Bureaucracy* (London: Melville House, 2015), p. 20.

20 Graeber, *Rules*, p. 20.

21 Joseph A. Schumpeter, *The Theory of Economic Development*, trans. Redvers Opie (London: Routledge, 2021), pp. 49–84. See also A.M. Ghannejh et al., 'A Qualitative Analysis of Product Innovation in Jordan's Pharmaceutical Sector', in *European Scientific Journal*, 11:4, 2015, pp. 474–503; Gouher Ahmed, 'Entrepreneurship in the United Arab Emirates', in *The Young Vision*, 3:5, 2014, pp. 15–28; Paul Samuelson, *Economics* (New York: McGraw-Hill, 1980), pp. 726–727).

22 Cited by Tariq Mehmood et al., 'Schumpeterian Entrepreneurship Theory: Evolution and Relevance', in *Academy of Entrepreneurship Journal*, 25:4, 2019, p. 5.

23 ActionCOACH, *12 Essential Characteristics of an Entrepreneur*: 12 Essential Characteristics of an Entrepreneur - ActionCOACH (yumpu.com).

24 Sari Pekkala Kerr, William R. Kerr, Tina Xu, *Personality Traits of Entrepreneurs: A Review of Recent Literature* (Boston: Now Publishers, 2018).

25 Hugh Willmott, 'Strength is Ignorance; Slavery is Freedom: Managing Culture in Modern Organizations', in *Journal of Management Studies*, 30:4, 1993, pp. 518–19.

26 Paul du Gay, 'Enterprise Culture and the Ideology of Excellence', in *New Formations*, 13, 1991, pp. 53–4.

27 Masa Higo, 'Surviving Death-Anxieties in Liquid Modern Times: Examining Zygmunt Bauman's Cultural Theory of Death and Dying', in *Omega*, 65:3, 2012, pp. 229–31; Louise Mansfield, *Gender, Power and Identities in the Fitness Gym: Towards a Sociology of the 'Exercise Body-Beautiful Complex'*, PhD Thesis (Loughborough: Loughborough University, 2005), pp. 4–5.

28   Barry Glassner, 'Fitness and the Postmodern Self', in *Journal of Health and Social Behavior*, 30, 1989, pp. 186–87.

29   Cheryl Cole, 'Body Studies in the Sociology of Sport', in *Handbook of Sport Studies*, ed. Jay J. Coakley, Eric Dunning (London: Sage, 2002), p. 438; Brian Turner, *The Body and Society* (London: Sage, 2996), p. 5.

30   Turner, *The Body*, p. 3.

31   Zygmunt Bauman, *Liquid Modernity* (Cambridge: Polity, 2000), pp. 77–8. Other insightful explanations of fitness are offered by Jennifer Smith Maguire and Barry Glassner. On the one hand, for Maguire, '"Being fit" is about possessing the appropriate capacities and resources to undertake the project of the self in a competent fashion, minimizing health risks, and maximizing market value. Fitness is a measure of aptitude for life in consumer culture and a service economy' (*Fit for Consumption: Sociology and the Business of Fitness* (Oxon: Routledge, 2008), p. 190. On the other hand, for Glassner, 'Fitness refers to the general state of a person's psycho-physical well-being – mind as well as body' ('Fitness and the Postmodern Self', in *Journal of Health and Social Behavior*, 30, 1989, p. 181).

32   Bauman, *Liquid Modernity*, p. 77.

33   Bauman, *Liquid Modernity*, pp. 77–8.

34   Mansfield, *Fitness Gym*, pp. 13, 16.

35   Glassner, 'Postmodern Self', pp. 185–86; Mansfield, *Fitness Gym*, pp. 266–67. Fitness is therefore more than just healthy eating, a routine exercise like jogging, a profession (as a fitness trainer or a sports player for instance), or a diet and/or physical regimen, although 'a fit life' or 'a fit person' is often related with such practices. As a consumerist identity-type, fitness is not a pastime. It denotes an enterprise that governs our life; a fulltime pursuit that emerges from the commitment to a very particular perspective.

36   Glassner, 'Postmodern Self', pp. 185–86; Mansfield, *Fitness Gym*, pp. 266–67.

37   Adrian Franklin, 'The Tourist Syndrome: An Interview with Zygmunt Bauman', in *Tourist Studies*, 3:2, 2003, pp. 205–17.

38   Adrian Franklin, 'The Tourism Ordering: Taking Tourism More Seriously as a Globalising Ordering', in *Civilisations: Revue internationale d'anthropologie et de sciences humaines*, 57:1–2, 2008, p. 35.

39   Franklin, 'The Tourism Ordering', p. 35.

40   Zygmunt Bauman, *Postmodern Ethics* (Oxford: Blackwell, 1993), pp. 168–69, 172, 180.

41   Zygmunt Bauman, 'Morality in the Age of Contingency', in *Detraditionalization: Critical Reflections on Authority and Identity*, ed. Paul Heelas, Scott Lash, Paul Morris (Oxford: Blackwell, 1996), pp. 52–3.

42   Bauman, *Postmodern Ethics*, p. 169.
43   Adrian Franklin, *Tourism: An introduction* (London: Sage, 2003).
44   Mauro Dujmović, Aljoša Vitasović, 'Postmodern Society and Tourism', in *Journal of Tourism and Hospitality Management*, 3:9–10, 2015, pp. 197–99.
45   Mauro Dujmović and Aljoša Vitasović, 'Postmodern Society', p. 198.
46   Mauro Dujmović and Aljoša Vitasović, 'Postmodern Society', p. 199.
47   Bauman, 'Tourist Syndrome', p. 213. To an extent, the tourist mindframe *in itself* regards the world from an aesthetic space. Its appropriation by corporate companies, however, means that the focus and investment is predominantly targeted toward this viewpoint at the expense of any other. In the options and packages they churn out, they tend to marginalize in significance all other potential mindframes in that they do not yield as much financial gain.
48   Dominika Motak, 'Postmodern Spirituality and the Culture of Individualism', in *Scripta Instituti Donneriani Aboensis*, 21, 2009, pp. 129–30.
49   Jennifer Rindfleish, 'Consuming the Self: New Age Spirituality as "Social Product" in Consumer Society', in *Consumption, Markets and Culture*, 8:4, 2005, pp. 345–46.
50   Gordon Lynch, *The New Spirituality: An Introduction to Progressive Belief in the Twenty-First Century* (London: I.B. Taurus, 2007), p. 44.
51   Lynch, *New Spirituality*, p. 53.
52   Graham Reside, 'Book Review: *The New Spirituality: An Introduction to Progressive Belief in the Twenty-First Century*', in *Conversations in Religion & Theology*, 8:1, 2010, pp. 64–5.
53   Guy Redden, 'Revisiting the Spiritual Supermarket: Does the Commodification of Spirituality Necessarily Devalue It?', in *Culture and Religion*, 17:2, 2016, p. 233; Paul Heelas, 'Challenging Secularization Theory: The Growth of "New Age" Spiritualities of Life', in *The Hedgehog Review*, 8:1–2, 2006, pp. 46–7.
54   Andrew Dawson, 'Consuming the Self: New Spirituality as "Mystified Consumption"', in *Social Compass*, 58:3, 2011, p. 311.
55   Redden, 'Spiritual Supermarket', pp. 233–35; Heelas, 'Secularization', p. 46.
56   Nevill Drury, *Exploring the Labyrinth: Making Sense of the New Spirituality* (St. Leonards: Allen & Unwin, 1999), p. 96; Jeremy R. Carrette, Richard King, *Selling Spirituality: The Silent Takeover of Religion* (East Sussex: Psychology, 2005).
57   Dan P. McAdams, 'The Psychology of Life Stories', in *Review of General Psychology*, ed. Gerianne M. Alexander, 5:2, 2001, p. 101. See also Jefferson A. Singer, 'Narrative Identity and Meaning Making Across the Adult Lifespan: An Introduction', in *Journal of Personality*,

72:3, 2004, pp. 437–60; Dan P. McAdams, Kate C. McLean, 'Narrative Identity', in *Current Directions in Psychological Science*, ed. Rendall W. Engle, 22:3, 2013, pp. 233–38.

58 These two examples are taken from McAdams, McLean, 'Narrative Identity', p. 234.
59 Bauman, 'History of Identity', p. 19.
60 Charles Taylor, *The Ethics of Authenticity* (London: Harvard University, 1991), pp. 31–42.
61 George Herbert Mead, *Mind, Self and Society* (Chicago: Chicago University, 1934).
62 Taylor, *Authenticity*, pp. 31–42.
63 Taylor, *Authenticity*, p. 91.
64 Taylor, *Authenticity*, pp. 34, 40.
65 Anthony Giddens, *Modernity and Self-Identity: Self and Society in the Late Modern Age* (Cambridge: Polity, 1991), p. 81.
66 Mike Featherstone, *Consumer Culture and Postmodernism* (London: Sage, 2007), p. 84.
67 Bauman, 'History of Identity', p. 26.
68 Rindfleish, 'Consuming the Self', p. 348.

II

The Refiguring Identity's Narrative Model

1 Jean Baudrillard, *The Consumer Society: Myths and Structures* (London: Sage, 1998), pp. 87–8.
2 Baudrillard, *Consumer Society*, p. 95.
3 Baudrillard, *Consumer Society*, p. 170.
4 Baudrillard, *Consumer Society*, p. 89.
5 Charles Taylor, *The Ethics of Authenticity* (London: Harvard University, 1991), p. 23.
6 Taylor, *Authenticity*, pp. 28–9.
7 Taylor, *Authenticity*, pp. 28–9.
8 Simon Critchley, *Infinitely Demanding:* Ethics of Commitment, Politics of Resistance (London: Verso, 2012), pp, 18, 39.
9 Paul Ricoeur, *Oneself as Another*, trans. Kathleen Blamey (London: University of Chicago, 1992), p. 355.
10 Steven Shaviro, *Passion and Excess: Blanchot, Bataille, and Literary Theory* (Tallahassee: Florida University, 1990), p. 113.
11 The ideas and coinage explored in this passage are mine.
12 Ricoeur, *Oneself as Another*, pp. 169–202. On a more originary level still, self-esteem in the refiguring identity entails the extent of my union with the Thou that calls me. My self-esteem is here a response

to the more elemental call to unify with the caller. It depends therefore on my willingness to surrender to the Thou's reality. The call to be with the Thou is especially intuited in episodes of extreme duress. See Chapter 9.

13 Ricoeur, *Oneself as Another*, pp. 21–3.
14 Ricoeur, *Oneself as Another*, pp. 169–202.
15 John Stuart Mill, *On Liberty* (New York: Dover, 2002), p. 10.
16 Ricoeur, *Oneself as Another*, pp. 171–80.
17 Ricoeur, *Oneself as Another*, p. 179.
18 Ricoeur, *Oneself as Another*, p. 179.
19 Ricoeur, *Oneself as Another*, p. 179.
20 See Ricoeur, *Oneself as Another*, p. 189, on the definition of goodness.
21 Ricoeur, *Oneself as Another*, p. 182.
22 Ricoeur, *Oneself as Another*, p. 190.
23 Ricoeur, *Oneself as Another*, p. 193.
24 Ricoeur, *Oneself as Another*, pp. 193–94.
25 Ricoeur, *Oneself as Another*, p. 194.
26 Ricoeur, *Oneself as Another*, p. 202.
27 Ricoeur, *Oneself as Another*, p. 194.
28 Ricoeur, *Oneself as Another*, pp. 195–96.
29 Ricoeur, *Oneself as Another*, pp. 194–202.

III
The Five Virtues of the Refiguring Identity

1 See for instance, Christopher Lasch, *The Culture of Narcissism: American Life in an Age of Diminishing Expectations* (London: W. W. Norton & Company, 1979); Anthony Giddens, *Modernity and Self-Identity: Self and Society in the Late Modern Age* (Cambridge: Polity, 1991); Zygmunt Bauman, *Postmodern Ethics* (Oxford: Blackwell, 1993).
2 Jean Baudrillard, *The Consumer Society: Myths and Structures* (London: Sage, 1998), pp. 100–1.
3 Baudrillard, *Consumer Society*, pp. 100–2.
4 Teresa Brennan, *History After Lacan* (London: Routledge, 1993), p. 37.
5 Gabriel Marcel, *Homo Viator: Introduction to a Metaphysic of Hope*, trans. Emma Craufurd (Chicago: Henry Regnery Company, 1951), p. 63.

IV
From Openness to Exposure

1   Zygmunt Bauman, *Liquid Modernity* (Cambridge: Polity, 2000), p. 77.

2   Zygmunt Bauman, 'From Pilgrim to Tourist – or a Short History of Identity', in *Questions of Cultural Identity*, ed. Stuart Hall, Paul du Gay (London: Sage, 1996), p. 24.

3   Bauman, *Liquid Modernity*, p. 77.

4   Jean Baudrillard, *The Consumer Society: Myths and Structures* (London: Sage, 1998), p. 182.

5   Mike Featherstone, *Consumer Culture and Postmodernism* (London: Sage, 2007), p. 94,

6   Featherstone, *Consumer Culture*, p. 103. See also Pierre Bourdieu, 'The Forms of Capital', in *Handbook of Theory and Research for the Sociology of Education*, ed. John G. Richardson (New York: Greenwood, 1986), p. 243.

7   Ian Munt, 'The "Other" Postmodern Tourism: Culture, Travel, and the New Middle Classes', in *Theory, Culture, and Society*, 11:3, 1994, pp. 101–23.

8   Zygmunt Bauman, 'The Self in a Consumer Society', in *The Hedgehog Review: Critical Reflections on Contemporary Culture*, ed. Jay Tolson, 11, 1999, p. 38.

9   Melanie K. Smith, 'New Leisure Tourism: Fantasy Futures', in *New Tourism Consumers, Products, and Industry: Present and Future Issues*, ed. Dimitrios Buhalis, Carlos Costa (Oxford: Butterworth-Heinemann, 2005), pp. 220–27.

10 Zygmunt Bauman, *Postmodern Ethics*, (Oxford: Blackwell, 1993), p. 180.

11 Adrian Franklin, 'The Tourist Syndrome: An Interview with Zygmunt Bauman', in *Tourist Studies*, 3:2, 2003, p. 208.

12 Franklin, 'The Tourist Syndrome', p. 208.

13 Bauman, *Postmodern Ethics*, pp. 241–42.

14 Cited by Gilles Lipovetsky, *The Empire of Fashion: Dressing Modern Democracy*, trans. Catherine Porter (Oxford: Princeton University, 1994) p. 104.

15 Georg Simmel, *Gesamtausgabe*, vol. 5 (Berlin: Suhrkamp, 1992).

16 Lipovetsky, *Fashion*, p. 79.

17 Lipovetsky, *Fashion*, p. 79.

18 Russell W. Belk, Melanie Wallendorf, John F. Sherry Jr., 'The Sacred and the Profane in Consumer Behavior: Theodicy on the Odyssey', in *Journal of Consumer Research*, 16, 1989, p. 9.

19 Andrew Dawson, *New Era New Religions: Religious Transformation in Contemporary Brazil* (Aldershot: Ashgate, 2007).

20   Wright Schermerhorn Jr., *Management*, 12 edn. (New York: Wiley, 2013), p. 155.

21   Sari Pekkala Kerr, William R. Kerr, Tina Xu, *Personality Traits of Entrepreneurs: A Review of Recent Literature* (Boston: Now Publishers, 2018).

22   Thomas Grebel, 'Neo-Schumpeterian Perspectives in Entrepreneurs Research', in *Elgar Companion to Neo-Schumpeterian Economics*, ed. Horst Hanusch, Andreas Pyka (Cheltenham: Edward Elgar, 2007) pp. 147–58; Christopher Freeman, *Technology Policy and Economic Performance: Lessons from Japan* (London: Frances Printer, 1987).

23   Hans-Georg Gadamer, *Truth and Method*, trans. Joel Weinsheimer, Donald G. Marshall (London: Bloomsbury, 2013), pp. 347–51.

24   Gadamer, *Truth*, p. 365.

25   Gadamer, *Truth*, p. 364.

26   Our 'horizon of understanding' or 'horizon of possibility' is Gadamer's term for our particular perception of existence as conditioned by our historically-determined situatedness. It entails an individual's idiosyncratic way of seeing, all the knowledge that constitutes a particular viewpoint on existence (Gadamer, *Truth*, pp. 313–17, 381–83).

27   Gadamer, *Truth*, p. 364.

28   The intimate relationship of exposure with our hope for the good life will be clarified once the virtue of hope is explored in Chapter 8.

29   Baudrillard, *Consumer Society*, pp. 79–80. See also Featherstone, *Consumer Culture*, p. 83.

30   Zygmunt Bauman, 'Identity – Then, Now, What For?', in *Polish Sociological Review*, 123, 1998, p. 209.

31   Jean Baudrillard, *Simulations*, trans. Paul Foss, Paul Patton, Philip Beitchman (New York: Semiotext(e), 1983).

32   Baudrillard, *Simulations*, p. 151.

33   Featherstone, *Consumer Culture*, p. 97.

34   Baudrillard, *Simulations*, p. 148.

35   To read the consumer culture's sign-values in many cases requires no reflective decoding as the signs themselves usually '*say it all*'. In their immediate aesthetic appeal is precisely the value they intend to communicate. By virtue of its appearance, the signifier here becomes itself the signified. An object's significance depends on the extent of how cool, sleek, exciting, mysterious . . . its look '*actually*' is. A moderate exposure to the images – and many of us are overexposed on a daily basis – will then educate us in a more 'nuanced' distinction of the levels of significance (or prestige and arousal) they insinuate. In focusing on appearances that everyone 'gets', consumer culture thrives on general consensus. Its commodity displays are often seduc-

tive for a majority. If the reality it propagates is intentionally tailor-made for the masses, then it cannot afford to be didactic or symbolic. Its signs cannot reference an external ideological system as this would compromise its instant comprehension for many. Nor must its signs refer to the outside world. To learn what signifieds they refer to would necessitate a preliminary education and discursive work that would complicate eligibility. To be truly universal, consumer culture reality must be understood with hardly any effort. It must elicit an impulsive appreciation of what most people regard as intense and estimable.

36 Baudrillard, *Consumer Society*, p. 132.
37 Barry Glassner, 'Fitness and the Postmodern Self', in *Journal of Health and Social Behavior* 30, 1989, p. 184. 180–191.
38 John Urry, *The Tourist Gaze* (London: Sage, 2002); Chris Rojek, 'Indexing, Dragging, and the Social Construction of Tourist Sights', in *Touring Cultures: Transformations of Travel and Theory*, ed. Chris Rojek, John Urry (London: Routledge, 1997), pp. 52–74; George Ritzer, *The McDonaldization Thesis: Explorations and Extensions* (London: Sage, 1998).
39 Chris Rojek, *Ways of Escape: Modern Transformations in Leisure and Travel* (London: Macmillan, 1993).
40 Emmanuel Levinas, *Totality and Infinity: An Essay on Exteriority*, trans. Alphonso Lingis (Pittsburgh: Duquesne University, 1969), p. 26. See also pp. 26–7, 281–82.
41 Maurice Blanchot, *The Writing of the Disaster*, trans. Ann Smock (London: University of Nebraska, 1995), p. 16.
42 See Chapter 5: 'The imaginative image (Ricoeur)' and Chapter 6: 'The dialectic of practical wisdom in the refiguring identity model (and its other functions)'; 'The type of knowledge that practical wisdom devises (Ricoeur)', for a further exploration of the relationship between exposure and the hermeneutics of imagination and practical wisdom respectively.

V
From Consumer Creativity to Imagination

1 Charles Taylor, *The Ethics of Authenticity* (London: Harvard University, 1991), p. 61.
2 Taylor, *Authenticity*, p. 62.
3 Taylor indicates that in fact we consider those people who have acquired some degree of originality in their life as 'creative' (*Authenticity*, p. 63).
4 Joseph A. Schumpeter, *Business Cycles: A Theoretical, Historical and*

Statistical Analysis of the Capitalist Process (New York, McGraw-Hill, 1939), p. 102.

5   Joseph A. Schumpeter, *The Theory of Economic Development*, trans. Redvers Opie (London: Routledge, 2021), pp. 1–84.

6   Joseph A. Schumpeter, *Capitalism, Socialism and Democracy* (London: George Allen & Unwin, 1976), p. 13.

7   Schumpeter, *Economic Development*, p. 76.

8   Jean Baudrillard, *The Consumer Society: Myths and Structures* (London: Sage, 1998), p. 192.

9   Meyer Schapiro, 'Style', in *Aesthetics Today*, ed. Morris Phillipson (London: Meridian Books, 1961), pp. 81–113.

10 Baudrillard, *Consumer Society*, pp. 88–90.

11 Baudrillard, *Consumer Society*, p. 61.

12 Baudrillard, *Consumer Society*, p. 61.

13 See Baudrillard, *Consumer Society*, p. 88.

14 See for instance, Jennifer Rindfleish, 'Consuming the Self: New Age Spirituality as "Social Product" in Consumer Society', in *Consumption, Markets and Culture*, 8:4, 2005, p. 349.

15 Andrew Dawson, 'Consuming the Self: New Spirituality as "Mystified Consumption"', in *Social Compass*, 58:3, 2011, pp. 310–11.

16 Mauro Dujmović and Aljoša Vitasović, 'Postmodern Society and Tourism', in *Journal of Tourism and Hospitality Management*, 3:9–10, 2015, pp. 194–97.

17 Auliana Poon, *Tourism, Technology, and Competitive Strategies* (Wallingford: CAB International, 1993).

18 Scott Lash and John Urry, *Economies of Signs and Space* (London: Sage, 1994).

19 Mike Featherstone, *Consumer Culture and Postmodernism* (London: Sage, 2007), p, 26.

20 Hanna Heidi, 'How to Use Physical Exercise as a Spiritual Practice': https://medium.com/thrive-global/how-to-use-physical-exercise-as-a-spiritual-practice-a05f9de1f5a8.

21 Clark Hamilton Depue, *Meditative Fitness: The Art and Practice of the Workout* (Irving: Sparkananda, 2015).

22 Andrew Dawson, 'Consuming the Self: New Spirituality as "Mystified Consumption"', in *Social Compass*, 58:3, 2011, p. 311.

23 Dawson, 'Consuming the Self'.

24 David Graeber, *The Utopia of Rules: On Technology, Stupidity, and the Secret Joys of Bureaucracy* (London: Melville House, 2015), p. 21.

25 The Young Entrepreneur Council, 'Ask the Entrepreneurs: 15 Ways to Incorporate Fitness into Your Company Culture': https://www.lifehack.org/articles/lifestyle/ask-the-

entrepreneurs-15-ways-to-incorporate-fitness-into-your-company-culture.html.

26 Charles Crawford, '9 Reasons Why Encouraging Fitness in the Office is Beneficial': https://www.business.com/articles/fitness-office-benefits/.

27 Mauro Dujmović and Aljoša Vitasović, 'Postmodern Society', p. 200.

28 Dujmović, Vitasović, 'Postmodern Society', pp. 199–201.

29 Zygmunt Bauman, *Liquid Modernity* (Cambridge: Polity, 2000), p. 78.

30 Bauman, *Liquid Modernity*, p. 78.

31 Dominika Motak, 'Postmodern Spirituality and the Culture of Individualism', in *Scripta Instituti Donneriani Aboensis*, 21, 2009, p. 136.

32 Rindfleish, 'Consuming the Self', p. 346.

33 Rindfleish, 'Consuming the Self', p. 357.

34 Rindfleish, 'Consuming the Self', p. 357.

35 See Bauman, *Liquid Modernity*, pp. 77–80.
    The fashionista's and traveller's goals are equally unclear in meaning. On the one hand, the emancipation fashionistas dream of through their appearance aesthetic remains a thin and incomplete backdrop ideal as focus is recurrently invested in the urgent fashion cycles that are supposed to realize it. By virtue of the cycles' continual renewal, the ideal is made ever more unreachable and abstract. On the other hand, the travellers' dream of accumulating as many authentic experiences as they can is often disappointed on account of the fact that their lifestyle discourses hardly ever provide a proper and stable definition of what 'authentic' or any other similar term actually mean. Normally absent in travel discourses are precise and stable criteria to distinguish the valuable from the not so valuable. As a result, various questions inevitably arise. How are authentic moments supposed to transform us? How can we tell that they are transforming us? What does 'transformation' even mean? And so on and so forth.

36 For thinkers such as I.A. Richards, Max Black, and Monroe C. Beardsley, the metaphorical meaning of a word is performed in specific contexts where it is opposed to the literal meanings of other words. Richards and Black present the metaphor as the site of a semantic tension between a tenor and a vehicle, between a focus and a frame, between a word and the sentence in which it is posited. Beardsley likewise perceives the metaphor as constituted by a procedure of self-contradiction, what he calls the 'metaphorical twist' (see I.A. Richards, *The Philosophy of Rhetoric* (London: Oxford University, 1964); Max Black, *Models and Metaphors: Studies in Language and Philosophy* (Ithaca: Cornell University, 1962); Monroe C. Beardsley, *Aesthetics: Problems in the Philosophy of Criticism*

(New York: Harcourt, 1958)). By the same token, Colin M. Turbayne rightly compares the dynamic of the metaphor with what Gilbert Ryle calls a 'category mistake', which is a mislocation of names and of predicates (see Colin M. Turbayne, *Myth of Metaphor* (Columbia: University of South Carolina, 1989)).

Ricoeur acknowledges the significance and influence of such thinkers on his view of the metaphor when he perceives it as a dialectical procedure that works on two different planes. Consider the following two examples: (1) Man is a wolf. (2) Time is a beggar. The first and more self-evident plane is the verbal plane. A semantic tension takes place because the predicate, 'wolf' or 'beggar', is used in an unusual manner. Its strange allocation instigates discordance between its meaning and the customary meaning of the subject, 'man' or 'time'. The two clauses are in semantic conflict with one another. A tension dramatizes both sentences. The same tension, however, in turn incites the imagination to link the two clauses. We are compelled to envision a way how assimilation can be brought about. An alternative insight into existence is revealed that is precisely based on a concordance of the former discordance. The possibility of a foreign new perception discloses itself. Within this potential worldview, 'man' or 'time' reappears *as* subsumed in a new meaningfulness. The metaphor defamiliarizes the familiar, evoking a different perspective from which to regard the world, therefore altering and enhancing our customary perspective (Paul Ricoeur, *From Text to Action: Essays in Hermeneutics, II*, trans. Kathleen Blamey, John B. Thompson (London: Athleen, 1991), pp. 171–73; 'Word, Polysemy, Metaphor: Creativity in Language', in *A Ricoeur Reader: Reflection and Imagination*, ed. Mario J. Valdés (Toronto: University of Toronto, 1991).

The same metaphor dialectic is seen to operate in the imaginative process of the refiguring identity but as a conflict and unification between our worldview and the foreign reality of experience.

37 In this role, the imagination is equivalent to the Kantian transcendental and its formative activity, whereby it synthesizes the chaotic data received through our senses into images in order to comprehend our environment.

38 Paul Ricoeur, 'Pastoral Praxeology, Hermeneutics, and Identity', in *Figuring the Sacred: Religion, Narrative, and Imagination*, ed. Mark I. Wallace, trans. David Pellauer (Minneapolis: Augsburg Fortress, 1995), pp. 220–23; Paul Ricoeur, 'Metaphor and the Main Problem of Hermeneutics', trans. David Pellauer, in Ricoeur, *Reader*, pp. 313–14; 'Poetry and Possibility', in Ricoeur, *Reader*, p. 452.

39 Ricoeur, 'Naming God', in *Sacred*, p. 222.

40 Ricoeur, 'Naming God', in *Sacred*, pp. 220–23; Ricoeur, 'Metaphor and the Main Problem of Hermeneutics', in *Reader*, pp. 313–34; Ricoeur, 'Poetry and Possibility', in *Reader*, p. 452.
41 Ricoeur, 'Poetry and Possibility', in *Reader*, p. 453.
42 Keats, John, *Keats: Selected Poems & Letters*, ed. Sarah Anstey (Oxford: Heinemann Educational Publishers, 1995), pp. 242–45.
43 Thomas McFarland, *The Masks of Keats: The Endeavour of a Poet* (Oxford: Oxford University, 2000), p. 224.
44 Refer for instance to McFarland, *Masks*, pp. 219–25, for a detailed analysis of how 'To Autumn's' worldview is brought into being.
45 Cormac McCarthy, *All the Pretty Horses* (New York: Alfred A. Knopf, 2000).

VI
From Instrumental Reason to Practical Widsom

1 Charles Taylor, *The Ethics of Authenticity* (London: Harvard University, 1991), p. 5.
2 Hugh Willmott, 'Postmodernism and Excellence: The De-differentiation of Economy and Culture', in *Journal of Organizational Change Management*, 5:1, 1992, pp. 58–68 ; Hugh Willmott, 'Strength is Ignorance; Slavery is Freedom: Managing Culture in Modern Organizations', in *Journal of Management Studies*, 30:4, 1993, pp. 515–52.
3 James H. Michelman, 'Some Ethical Consequences of Economic Competition', in *Journal of Business Ethics*, 2:2, 1983, p. 82.
4 Willmott, 'Postmodernism and Excellence', pp. 58–68 ; Willmott, 'Strength is Ignorance', pp. 515–52.
5 Michelman, 'Ethical Consequences', pp. 79–87.
6 René ten Bos, 'Business Ethics and Bauman Ethics', in *Organization Studies*, 18, 1997, pp. 1003–4.
7 Ten Bos, 'Business Ethics', p. 1003.
8 Michelman, 'Ethical Consequences, p. 84.
9 Gary Hamel, Coimbatore K. Prahalad, *Competing for the Future: Breakthrough Strategies for Seizing Control of Your Industry and Creating the Markets of Tomorrow* (Cambridge: Harvard Business School, 1994), p. 37.
10 Michelman, 'Ethical Consequences', pp. 85–6.
11 Peter Vardy, Paul Grosch, *The Puzzle of Ethics* (London: HarperCollins, 1999), pp. 103–4. Objectifying anything as a potential source of manipulation, however, is not a modus operandi that is feasible at all times. In *Ethics in the Conflicts of Modernity* (2016),

Alasdair MacIntyre writes that it is also often in the business' best interest to commit itself to other people – but only insofar as these others have some foreseen value for it. Relationships of loyalty and trust are thus reserved for those parties that are currently or will possibly be in some negotiating relationship with the business as well as those on whose goodwill the business has to depend owing to certain benefits it might receive (power, skills, influence, etcetera). Entrepreneurs invest in relationships only insofar as they align with the interests of their company (*Ethics in the Conflicts of Modernity: An Essay on Desire, Practical Reasoning, and Narrative* (Cambridge: Cambridge University, 2016), pp. 186–88). The same logic is evident in business humanitarian interventions. Gilles Lipovetsky remarks that one of the central goals of business ethics 'is to improve companies' performance ("ethics pays") through the management and marketing of values: ethical codes, sponsorship, participation, institutional communication of an ethical nature' (Gilles Lipovetsky, *The Empire of Fashion: Dressing Modern Democracy*, trans. Catherine Porter (Oxford: Princeton University, 1994), p. 249). Ethics in the entrepreneurial world, if existent at all, is a strictly functional procedure.

12   Norbert Elias, *The Court Society* (Oxford: Blackwell, 1983); Norbert Elias, *The Society of Individuals* (Oxford: Blackwell, 1991); Norbert Elias, *The Civilising Process: Sociogenetic and Psychogenetic Investigations* (Oxford: Blackwell, 2000).

13   Louise Mansfield, *Gender, Power and Identities in the Fitness Gym: Towards a Sociology of the 'Exercise Body-Beautiful Complex'*, PhD Thesis (Loughborough: Loughborough University, 2005), pp. 174, 265–66; Chris Shilling, *The Body and Social Theory* (London: Sage, 1993), p. 159.

14   Jean Baudrillard, *The Consumer Society: Myths and Structures* (London: Sage, 1998), p. 80.

15   Baudrillard, *Consumer Society*, p. 80.

16   Baudrillard, *Consumer Society*, p. 80.

17   Baudrillard, *Consumer Society*, p. 80. Among all the consumerist life-strategies, it is perhaps in the life-strategy of travel that the fun morality is most evidently witnessed. The travellers' aesthetic space turns places, people, and circumstances into resources from which it can draw a spectrum of exhilarating sensations such as excitement, a sense of danger, awe, mystery, and so on. Entertainment is the predominant compass guiding travellers on their journeys.

18   See Chapter 4 for a detailed study of 'open-mindedness' as a prominent quality in consumer culture.

19   Baudrillard, *Consumer Society*, p. 80.

20 Zygmunt Bauman, *Liquid Modernity* (Cambridge: Polity, 2000), p. 78.
21 Margaret Carlisle Duncan, Lori A. Klos, 'Paradoxes of the Flesh: Emotion and Contradiction in Fitness/Beauty Magazine Discourses', in *Journal of Sport and Social Issues* 38:3, 2014, pp. 248–59. Though they do not mention the element of willpower as unequivocally as fitness, the discourses of the other life-strategies are also predicated on its uncompromising freedom. Each one in its own way insists that our progress depends only on us. For those who are determined, there are no limits they cannot surpass. Consequently, to make a mistake, to earn a much lesser reward than was expected (or to earn no reward at all), to find it close to impossible or just impossible to go on because of some immutable force in opposition, *is no excuse*. If we gain weight despite our strict regimes, if we opt for a look that is too distinctive or standard for the appreciation of our viewership, if our spiritual exercises, vegan diet, or workout barely has any payoff – it is ultimately on us.
22 Bauman, *Liquid Modernity*, p. 118.
23 Frederic Jameson, 'The Cultural Logic of Late Capitalism', in *Postmodernism, Or the Cultural Logic of Late Capitalism* (Durham: Duke University, 1991), pp. 25–6.
24 Cited by Mike Featherstone, *Consumer Culture and Postmodernism* (London: Sage, 2007), p. 57.
25 See Zygmunt Bauman, *Liquid Modern Challenges to Education* (Padova: Padova University, 2011). 'Nowist culture' has been coined by Stephen Bertman in reference to the way we live in contemporary times (See Stephen Bertman, *Hyperculture: The Human Cost of Speed*, Westport: Praeger, 1998).
26 Bauman, *Liquid Modernity*, pp. 118–29. See also Bauman, *Education* (Padova: Padova University, 2011).
27 See for instance Bauman, *Liquid Modernity*, pp. 118–29; Bauman, *Education*.
28 Bauman, 'From Linear to Pointillist Time', in *Liquid Modern Challenges to Education* (Padova: Padova University, 2011).
29 Bauman, 'From Linear to Pointillist Time', in *Education*.
30 Bauman, 'From Linear to Pointillist Time', in *Education*.
31 As consumers, our penchant to start new experiences to abandon them soon after tends to increasingly condense our now to a point that hardly progresses anywhere any further. A point has no dimensionality and yet it holds the potential to develop into anything. 'Points have no length, width, or depth', Bauman points out. '[T]hey exist, one is tempted to say, *before* the space and time; both space and time are yet to begin. [But] each point is presumed to contain an infinite potential to expand and the infinity of possibilities waiting to

explode if properly ignited' ('From Linear to Pointillist Time', in Bauman, *Education*). Bauman therefore also fittingly calls this kind of life 'pointillist' after the neo-impressionist technique in painting using tiny dots of various pure colours, which appear as blended to the viewers' gaze from a certain distance.

32 The notion of solicitude has been explained in depth in Chapter 2: 'The three constituents of the good life schema', in connection to the refiguring identity's schematic definition of the good life.

33 John Wall, 'Phronesis, Poetics, and Moral Creativity', in *Ethical Theory and Moral Practice*, 6, 2003, p. 324.

34 Ricoeur, *Oneself as Another*, p. 177.

35 Ricoeur, *Oneself as Another*, p. 273.

36 Ricoeur, *Oneself as Another*, p. 280.

37 Ricoeur, *Oneself as Another*, pp. 203–339.

38 Stelios Virvidakis, 'Reflective Equilibrium', in *International Encyclopedia of the Social & Behavioral Sciences*, ed. James D. Wright, vol. 20 (Oxford: Elsevier, 2015), pp. 77–81.

39 Virvidakis, 'Reflective Equilibrium', pp. 77–81.

40 Ricoeur, *Oneself as Another*, pp. 262–73.

41 See Chapter 2: 'Authenticity as the call of conscience', for a more detailed definition of Ricoeur's concept of 'self-esteem'.

42 Ricoeur, *Oneself as Another*, p. 170.

43 Ricoeur, *Oneself as Another*, p. 170.

44 Ricoeur, *Oneself as Another*, p. 170.

45 Ricoeur, *Oneself as Another*, pp. 283–90; Wall, 'Phronesis', pp. 324–26.

46 Wall, 'Phronesis, pp. 324–25.

47 Wall, 'Phronesis', p. 330.

48 'Conviction' as explained here is a liberal adaptation of Ricoeur's version of 'conviction' and it is therefore not meant to reference the latter.

49 In *Oneself as Another*, Ricoeur does not explore the universalizing potential of the universals in context and therefore this explanation is entirely my own.

50 Zygmunt Bauman, 'The Self in a Consumer Society', in *The Hedgehog Review: Critical Reflections on Contemporary Culture*, ed. Jay Tolson, 11, 1999, p. 39.

51 Ten Bos, 'Business Ethics', p. 998.

52 Ten Bos, 'Business Ethics', pp. 997–1000.

53 Zygmunt Bauman, *Postmodern Ethics*, (Oxford: Blackwell, 1993), p. 80.

54 Bauman, *Postmodern Ethics*, p. 77.

55 Bauman, *Postmodern Ethics*, p. 80.

56   Bauman, *Postmodern Ethics*, p. 125.
57   Ten Bos, 'Business Ethics', p. 1003.
58   Ten Bos, 'Business Ethics', pp. 1004–6. See also Tom Peters, *Liberation Management* (New York: Macmillan, 1992); Gary Hamel, Coimbatore K. Prahalad, *Competing for the Future: Breakthrough Strategies for Seizing Control of Your Industry and Creating the Markets of Tomorrow* (Cambridge: Harvard Business School, 1994).
59   Ten Bos, 'Business Ethics', pp. 1004–6.

VII
From Surrender to Acceptance

1   See Shiva Rea, 'Ishvara Pranidhana: The Practice of Surrender': Ishvara Pranidhana: The Practice of Surrender (yogajournal.com).
2   Marianne Robinson, *A Return to Love: Reflections on the Principles of 'A Course in Miracles'* (San Francisco: HarperOne, 1996); Kathy Cordova, *Let Go, Let Miracles Happen: The Art of Spiritual Surrender* (York Beach: Conari, 2003).
3   Sally Kempton, 'Learn the Value of Spiritual Surrender': Learn the Value of Spiritual Surrender (yogajournal.com)
4   Kempton, 'Spiritual Surrender': Learn the Value of Spiritual Surrender (yogajournal.com)
5   'The Art of Not Planning': The art of not planning | Road trips | The Guardian.
6   Rick Steves, 'The Beauty of Spontaneous Travel': The Beauty of Spontaneous Travel by Rick Steves.
7   Dean Seguin, 'The Key to Happiness? Travel More Spontaneously, says a Travelzoo Study': The Key to Happiness? Travel More Spontaneously, says a Travelzoo Study | Travelzoo.
8   Seguin, 'The Key to Happiness?': The Key to Happiness? Travel More Spontaneously, says a Travelzoo Study | Travelzoo; 'How to Ace Spontaneous Travel': https://www.travelsupermarket.com/en-gb/blog/travel-advice/how-to-ace-spontaneous-travel/
9   Christopher Lasch, *The Culture of Narcissism: American Life in an Age of Diminishing Expectations* (London: W.W. Norton & Company, 1979), pp. 7, 13.
10 Cited by Lash, *Narcissism*, p. 6.
11 See Chapter 4: 'Exposure is the readiness to see the foreign in experience', for a study of the exposure mindset as an intrinsic attribute of Gadamer's view of experienced persons.
12 Hans-Georg Gadamer, *Truth and Method*, trans. Joel Weinsheimer, Donald G. Marshall (London: Bloomsbury, 2013), p. 365.

13   Gadamer, *Truth and Method*, p. 365.
14   Richard Kearney, *On Stories* (London: Routledge, 2002), pp. 137–39.
15   *Hellenistic Philosophy: Introductory Readings*, trans. Brad Inwood, L.P. Gersoon (Cambridge: Hackett, 1997), I-22.
16   Peter Preuss, *Epicurean Ethics: Katastematic Hedonism* (Lewiston: Edwin Mellen, 1994), p. 172.
17   William Shakespeare, *King Lear*, ed. Burton Raffel (London: Yale University, 2007).
18   John Millington Synge, *The Playboy of the Western World and Riders to the Sea* (London: Routledge, 2003), p. 92.
19   Synge, *Riders*, p. 93.
20   Elizabeth S. Belfiore, *Tragic Pleasures: Aristotle on Plot and Emotion* (Princeton: Princeton University, 2014), pp. 346–50.
21   Maurice Blanchot, *The Instant of My Death*, and Jacques Derrida, *Demeure: Fiction and Testimony*, trans. Elizabeth Rottenberg (Stanford: Stanford University, 2000), p. 5.
22   Blanchot, *Instant of My Death*, pp. 7–8.
23   Johan C. Thom, *The Pythagorean Golden Verses* (Leiden: E.J. Brille, 1995), p. 137.
24   Pierre Hadot, *What Is Ancient Philosophy?* trans. Michael Chase (London: Harvard University, 2002), pp. 96, 85.
25   Adelmo Barigazzi, 'Uomini e dei in Epicuro', in *Acme,* 8, 1955, p. 41 (my translation). See also Adelmo Barigazzi, 'Atomo e provvidenza divina', in *L'atomo fra scienza e letteratura* (Genoa: University of Genoa, 1983) p. 55.

VIII
From Consumer Desire to Hope

1   Russell W. Belk, Søren Askegaard, Guliz Ger, 'The Fire of Desire: A Multisited Inquiry into Consumer Passion', in *Journal of Consumer Research*, 30, 2003, pp. 326–29.
2   Julien Freund, 'Théorie du besoin', in *L'anné sociologique* (Paris: Presses Universitaires de France, 1971), pp. 13–64.
3   Russell W. Belk, Søren Askegaard, Guliz Ger, 'Metaphors of Consumer Desire', in *Advances in Consumer Research*, ed. Kim P. Corfman, John G. Lynch Jr., vol. 23 (Provo: Association for Consumer Research, 1996), pp. 368–73.
4   Belk et al., 'Fire of Desire', p. 333.
5   Russell Belk, Søren Askegaard, Guliz Ger, 'Consumer Desire in Three Cultures: Results from Projective Research', in *Advances in Consumer Research*, ed. Merrie Brucks, Debbie MacInnis,

vol. 24 (Provo: Association for Consumer Research, 1997), pp. 24–8.

6   Belk et al., 'Fire of Desire', p. 344.

7   Jean Baudrillard, *Seduction*, trans. Brian Singer (Montréal: New World Perspectives, 1991), p. 98.

8   Pasi Falk, *The Consuming Body* (London: Sage, 1994).

9   Gabriel Marcel, *Being and Having: An Existentialist Diary* (New York: Harper & Row, 1965), p. 162; *The Mystery of Being*, vol. 2: *Faith & Reality*, trans. George S. Fraser (Chicago: Henry Regnery, 1960), pp. 176–77, 181; 'Desire and Hope', in *Readings in Existential Phenomenology*, ed. Nathaniel Lawrence, Daniel O'Connor (Englewood Cliffs: Prentice-Hall, 1967), pp. 277–85; *Presence and Immortality*, trans. Michael A. Machado (Pittsburgh: Duquesne University, 1967), pp. 231–32.

10 Marcel, 'Desire and Hope', p. 280.

11 See also Chapter 4: 'Openness for arousal and status' and Chapter 6: '"You must have fun (or else you are to blame)"', on the prominence of the new experience in consumer culture lifestyles.

12 Zygmunt Bauman, *Liquid Modernity* (Cambridge: Polity, 2000), p. 72.

13 Zygmunt Bauman, 'From Pilgrim to Tourist – or a Short History of Identity', in *Questions of Cultural Identity*, ed. Stuart Hall, Paul du Gay (London: Sage, 1996), p. 18.

14 See for instance Zygmunt Bauman, *Culture in a Liquid Modern World*, trans. Lydia Bauman (Cambridge: Polity, 2011), p. 21; Adrian Franklin, 'The Tourist Syndrome: An Interview with Zygmunt Bauman', in *Tourist Studies*, 3:2, 2003, p.207.

15 Bauman, *Liquid Modernity,* pp. 72–80.

16 Bauman, *Culture*, p. 27.

17   See Bauman, *Liquid Modernity,* pp. 123–26.

18 Georg Simmel, *The Philosophy of Money*, trans. Tom Bottomore, David Frisby (London: Routledge & Kegan Paul, 1978); Dean MacCannell, '"Sex Sells": Comment on Gender Images and Myth in Advertising', in *Marketing and Semiotics: New Directions in the Study of Signs for Sale*, ed. Jean Sebeok (Berlin: de Gruyter, 1987), pp. 521–31; Colin Campbell, *The Romantic Ethic and the Spirit of Modern Consumerism* (London: Blackwell, 1987).

19 Simmel, *Money*, p. 67.

20 See also Belk et al, 'Fire of Desire', pp. 342–43.

21 Belk et al., 'The Fire of Desire', p. 342.

22 Bauman, *Liquid Modernity*, pp. 73, 88.

23 Joseph J. Godfrey, *A Philosophy of Human Hope* (Lancaster: Martinus Nijhoff, 1987), pp. 11–4, 47–9, 127–29.

24 Godfrey, *Hope*, p. 139. See also p. 138.

25 Gabriel Marcel, *Homo Viator: Introduction to a Metaphysic of Hope*, trans. Emma Craufurd (London: Victor Gollancz, 1951), p. 36. See also Marcel, 'Desire and Hope', in *Readings in Existential Phenomenology*, ed. Nathaniel Lawrence, Daniel O'Connor (Englewood Cliffs: Prentice-Hall, 1967), p. 278; *The Philosophy of Existentialism*, trans. Manya Harari (New York: Citadel Press, 1971), p. 28.

26 'Hope and the Structure of Philosophical Systems', in Paul Ricoeur, *Figuring the Sacred: Religion, Narrative, and Imagination*, ed. Mark I. Wallace, trans. David Pellauer, (Minneapolis: Augsburg Fortress, 1995), pp. 207, 206.

27 Ricoeur, 'Hope', p. 207. See also pp. 205–7.

28 William Desmond, *Beyond Hegel and Dialectic: Speculation, Cult and Comedy* (New York: State University of New York, 1992), pp. 238–39.

29 Godfrey, *Hope*, p. 108.

30 Marcel, *Homo Viator*, p. 39.

31 Belk et al., 'Fire of Desire', p. 335.

32 Bauman, *Culture*, p. 29.

33 Godfrey, *Hope*, p. 108. See also pp. 108–110.

34 Marcel, *Homo Viator*, pp. 30, 49–50, 61; *Being and Having*, pp. 75, 80; 'Desire and Hope', p. 283; *Existentialism*, p. 28.

35 Marcel, 'Desire and Hope', p. 285.

36 Godfrey, *Hope*, p. 114.

37 Marcel, *Homo Viator*, p. 36.

38 Marcel, *Homo Viator*, p. 45.

39 Marcel, *Existentialism*, p. 28.

IX
The Case of Limit-Experiences

1 The reflections that follow are predominantly an extension of Paul Ricoeur's hermeneutic-phenomenology on the call of conscience, which, as already illustrated, has been adapted for the refiguring self-narrative schema.

2 Michel Foucault, 'The "Experience Book"', in *Remarks on Marx: Conversations with Duccio Trombadori*, trans. R. James Goldstein, James Cascaito (New York: Semiotext(e), 1991), pp. 30–1. See also for instance, Georges Bataille, *Inner Experience*, trans. Leslie Anne Boldt (New York: State University of New York, 1988); Maurice Blanchot, *The Space of Literature*, trans. Ann Smock (London: Nebraska University, 1982); *The Writing of the Disaster*, trans. Ann

Smock (London: Nebraska University, 1995); John D. Caputo, *The Prayers* and *Tears of Jacques Derrida: Religion without Religion* (Bloomington: Indiana University Press, 1997).

3   Charles Taylor, *A Secular Age* (Cambridge: Harvard University, 2007), p. 5.

4   Jacques Lacan, *Ecrits: A Selection*, trans. Alan Sheridan (London: Routledge, 1997), p. 192.

5   Nonetheless, the writings on limit-experiences are often characterized by an implicit sense of fascination and awe that seem to imply that there is an insuperable value in our unreserved exposure to these experiences. The authors on the subject often seem to insist on the inherent falsity of our subjective reality, with its obsessive focus on empowering our ego. The invaluable element of limit-experiences seems to be derived from their capacity to break us out of our self-centred illusion to expose ourselves to an unknown that is seen to be in some irreducible sense a much 'truer' reality than our own. Opening ourselves without reservations to limit-experiences is considered to be emancipatory.

6   For references to 'signifying' and 'signifyingness', see for instance Emmanuel Levinas, *Totality and Infinity*, trans. Alphonso Lingis (Pittsburgh: Duquesne University, 1969), pp. 66, 259–61. See also pp. 92, 206–7, 218–19, 297.

7   Gabriel Marcel, *Homo Viator: Introduction to a Metaphysic of Hope*, trans. Emma Crauford (Chicago: Henry Regnery Company), pp. 37–8, 66–7, 114–16; *The Mystery of Being*, vol. 2: *Faith & Reality*, trans. George S. Fraser (Chicago: Henry Regnery, 1960), pp. 176–82. See also Joseph J. Godfrey, *A Philosophy of Human Hope* (Lancaster: Martinus Nijhoff, 1987), pp. 37–40.

8   Marcel, *Homo Viator*, p. 60.

9   Godfrey, *Hope*, p. 39.

10   Godfrey, *Hope*, p. 39.

11   See for instance, Steven Shaviro, *Passion and Excess: Blanchot, Bataille, and Literary Theory* (Tallahassee: Florida University Press, 1990), pp. 107, 124–25.

12   Citation originally from Jacques Derrida, '*Khora*', in *On the Name*, trans. D. Wood, J. P. Leavey, I. McLeod (Stanford: Stanford University Press), 1995, p. 125.

13   Richard Kearney, *Strangers, Gods and Monsters: Interpreting Otherness* (London: Routledge, 2003), pp. 201–2.

14   Kearney, *Strangers*, pp. 198–200. The relationship between limit-experiences and faith is here only briefly indicated in order to stress the extent of the (uncanny) congruence between the attitude evoked by the refiguring narrative model and the limit-experience. To avoid

digression, various aspects and details of the relationship are either omitted or presented as an overview.

15   Cited by Kearney, *Strangers*, p. 211.

16   Kearney, *Strangers*, p. 211.

CONCLUSION

1   As already indicated in Chapter 6: 'Entrepreneurial and fitness rationality', n11, however, the humanitarian interventions of companies are often not as altruistic as they might seem, and a certain degree of caution is always required in interpreting their true motive.

Bibliography

ActionCOACH, *12 Essential Characteristics of an Entrepreneur*: 12 Essential Characteristics of an Entrepreneur - ActionCOACH (yumpu.com).

Adelman, Irma, *Theories of Economic* (California: Stanford University, 1961).

Ahmed, Gouher, 'Entrepreneurship in the United Arab Emirates', in *The Young Vision*, 3:5, 2014, pp. 15–28.

Barigazzi, Adelmo, 'Atomo e provvidenza divina', in *L'atomo fra scienza e letteratura* (Genoa: University of Genoa, 1983), pp. 55–73.

—— 'Uomini e dei in Epicuro', in *Acme*, 8, 1955, pp. 37–56.

Bataille, Georges, *Inner Experience*, trans. Leslie Anne Boldt (New York: State University of New York, 1988).

Baudelaire, Charles, *Oeuvres complètes* (Paris: Gallimard, 1980).

Baudrillard, Jean, *Seduction*, trans. Brian Singer (Montréal: New World Perspectives, 1991).

—— *Simulations*, trans. Paul Foss, Paul Patton, Philip Beitchman (New York: Semiotext(e), 1983).

—— *The Consumer Society: Myths and Structures* (London: Sage, 1998).

Bauman, Zygmunt, *Culture in a Liquid Modern World*, trans. Lydia Bauman (Cambridge: Polity, 2011).

—— 'From Pilgrim to Tourist – or a Short History of Identity', in *Questions of Cultural Identity*, ed. Stuart Hall, Paul du Gay (London: Sage, 1996), pp. 18–36.

—— *Globalization: The Human Consequences* (Oxford: Polity, 1998).

—— 'Identity – Then, Now, What For?', in *Polish Sociological Review*, 123, 1998, pp. 205–16.

—— *Liquid Modernity* (Cambridge: Polity, 2000).

—— *Liquid Modern Challenges to Education* (Padova: Padova University, 2011).

—— 'Morality in the Age of Contingency', in *Detraditionalization: Critical Reflections on Authority and Identity*, ed. Paul Heelas, Scott Lash, Paul Morris (Oxford: Blackwell, 1996), pp. 49–59.

—— *Postmodern Ethics* (Oxford: Blackwell, 1993).

—— *The Art of Life* (Cambridge: Polity, 2008).

Bibliography

—— 'The Self in a Consumer Society', in *The Hedgehog Review: Critical Reflections on Contemporary Culture*, ed. Jay Tolson, 11, 1999, pp. 35–40.

Beardsley, Monroe C., *Aesthetics: Problems in the Philosophy of Criticism* (New York: Harcourt, 1958).

Belfiore, Elizabeth S., *Tragic Pleasures: Aristotle on Plot and Emotion* (Princeton: Princeton University, 2014).

Belk, Russell W., Askegaard, Søren, Ger, Guliz, 'Consumer Desire in Three Cultures: Results from Projective Research', in *Advances in Consumer Research*, ed. Merrie Brucks, Debbie MacInnis, vol. 24 (Provo: Association for Consumer Research, 1997), pp. 24–8.

—— 'Metaphors of Consumer Desire', in *Advances in Consumer Research*, ed. Kim P. Corfman, John G. Lynch Jr., vol. 23 (Provo: Association for Consumer Research, 1996), pp. 368–73.

—— 'The Fire of Desire: A Multisited Inquiry into Consumer Passion', in *Journal of Consumer Research*, 30, 2003, pp. 326–29.

Belk, Russell W., Wallendorf, Melanie, Sherry Jr., John F., 'The Sacred and the Profane in Consumer Behavior: Theodicy on the Odyssey', in *Journal of Consumer Research*, 16, 1989, pp. 1–38.

Bertman, Stephen, *Hyperculture: The Human Cost of Speed* (Westport: Praeger, 1998).

Black, Max, *Models and Metaphors: Studies in Language and Philosophy* (Ithaca: Cornell University, 1962).

Blanchot, Maurice, *The Instant of My Death*, and Derrida, Jacques, *Demeure: Fiction and Testimony*, trans. Elizabeth Rottenberg (Stanford: Stanford University, 2000).

—— *The Space of Literature*, trans. Ann Smock (London: Nebraska University, 1982).

—— *The Writing of the Disaster*, trans. Ann Smock (London: Nebraska University, 1995).

Bos, René ten, 'Business Ethics and Bauman Ethics', in *Organization Studies*, 18, 1997, pp. 997–1014.

Bourdieu, Pierre, 'The Forms of Capital', in *Handbook of Theory and Research for the Sociology of Education*, ed. John G. Richardson (New York: Greenwood, 1986), pp. 241–58.

Brennan, Teresa, *History After Lacan* (London: Routledge, 1993).

Campbell, Colin, *The Romantic Ethic and the Spirit of Modern Consumerism* (London: Blackwell, 1987).

Caputo, John D., *The Prayers and Tears of Jacques Derrida: Religion without Religion* (Bloomington: Indiana University Press, 1997).

Carrette, Jeremy R., King, Richard, *Selling Spirituality: The Silent Takeover of Religion* (East Sussex: Psychology, 2005).

Cole, Cheryl L., 'Body Studies in the Sociology of Sport', in *Handbook of*

Sport Studies, ed. Jay J. Coakley, Eric Dunning (London: Sage, 2002), pp. 439–60.

Cordova, Kathy, *Let Go, Let Miracles Happen: The Art of Spiritual Surrender* (York Beach: Conari, 2003).

Crawford, Charles, '9 Reasons Why Encouraging Fitness in the Office is Beneficial': https://www.business.com/articles/fitness-office-benefits/.

Critchley, Simon, *Infinitely Demanding: Ethics of Commitment, Politics of Resistance* (London: Verso, 2012).

Dalgliesh, Bregham, 'Zygmunt Bauman and the Consumption of Ethics by the Ethics of Consumerism', in *Theory, Culture & Society*, 31:4, pp. 97–118.

Dawson, Andrew, 'Consuming the Self: New Spirituality as "Mystified Consumption"', in *Social Compass*, 58:3, 2011, pp. 309–315.

—— *New Era – New Religions: Religious Transformation in Contemporary Brazil* (Aldershot: Ashgate, 2007).

Depue, Clark Hamilton, *Meditative Fitness: The Art and Practice of the Workout* (Irving: Sparkananda, 2015).

Derrida, Jacques, '*Khora*', in *On the Name*, trans. D. Wood, J. P. Leavey, I. McLeod (Stanford: Stanford University Press), 1995, pp. 89–130.

Desmond, William, *Beyond Hegel and Dialectic: Speculation, Cult and Comedy* (New York: State University of New York, 1992).

Donohue, Joseph, 'Salome and the Art of Wildean Theatre', in *Modern Drama*, 37:1, 1994, pp. 84–103

Drury, Nevill, *Exploring the Labyrinth: Making Sense of the New Spirituality* (St. Leonards: Allen & Unwin, 1999).

Du Gay, Paul, 'Enterprise Culture and the Ideology of Excellence', in *New Formations*, 13, 1991, pp. 45–61.

Dujmović, Mauro, Vitasović, Aljoša, 'Postmodern Society and Tourism', in *Journal of Tourism and Hospitality Management*, 3:9–10, 2015, pp. 192–203.

Duncan, Margaret Carlisle, Klos, Lori A., 'Paradoxes of the Flesh: Emotion and Contradiction in Fitness/Beauty Magazine Discourses', in *Journal of Sport and Social Issues* 38:3, 2014, pp. 245–262.

—— Elias, Norbert, *The Society of Individuals* (Oxford: Blackwell, 1991).

—— *The Civilising Process: Sociogenetic and Psychogenetic Investigations* (Oxford: Blackwell, 2000).

—— *The Court Society* (Oxford: Blackwell, 1983).

Falk, Pasi, *The Consuming Body* (London: Sage, 1994).

Featherstone, Mike, *Consumer Culture and Postmodernism* (London: Sage, 2007).

Foucault, Michel, *Remarks on Marx: Conversations with Duccio Trombadori*, trans. R. James Goldstein, James Cascaito (New York: Semiotext(e), 1991).

Bibliography

Franklin, Adrian, 'The Tourism Ordering: Taking Tourism More Seriously as a Globalising Ordering', in *Civilisations: Revue internationale d'anthropologie et de sciences humaines*, 57:1–2, 2008, pp. 25–39.

—— 'The Tourist Syndrome: An Interview with Zygmunt Bauman', in *Tourist Studies*, 3:2, 2003, pp. 205–17.

—— *Tourism: An introduction* (London: Sage, 2003).

Freeman, Christopher, *Technology Policy and Economic Performance: Lessons from Japan* (London: Frances Printer, 1987).

Freund, Julien, 'Théorie du besoin', in *L'anné sociologique* (Paris: Presses Universitaires de France, 1971), pp. 13–64.

Fromm, Erich, *The Fear of Freedom* (Oxon: Routledge, 1942).

Gadamer, Hans-Georg, *Truth and Method*, trans. Joel Weinsheimer, Donald G. Marshall (London: Bloomsbury, 2013).

Ghannejh, A.M. et al., 'A Qualitative Analysis of Product Innovation in Jordan's Pharmaceutical Sector', in *European Scientific Journal*, 11:4, 2015, pp. 474–503.

Giddens, Anthony, *Modernity and Self-Identity: Self and Society in the Late Modern Age* (Cambridge: Polity, 1991).

Glassner, Barry, 'Fitness and the Postmodern Self', in *Journal of Health and Social Behavior*, 30, 1989, pp. 180–191.

Godfrey, Joseph J., *A Philosophy of Human Hope* (Lancaster: Martinus Nijhoff, 1987).

Graeber, David, *The Utopia of Rules: On Technology, Stupidity, and the Secret Joys of Bureaucracy* (London: Melville House, 2015).

Grebel, Thomas, 'Neo-Schumpeterian Perspectives in Entrepreneurs Research', in *Elgar Companion to Neo-Schumpeterian Economics*, ed. Horst Hanusch, Andreas Pyka (Cheltenham: Edward Elgar, 2007), pp. 147–58.

Hadot, Pierre, *What Is Ancient Philosophy?* trans. Michael Chase (London: Harvard University, 2002).

Hamel, Gary, Prahalad, Coimbatore K., *Competing for the Future: Breakthrough Strategies for Seizing Control of Your Industry and Creating the Markets of Tomorrow* (Cambridge: Harvard Business School, 1994).

Heelas, Paul, 'Challenging Secularization Theory: The Growth of "New Age" Spiritualities of Life', in *The Hedgehog Review*, 8:1–2, 2006, pp. 46–58.

Heidi, Hanna, 'How to Use Physical Exercise as a Spiritual Practice': https://medium.com/thrive-global/how-to-use-physical-exercise-as-a-spiritual-practice-a05f9de1f5a8.

Hellenistic Philosophy: Introductory Readings, trans. Brad Inwood, L.P. Gersoon (Cambridge: Hackett, 1997).

Higo, Masa, 'Surviving Death-Anxieties in Liquid Modern Times:

Bibliography

Examining Zygmunt Bauman's Cultural Theory of Death and Dying', in *Omega*, 65:3, 2012, pp. 221–238.

Horace, *The Complete Odes and Epodes with the Centennial Hymn*, trans. W.G. Shepherd (Harmondsworth: Penguin, 1983).

'How to Ace Spontaneous Travel': https://www.travelsupermarket.com/en-gb/blog/travel-advice/how-to-ace-spontaneous-travel/.

Jameson, Frederic, 'The Cultural Logic of Late Capitalism', in *Postmodernism, Or the Cultural Logic of Late Capitalism* (Durham: Duke University, 1991), pp. 1–54.

Kearney, Richard, *On Stories* (London: Routledge, 2002).

—— *Strangers, Gods and Monsters: Interpreting Otherness* (London: Routledge, 2003).

Keats, John, *Keats: Selected Poems & Letters*, ed. Sarah Anstey (Oxford: Heinemann Educational Publishers, 1995).

Kempton, Sally, 'Learn the Value of Spiritual Surrender': Learn the Value of Spiritual Surrender (yogajournal.com).

Kerr, Sari Pekkala, Kerr, William R., Xu, Tina, *Personality Traits of Entrepreneurs: A Review of Recent Literature* (Boston: Now Publishers, 2018).

Lacan, Jacques, *Ecrits: A Selection*, trans. Alan Sheridan (London: Routledge, 1997).

Lasch, Christopher, *The Culture of Narcissism: American Life in an Age of Diminishing Expectations* (London: W. W. Norton & Company, 1979).

Lash, Scott, Urry, John, *Economies of Signs and Space* (London: Sage, 1994).

Levinas, Emmanuel, *Totality and Infinity: An Essay on Exteriority*, trans. Alphonso Lingis (Pittsburgh: Duquesne University, 1969).

Lipovetsky, Gilles, *Hypermodern Times*, trans. Andrew Brown (Cambridge: Polity, 2005).

—— *The Empire of Fashion: Dressing Modern Democracy*, trans. Catherine Porter (Oxford: Princeton University, 1994).

Lynch, Gordon, *The New Spirituality: An Introduction to Progressive Belief in the Twenty-First Century* (London: I.B. Taurus, 2007).

Lyotard, Jean-François Lyotard in *The Postmodern Condition: A Report on Knowledge*, trans. Geoff Bennington, Brian Massumi (Manchester: Manchester University, 1984).

MacCannell, Dean, '"Sex Sells": Comment on Gender Images and Myth in Advertising', in *Marketing and Semiotics: New Directions in the Study of Signs for Sale*, ed. Jean Sebeok (Berlin: de Gruyter, 1987), pp. 521–31.

MacIntyre, Alasdair, *Ethics in the Conflicts of Modernity: An Essay on Desire, Practical Reasoning, and Narrative* (Cambridge: Cambridge University, 2016).

Bibliography

Maguire, Jennifer Smith, *Fit for Consumption: Sociology and the Business of Fitness* (Oxon: Routledge, 2008).

Mansfield, Louise, *Gender, Power and Identities in the Fitness Gym: Towards a Sociology of the 'Exercise Body-Beautiful Complex'*, PhD Thesis (Loughborough: Loughborough University, 2005).

Marcel, Gabriel, *Being and Having: An Existentialist Diary* (New York: Harper & Row, 1965).

—— 'Desire and Hope', in *Readings in Existential Phenomenology*, ed. Nathaniel Lawrence, Daniel O'Connor (Englewood Cliffs: Prentice-Hall, 1967), pp. 277–85.

—— *Homo Viator: Introduction to a Metaphysic of Hope*, trans. Emma Craufurd (Chicago: Henry Regnery Company, 1951).

—— *Presence and Immortality*, trans. Michael A. Machado (Pittsburgh: Duquesne University, 1967).

—— *The Mystery of Being*, vol. 2: *Faith & Reality*, trans. George S. Fraser (Chicago: Henry Regnery, 1960).

—— *The Philosophy of Existentialism*, trans. Manya Harari (New York: Citadel Press, 1971).

McAdams, Dan P., 'The Psychology of Life Stories', in *Review of General Psychology*, ed. Gerianne M. Alexander, 5:2, 2001, pp. 100–22.

McAdams, Dan P., McLean, Kate C., 'Narrative Identity', in *Current Directions in Psychological Science*, ed. Rendall W. Engle, 22:3, 2013, pp. 233–38.

McCarthy, Cormac, *All the Pretty Horses* (New York: Alfred A. Knopf, 2000).

McFarland, Thomas, *The Masks of Keats: The Endeavour of a Poet* (Oxford: Oxford University, 2000).

Mead, George Herbert, *Mind, Self and Society* (Chicago: Chicago University, 1934).

Mehmood, Tariq et al., 'Schumpeterian Entrepreneurship Theory: Evolution and Relevance', in *Academy of Entrepreneurship Journal*, 25:4, 2019, pp. 1–10.

Mellor, Philip A., Shilling, Chris, 'Modernity, Identity and the Sequestration of Death' in *Sociology*, 27:3 (1993), pp. 411–431.

Michelman, James H., 'Some Ethical Consequences of Economic Competition', in *Journal of Business Ethics*, 2:2, 1983, pp. 79–87.

Mill, John Stuart, *On Liberty* (New York: Dover, 2002).

Motak, Dominika, 'Postmodern Spirituality and the Culture of Individualism', in *Scripta Instituti Donneriani Aboensis*, 21, 2009, pp. 129–41.

Munt, Ian, 'The "Other" Postmodern Tourism: Culture, Travel, and the New Middle Classes', in *Theory, Culture, and Society*, 11:3, 1994, pp. 101–23.

Bibliography

Packard, Vance, *The Waste Makers* (New York: David McKay, 1960).

Peters, Tom, *Liberation Management* (New York: Macmillan, 1992).

Poon, Auliana, *Tourism, Technology, and Competitive Strategies* (Wallingford: CAB International, 1993).

Preuss, Peter, *Epicurean Ethics: Katastematic Hedonism* (Lewiston: Edwin Mellen, 1994).

Rea, Shiva, 'Ishvara Pranidhana: The Practice of Surrender': Ishvara Pranidhana: The Practice of Surrender (yogajournal.com).

Redden, Guy, 'Revisiting the Spiritual Supermarket: Does the Commodification of Spirituality Necessarily Devalue It?', in *Culture and Religion*, 17:2, 2016, pp. 231–49.

Reside, Graham, 'Book Review: *The New Spirituality: An Introduction to Progressive Belief in the Twenty-First Century*', in *Conversations in Religion & Theology*, 8:1, 2010, pp. 60–77.

Richards, I. A., *The Philosophy of Rhetoric* (London: Oxford University, 1964).

Ricoeur, Paul, *A Ricoeur Reader: Reflection and Imagination*, ed. Mario J. Valdés (Toronto: University of Toronto, 1991).

—— *Figuring the Sacred: Religion, Narrative, and Imagination*, ed. Mark I. Wallace, trans. David Pellauer (Minneapolis: Augsburg Fortress, 1995).

—— *From Text to Action: Essays in Hermeneutics, II*, trans. Kathleen Blamey, John B. Thompson (London: Athleen, 1991).

—— *Oneself as Another*, trans. Kathleen Blamey (London: University of Chicago, 1992).

Rindfleish, Jennifer, 'Consuming the Self: New Age Spirituality as "Social Product" in Consumer Society', in *Consumption, Markets and Culture*, 8:4, 2005, pp. 343–60.

Ritzer, George, *The McDonaldization Thesis: Explorations and Extensions* (London: Sage, 1998).

Robinson, Marianne, *A Return to Love: Reflections on the Principles of 'A Course in Miracles'* (San Francisco: HarperOne, 1996).

Rojek, Chris, 'Indexing, Dragging, and the Social Construction of Tourist Sights', in *Touring Cultures: Transformations of Travel and Theory*, ed. Chris Rojek, John Urry (London: Routledge, 1997), pp. 52–74.

—— *Ways of Escape: Modern Transformations in Leisure and Travel* (London: Macmillan, 1993).

Samuelson, Paul, *Economics* (New York: McGraw-Hill, 1980).

Sartre, Jean-Paul, *Existentialism and Humanism*, trans. Philip Mairet (London: Methuen, 1948).

Schapiro, Meyer, 'Style', in *Aesthetics Today*, ed. Morris Phillipson (London: Meridian Books, 1961), pp. 81–113.

Schermerhorn Jr., Wright, *Management*, 12 edn (New York: Wiley, 2013).

Bibliography

Schumpeter, Joseph A., *Business Cycles: A Theoretical, Historical and Statistical Analysis of the Capitalist Process* (New York, McGraw-Hill, 1939).

—— *Capitalism, Socialism and Democracy* (London: George Allen & Unwin, 1976).

—— *The Theory of Economic Development*, trans. Redvers Opie (London: Routledge, 2021).

Seguin, Dean, 'The Key to Happiness? Travel More Spontaneously, says a Travelzoo Study': The Key to Happiness? Travel More Spontaneously, says a Travelzoo Study | Travelzoo.

Shakespeare, William, *King Lear*, ed. Burton Raffel (London: Yale University, 2007).

Shaviro, Steven, *Passion and Excess: Blanchot, Bataille, and Literary Theory* (Tallahassee: Florida University Press, 1990).

Shilling, Chris, *The Body and Social Theory* (London: Sage, 1993).

Simmel, Georg, *Gesamtausgabe*, vol. 5 (Berlin: Suhrkamp, 1992).

—— *The Philosophy of Money*, trans. Tom Bottomore, David Frisby (London: Routledge & Kegan Paul, 1978).

Singer, Jefferson A., 'Narrative Identity and Meaning Making Across the Adult Lifespan: An Introduction', in *Journal of Personality*, 72:3, 2004, pp. 437–60.

Smith, Melanie K., 'New Leisure Tourism: Fantasy Futures', in *New Tourism Consumers, Products, and Industry: Present and Future Issues*, ed. Dimitrios Buhalis, Carlos Costa (Oxford: Butterworth-Heinemann, 2005), pp. 220–27.

Steves, Rick, 'The Beauty of Spontaneous Travel': The Beauty of Spontaneous Travel by Rick Steves.

Synge, John Millington, *The Playboy of the Western World and Riders to the Sea* (London: Routledge, 2003).

Taylor, Charles, *A Secular Age* (Cambridge: Harvard University, 2007).

—— *The Ethics of Authenticity* (London: Harvard University, 1991).

'The Art of Not Planning': The art of not planning | Road trips | The Guardian.

The Young Entrepreneur Council, 'Ask the Entrepreneurs: 15 Ways to Incorporate Fitness into Your Company Culture': https://www.life-hack.org/articles/lifestyle/ask-the-entrepreneurs-15-ways-to-incorpora te-fitness-into-your-company-culture.html.

Thom, Johan C., *The Pythagorean Golden Verses* (Leiden: E.J. Brille, 1995).

Turbayne, Colin M., *Myth of Metaphor* (Columbia: University of South Carolina, 1989).

Turner, Brian, *The Body and Society* (London: Sage, 1996).

Urry, John, *The Tourist Gaze* (London: Sage, 2002).

Vardy, Peter, Grosch, Paul, *The Puzzle of Ethics* (London: HarperCollins, 1999).

Virvidakis, Stelios, 'Reflective Equilibrium', in *International Encyclopedia of the Social & Behavioral Sciences*, ed. James D. Wright, vol. 20 (Oxford: Elsevier, 2015), pp. 77–81.

Wall, John, 'Phronesis, Poetics, and Moral Creativity', in *Ethical Theory and Moral Practice*, 6, 2003, pp. 317–41.

Willmott, Hugh, 'Postmodernism and Excellence: The De-differentiation of Economy and Culture', in *Journal of Organizational Change Management*, 5:1, 1992, pp. 58–68.

—— 'Strength is Ignorance; Slavery is Freedom: Managing Culture in Modern Organizations', in *Journal of Management Studies*, 30:4, 1993, pp. 515–52.

Index

absorptiveness: quality of, 52, 136
acceptance as a refiguring identity
virtue, 44, 47–51, 102, 109–19
passim, 132, 136–38, 141, 148,
149; facticity of existence and
the, 109–11; future and its, 111;
dialogue with the other virtues
and its, 117–19; exposure and,
118–19 *passim*, 132, 136–38,
141
achievement in consumer culture.
See status in consumer culture
adjustability: quality of, 52, 136
aesthetic space the (Bauman), 20–2,
54–5, 155n47, 165n17
All the Pretty Horses (McCarthy),
83–4
alterity in experience. *See* foreign in
experience the
Aristotle, 37, 38, 39, 94, 112
arousal/enjoyment/happiness/well-
being in consumer culture, 4,
10, 20, 29, 46, 52, 53–7 *passim*,
60, 61, 62, 63, 64, 74, 75, 78,
79, 88–9 *passim*, 90, 91, 92, 93,
104, 105, 109, 120, 121, 122,
123, 124, 125, 126, 146, 150,
159n35; desire as, 120, 121,
122, 123, 124, 125, 126; entrepreneurship in, 56–7; fashion in,
55; fitness in, 78; fun morality
and the, 88–9, 90, 109; hyperreal and the, 60, 61, 63; novelty
and, 53–7, 89, 93; 'nowist time'
and, 91, 92, 93; self-spirituality
in, 55–6, 109; travel in, 20,
54–5, 107–8. *See also* status in
consumer culture

ataraxia. *See* Epicureanism
authenticity or being authentic in our
times, 3, 7, 9, 11, 12, 26 *passim*,
29–31, 32–6 *passim*, 42, 43, 44,
62, 68–9 *passim*, 70, 79, 138

Baudrillard, Jean, 8, 32–3, 45–6, 52,
60, 61–2, 69–71, 88–9, 121,
152n2; *Simulacra and
Simulations*, 61–2; *The
Consumer Society: Myths and
Structures*, 32–3, 45–6, 52, 60,
62, 69–71, 88–9, 152n2
Bauman, Zygmunt, 3, 4, 6, 8, 12, 14,
18–21, 22, 25–6, 30, 44–5, 52,
53, 54–5, 61, 75–6, 86, 89–90,
91, 92, 93, 101, 102 *passim*,
103 *passim*, 122–23, 124, 125,
129, 166–67n31; 'Business
Ethics and Bauman Ethics', 86,
101, 102, 103 *passim*; *Culture in
a Liquid Modern World,* 14,
124, 129; 'From Pilgrim to
Tourist – or a Short History of
Identity', 6, 12, 19–20, 25–6,
30, 123; *Globalization*, 19–20;
'Identity – Then, Now, What
For?', 61; *Liquid Modern
Challenges to Education*, 92, 93,
166–67n31; *Liquid Modernity*,
18–19, 52, 75–6, 89–90, 91, 92,
122–23, 125; *Modernity and the
Holocaust*, 101; 'Morality in the
Age of Contingency', 20;
Postmodern Ethics, 3, 20–1,
54–5, 101, 102 *passim*; *The Art
of Life*, 4; 'The Self in a
Consumer Society', 53, 101;

choices and its, 72, 74; individualism and its, 54–5, 75, 90,
109; intensity and its, 53–5,
162n35, 108; novelty and its,
53–5, 108; status and its, 53, 90.
See also new leisure tourism;
simulational tourism; spontaneous travelling

universals in context/potential or
inchoate universals of practical
wisdom the (Ricoeur), 98–100
passim, 167n49
unknown in experience the. *See*
foreign in experience the

vagueness of consumerist lifestyle
goals the, 75–8; fitness in, 77–8;
self-spirituality in, 76–7
values of consumerist life-strategies
the (in general), 7, 44–7, 50,
146, 147, 148, 149
virtues of the refiguring identity
model the (in general), 9, 10,
43–4, 45, 47–51, *passim*, 111,

131, 133, 134, 135–37, 147–50;
affirmations of the foreign in
experience as, 44, 47; aspects of
the refiguring decision as,
49–50; dialogue with the
consumerist life-strategies and
their, 147–150; limit-experiences and, 134, 135–37;
reciprocity of influence and
their, 10, 49–50. *See also* gifts:
the virtues as; humility in the
virtues of the refiguring identity
model
voice of conscience the. *See* call of
conscience the

*Ways of Escape: Modern
Transformations in Leisure and
Travel* (Rojek), 63
Willmott, Hugh, 17, 85;
'Postmodernism and Excellence:
The De-differentiation of
Economy and Culture', 85;
'Strength is Ignorance: Slavery is
Freedom', 17, 85

Printed and bound by CPI Group (UK) Ltd, Croydon, CR0 4YY

16/04/2025

14658575-0001